UNTAMED

UNTAMED

*The Wildest Woman in America
and the
Fight for Cumberland Island*

Will Harlan

Grove Press
New York

Published simultaneously in Canada
Printed in the United States of America

FIRST EDITION

ISBN 978-0-8021-2258-2
eISBN 978-0-8021-9262-2

Grove Press
an imprint of Grove/Atlantic, Inc.
154 West 14th Street
New York, NY 10011

Distributed by Publishers Group West

www.groveatlantic.com

14 15 16 10 9 8 7 6 5 4 3 2 1

for caretta

contents

Cumberland Island

LITTLE CUMBERLAND ISLAND

Long Point

Hush Your Mouth

First African Baptist Church

Terrapin Point

Half Moon Bluff

Candler Estate

North Cut Trail

Lake Whitney

South Cut Trail

BRICKHILL RIVER

Table Point

Main Road

Sweetwater Lakes

Original Wilderness Area Boundary

ATLANTIC OCEAN

Plum Orchard Mansion

Ashley Pond

Duck House

Lake Retta

Willow Pond

Stafford Mansion

Slave Chimneys

Stafford Field

Kings Bay Nuclear Submarine Base

Davisville

SOUND

Greyfield Inn

Sea Camp Dock

Dungeness Dock

CUMBERLAND

Dungeness Ruins

The Grange

Raccoon Keys

ST. MARYS RIVER

Jetty

GEORGIA

FLORIDA

	Trail
	Beach and dunes
	Maritime forest
	Salt marsh
	Wilderness area boundary
◣	Campground
▲	Primitive backcountry campsite
⁞	Dune crossing marker

Illustration by Wade Mickley

prologue

bareback through the ocean

Carol shot the wild hog roaming the dunes and gutted it on the beach. She cooked the meat over a campfire as the first pinpricks of starlight pierced the sky. She had not slept in two days, and her eyelids grew heavy as the food settled in.

She felt safe on the wide-open, windswept beach. Anything was better than being holed up in her cabin waiting for a bullet. The thrum of the tides calmed her jangled nerves.

Then she spotted a wet-backed glint of moonlight moving through the curling breakers. A giant sea turtle heaved her ancient body out of the water and onto the dark island beach. She crawled into the dunes, dug a nest with her flippers, and began dropping Ping-Pong-ball-sized eggs into the hole. Gooey tears dripped from the turtle's eyes.

Carol crept closer. She waited until the turtle had finished burying her eggs. Then she grabbed the turtle by the rim of her shell, hoisted the edge of her three-hundred-pound body skyward, and flipped her onto her back. The turtle hissed.

"I know, darlin'. This won't take long."

Carol stapled identification tags into the turtle's flippers and measured her shell: 219 centimeters, one of the largest ever recorded on Cumberland Island. The turtle's liquid brown eyes followed Carol.

"Don't fret, mama. I'll keep an eye on your nest."

The giant sea turtle crawled back into the ocean. As Carol watched, a lonely trickle of wind grazed her cheek. The beach was dark and deserted, and so was she. Feverishly, Carol stripped off her clothes and waded out to the turtle, still awash in the surf.

She straddled the turtle's massive shell and held on to the front edge, riding bareback into the wild waters. The sea turtle—slow and

heavy on land—was swift and buoyant in the ocean. Carol felt lighter, too. Her fears lifted. The dread that had shadowed her for months washed away as the turtle carried her farther from shore.

Then the turtle began to dive. Carol gulped one last lungful of air and pressed herself against the turtle's shell as they went underwater together.

She and the turtle skimmed the ocean floor. It was quiet, the water was inky, and Carol's lungs burned, but she held on and went deeper still. Down here, she felt raw and real. She tightened her grip on the turtle's shell and held on as long as she could.

Ahead, the ocean floor dropped off sharply. The turtle plunged into the abyss, and Carol finally let go. She clawed frantically toward the moonlit surface and finally popped out into the night air, gasping and wheezing. She floated on her back, chest heaving, the summer stars whirling overhead.

"Hooo-weee!" she howled. She drifted naked in the ocean, tossed by the waves, her oxygen-starved lungs still on fire.

Then she noticed a different burning—gory gashes along her legs that had ripped open when she slid off the turtle's barnacled back. A cloud of bloody water engulfed her bare body. She could not see the shore.

Electric fear shot through her veins like lightning. She was swimming through one of the largest shark nurseries in the eastern Atlantic. Sand tigers, hammerheads, and spinner sharks bred and fed in the fecund waters. Carol swam hard and steady, trying not to flail or thrash. A trail of blood followed in her wake. Salt stung her open wounds. With each stroke, one thought rattled around her skull: "I'm bait!"

Carol lifted her head to scan the waves for fins but saw only scattered moonlight across the rolling ocean. The tide carried her closer to shore. Finally, her fingers brushed the sandy bottom. She stumbled out of the surf and collapsed onto the beach, her body shaking, her adrenaline-buzzed brain soaring with wild delight.

Carol pressed her bandana against the bloodiest of her gashes. The night breeze dried her. About a half mile out, she saw the giant turtle surface for air and then disappear into the deep.

She stepped back into her jeans, buttoned her flannel shirt, and shouldered her pack. Her hair was still wet, so she stopped to wring out the ocean from her braids. That's when she looked down at the sand: another pair of boot prints followed hers. Carol felt eyes watching her from the forest.

Carol Ruckdeschel is the wildest woman in America. She eats roadkill, wrestles alligators, and dissects dead sea turtles that wash ashore. She lives on a wilderness island in a ramshackle cabin that she built herself, and she eats mostly what she hunts, gathers, and grows. She is a hard-drinking, gun-toting, modern-day Thoreau who is even more outspoken in protecting her Waldenesque island.

A self-taught scientist with only a high school diploma, she knows more about sea turtles than most PhD biologists. She is the Jane Goodall of sea turtles and a voice for wilderness, especially on Cumberland Island, a national park along the Georgia coast that Carol calls home. Cumberland is one of the most biologically diverse islands in the world—the United Nations named it a global biosphere reserve because it shelters so much rare and endangered wildlife. Alligators slide through primordial swamps, while bald eagles soar overhead, and horses roam free. Dense flocks of wood storks nest in old-growth live oaks strewn with beards of Spanish moss. Its bone-colored beaches are pristine and unspoiled, and its dunes are still covered with sea oats instead of beachfront hotels. Hundreds of sea turtles nest on the eighteen-mile-long barrier island each summer, as they have for millennia.

Turtles aren't the only creatures that dig Cumberland. Even before John F. Kennedy Jr. and Carolyn Bessette married there in 1996, Cumberland Island has attracted its share of lovers. It was a coveted Gilded Age playground for the Carnegie and Rockefeller families. In 1972, it became one of the country's most beloved national parks. Today, artists set up easels atop its towering dunes, backpackers trek through the island's mystical maritime forests, and kayakers paddle through a labyrinth of creeks fingering through its emerald marshes. It's one of the last and largest wilderness islands in the country.

It's also one of the most controversial. Cumberland Island, originally named *tacatacuru*—"place of fire," has ignited human passions for centuries. Native Americans slaughtered the island's first Christian missionaries and were soon decimated by conquistadors. Later, the marshes ran red with blood as European commanders feuded over the island.

However, for most of Cumberland's recent history, it's been fierce females who have fought to protect the island. In the past century, bold island matriarchs chased off developers and saved the island from strip mining.

Today, the fight over Cumberland Island pits influential Carnegie and Rockefeller heirs against a scrappy turtle biologist who rides bareback in shark-infested waters. Will one of the wealthiest families in America be stopped by a dirt-poor naturalist with turtle guts beneath her fingernails?

Carol has made some enemies. They have described her as a "pseudo-scientist who smells like death" and a "manipulative, murderous whore who cares more about turtles than people." She's had three husbands and many lovers. She is an exiled island outcast— ostracized by the wealthy, vilified by government officials, and even stalked like prey.

Not surprisingly, she mostly prefers the companionship of wild creatures to human ones. Carol tromps the island in search of alligator dens and turtle nests. She likes a hard drink every evening. She is as tough as the sea turtle carapaces that line her museum. But beneath that hardened shell is a soft, bruised being.

I began hearing stories about Carol as soon as I arrived on Cumberland Island nineteen years ago. I was working as a ranger for the National Park Service on Cumberland Island, and visitors inevitably asked about "Carrion Carol."

"Have you met the wicked witch of the wilderness?"

"Does her breath smell like roadkill?"

"Is she hiding out from the law?"

"Does she fight with the vultures over turtle carcasses?"

"Carol comes tearing ass down the beach on her motorcycle, pigtails flying in the wind," one fellow park ranger told me. "People stand with their mouths open and gawk. She is not unaware of the effect she has on people—especially men."

After a few weeks, I asked my boss, the chief ranger of Cumberland Island, about Carol. His eyes narrowed, his lips curled, and he grumbled, "We don't talk about her."

But the maintenance guys down at the park garage were more than happy to oblige.

"Carol eats dead things off the road."

"She rides horses buck naked down the beach, carryin' a bottle of Jack Daniel's in one hand and firin' a pistol with the other."

"I seen her smashin' ticks between her teeth. She just picks 'em off her legs and mashes 'em in her mouth, then spits out the juice."

Inevitably, the banter ended with a long pause, followed by a cold, eyebrow-raised murmur: "You know, she killed a man."

Island families were less vague: "She killed her boyfriend so she could live here," a Carnegie islander told me. "She slept her way onto the island."

"Carol likes animals and hates people," said another Carnegie heiress. "That's why all of her husbands end up dead." More than once, I was warned by island families to stay away from her or I'd end up with my throat slit.

At an island meeting, Gogo Ferguson warned me not to get too close to Carol, and that wilderness was the most important thing to her. Gogo, the great-granddaughter of Thomas Carnegie, is a jewelry designer who helped run her family's private inn on Cumberland Island. Gogo and Carol were once close friends, but later became bitter rivals.

As a Cumberland Island ranger, I hiked through snake-filled swamps and wetlands thick with alligators, but after hearing stories from rangers and island families, I was more nervous about crossing paths with Carol.

Then, quite unexpectedly one afternoon, I stumbled onto her, elbow-deep in the bowels of a dead sea turtle that had washed ashore. I approached cautiously.

"Wanna see what she ate for breakfast?" Carol asked, without lifting her head.

She reached into the turtle's long white fire hose of intestines, which were a diary of its life. Olive goop spilled onto the beach. She sorted through the slop to find the remains of crabs, snails, and shrimp.

Then Carol opened the turtle's chest. Its nerves twitched, and its heart was still beating. A turtle's heart can continue throbbing hours after it has been butchered. Carol held the pumping fist of flesh in her bare, bloodstained hands.

"I have a heart like you," she whispered.

She slid the beating heart into a plastic sack. Then she sliced off the turtle's head and loaded it onto her four-wheeler. She dragged the remaining carcass into the dunes and whistled. A pair of black vultures appeared overhead. She knew the vultures by name, and she could tell which ones had followed her from her cabin fourteen miles to the north.

"The bird pickin' at the turtle's bowels—that's Big Man. He steals mullet out of my cat's food bowl every morning."

Carol's soil-brown eyes wrinkled at the corners when she smiled, and her teeth were radiant and white. With her high cheekbones, dark hair, and tanned skin, she could have passed for Native American. She was trim and fit, with calloused hands and a lean, strong frame. The sleeves of her button-down flannel were rolled up to her elbows, and her baggy jeans were smudged with turtle flesh. Tied to her horse-leather belt were a steel knife, bandana, and a timepiece. Her jeans were stuffed into white rubber boots, which she wore to keep her sockless feet dry and to protect her from snakes and ticks.

Her five-foot-six, 120-pound frame was lithe and agile, like a gymnast's. She could stand on one hand and drink a shot of whiskey with the other. She could climb any tree on the island and catch any animal.

She invited me up to see her homestead on the island's north end. Despite all of the dire warnings I had received, I hopped aboard her four-wheeler, wedged between Carol and a rotting turtle skull in a wet cardboard box.

Her cabin was nestled deep in the wilderness, surrounded by an old-growth forest of live oaks and longleaf pines. She had rebuilt the cabin years ago by dragging planks of driftwood from the beach. Wood was still piled everywhere.

"I couldn't drive to the hardware store, so I brought it to me," she said.

The inconvenience of living on a bridgeless barrier island also explained the stacks of hats, clothes, and tools strewn about. A trip to the grocery store took a full day, since the twice-a-day ferry was her only way to the mainland. So Carol collected goods that washed ashore on her weekly beach surveys, even bottled beer, canned food, and seaworthy fruits and vegetables. She had furnished most of her cabin with scavenged tables, benches, and rocking chairs. Her homestead was a chaotic collection of packrat practicality. She saved everything from auto parts to worn shoes.

Strewn about the yard were dozens of plastic buckets, each with macerated turtle skulls in various states of decay. The stench blended into a background of other aromas: citrus, smoked cedar, tomato, pine.

Black vultures lined the apex of her rusted tin roof, heads tilted, waiting to peck at the fresh turtle skull on the four-wheeler. One vulture drank from a sun-warmed ceramic bathtub—her "redneck Jacuzzi"—plopped in the middle of the yard. Her free-ranging hens *bawk-bawked* from the edge of the forest.

She'd had no job or steady income in three decades, so she lived frugally using the island's plentiful—and free—natural resources. Her water came from a naturally flowing artesian well. She heated and often cooked with wood that she hauled and split herself. Grapefruit and fig trees flanked the cabin, and a bedraggled wire fence surrounded a garden of tomatoes, okra, squash, greens, and melons. She had electricity, which she used primarily for food storage. Her

freezer was stocked with meats from island wildlife—hog, deer, coon, armadillo, gator, horse.

"I never go hungry," she said. "But dang, what I wouldn't give for some ice cream."

She had plenty of living creatures surrounding her, too. In addition to a wild horse she had tamed, she had a dozen chickens, four cats, six pigs, two snakes, an otter and an orphaned duckling. In a cage behind her cabin, she was nursing an injured red-shouldered hawk back to health. She had bottle-fed wounded otters and rescued bobcat cubs.

"I've always felt close to animals," she said. "They don't let you down."

Carol's kinship with the wild was as refreshingly simple as her bare-bones life in the woods. Her relationship with her fellow *Homo sapiens*, however, was a bit more complicated, as I soon learned.

I ended up shadowing Carol for the next two decades. I've been alongside her dissecting dead sea turtles on the beach and sipping cocktails in Carnegie mansions. I've waded into gator dens and chased wildfires with her. She has shared her extensive field notes, journals, photographs, correspondence, and, most importantly, her heart.

It's a heart that is tempestuous and tormented, a crucible of conflict. She is haunted by her past and hated by many of her island neighbors. She violates the wilderness she loves most by living in it. Yet she is also deeply committed to the wild island and has risked her life to defend it.

Her unflinching defense of the wilderness has put her at odds with island families and park managers. Neither of them likes a penniless, pigtailed carcass collector standing in the way of their plans. When a tourist resort is proposed for the island, Carol stops the development. And when hundreds of dead sea turtles inexplicably begin washing ashore, her turtle autopsies help solve the mystery. As she searches for clues, she also discovers something else: herself. A lost and lonely girl finds her way home—and fights like hell to save it.

part one

wild child

1

On a gray winter morning in 1946 in upstate New York, Carol walked to church with her parents. The lacy frills of her dress made her legs itch. They passed the manicured lots of her square-block neighborhood in silence. As they crossed Titus Avenue, her father clasped her five-year-old hand tight.

"Stop scratching," he warned her. "You're worse than a fleabag mutt."

Two cans of tuna were tucked beneath her dress. Her parents did not hear the metal cans thunking as they marched up the steps of United Congregational Church, a red brick edifice with colonial pillars and a domed steeple. Just before the church bell clanged, Carol and her parents scooted into a pew near the back. She fidgeted through the preacher's sermon, which was about a man feeding fish to a hungry crowd. Wedged between her parents, it smelled like roses and bleach.

"Can I go to Sunday School now?" Carol asked.

Her mother frowned. "Go on, then."

Carol dashed down the aisle, but instead of turning down the hall to the classrooms, she creaked open the heavy wooden doors and tiptoed out of the church.

Outside, the wind tussled her dress. She headed straight for the boarded-up high school behind the church. In the empty parking lot, she opened the tuna cans and sat on the curb.

A scrawny black tomcat crept out of a broken window. He was little more than a patchy, threadbare mat of fur draped over a cage of bones, and he devoured the tuna with big bites. As Carol rubbed her hand down his back, he arched his spine and flicked his wiry tail. A low purr rumbled between mouthfuls.

"That's a good boy," she said.

Four more feral cats climbed out of the school windows and jostled for position around the tuna cans. Carol pulled her dress over

her knees to keep out the cold wind. A slant of winter sunlight broke through the tattered clouds, and she felt it warm her cheeks. She didn't need to hear sermons about feeding the hungry. She was doing it.

Then Carol smelled smoke curling from the church chimney and followed its trail down a narrow flight of stairs into the church basement. Carol peered around the corner of the doorway. A silver-haired groundskeeper was tending to a fire in the hearth of the church chimney. The wheelbarrow beside him was loaded with the carcasses of feral cats. One by one, he lifted dead cats by their tails and tossed them into the flames. The fire sparked and popped. She watched the charred flesh of a tabby cat smolder and then ignite until all that remained was the bony skeleton swallowed in orange flames. She wanted to cry. But she also wanted to get closer.

When the groundskeeper left the room, she crept up to the fire. A scorched skull lay buried in the ashes. It seemed shockingly small and naked to Carol, and its exposed teeth made it look more vicious. Is that what she looked like under her skin? She stared into its empty eye sockets for a long time.

Carol was late returning to church. Her parents were waiting for her outside the empty Sunday School classroom. Her father grabbed her hand and yanked her down the hall.

"You smell like barbecue! And your dress is filthy. Where the hell have you been?"

Carol Anne Ruckdeschel was born in Rochester, New York, on December 3, 1941, four days before the Japanese attacked Pearl Harbor. Her parents, Earl and Anne, beamed over their daughter, with chocolate brown eyes and a tangle of brown hair.

Raising a child during World War II was stressful for the young couple. Anne planted a victory garden, and Earl amassed an arsenal of guns. Earl and Anne decided to wait until after the war to have more kids, but when the Japanese surrendered in 1945 they were too exhausted from chasing after their rowdy four-year-old to consider having another. Carol would be an only child, just like her father.

Earl's parents had died of tuberculosis when Earl was barely a toddler. He was raised by his Aunt Mabel and Uncle Free, who themselves never had children. Uncle Free worked as a chemist for Kodak, and despite the Depression-era job shortages he begged his boss to hire Earl as a messenger boy at age fourteen. From the very bottom rung, Earl worked his way up the corporate ladder and became a lab manager for Kodak. "I went up the ranks by following orders and respecting authority," Earl said. "My daughter took a different approach."

Earl was a tall, commanding authoritarian of German descent. His chestnut-brown hair cleanly parted to the right, and his face was chiseled by sharp cheekbones and a wide brow. Despite his stern appearance, he was a lively entertainer, engaging conversationalist, and the life of a party. After a few drinks, Earl could match wits with anyone in the room.

On his way to a meeting with his boss one afternoon, Earl passed by the desk of twenty-four-year-old Anne Rogers, a secretary at Kodak. Short and slender, Anne was dark skinned with round amber eyes, a button nose, and a wide, warm smile. Over the next few weeks, he invented more excuses to visit his boss and eventually asked Anne on a date. One year later, they were married. They moved into a small, two-story suburban box on the same block where Earl's family lived.

Quiet and curious, Anne steadfastly played the role of house-wife but longed for more creative outlets. On summer afternoons, Anne unfurled a blanket beneath a backyard maple tree for her infant daughter while she staked tomatoes and harvested squash from her postage-stamp garden. Later, Anne let her five-year-old daughter roam the neighborhood and play tackle football with older neighborhood boys, despite whispers from neighbors about her uncouth tomboy of a daughter. Anne often took Carol to a nearby creek, where Carol waded in her underwear and caught minnows and tadpoles.

Her mother's leniency stiffened at the end of each day when Earl arrived home from work. He expected a tidy house, a cocktail at five o'clock sharp, and dinner on the table by six. Anne dutifully complied.

Earl prided himself on precision. His grandfather had been a diamond cutter in Germany, and Earl inherited his obsession with intricacy. He tinkered with watches and built his own stonecutting tools so he could transform uncut semiprecious minerals into gems of polished perfection.

But his lifelong passion was guns. Every evening after dinner, he cleaned gun barrels and refashioned stocks to fire with pinpoint accuracy. He collected World War II rifles and pistols, and he taught Carol how to shoot when she was a toddler.

Once, when Earl took Carol to the rifle range, she wandered out onto the range, directly beneath her father's gun. He fired, and the deafening discharge knocked his two-year-old daughter backward. She curled into a ball, clutching her bleeding ear and sobbing. Carol lost 50 percent of her hearing in her right ear that day. It only sharpened her other senses.

Her acuity became apparent one autumn morning when she was five. Carol had feigned illness to stay home from school. Her mom brought in a bowl of tomato soup and a washcloth while Carol looked out the bedroom window. She saw a dark object on the road.

"Look, Ma. It's a turtle."

Anne squinted. "That's just a fallen leaf."

Carol smelled diesel and heard—through her left ear—a distant engine rumble. She sprang out of bed, spilling her soup, and dashed out the front door.

Her mother shouted after her, but Carol was already scampering down the road toward the turtle. Seconds after she plucked him off the pavement, a tow truck rounded the curve. Carol hopped to the shoulder of the road as it barreled past.

Carol filled an old washtub with water and fed the turtle lettuce leaves from their garden. She named the turtle Coon, beginning a lifelong habit of naming pets after other animal species.

Coon would soon have company in the Ruckdeschel basement. With no siblings and few neighborhood children to play with, Carol turned to animals for companionship. By age seven, she was riding her bike to a nearby pond to catch crayfish, frogs, and turtles. She

waded alone into neck-deep water, probing the bottom with her bare feet. One afternoon, her toes bumped something hard in the mud. She dove down into the brown water and scoured the bottom. Suddenly, something pinched her hand sharply and let go. She screamed underwater, sending a torrent of bubbles to the surface. But she still had enough oxygen in her lungs to go back for a closer look. Bedded down in the mud was the largest snapping turtle she had ever seen.

She popped up for air, grabbed a hefty tree branch, and pried up the giant turtle from the bottom of the pond. It was nearly two feet long, with horned ridges on its back. As she lifted it from the mud, she felt like she was unearthing a prehistoric creature, with its long claws, hooked beak, and horned shell. She lifted it by its tail and balanced it headfirst on the handlebars of her bike. At home she filled up the bathtub and kept it hidden for nearly a week. Finally, Earl demanded that she take a bath.

"I don't need to, really. I got clean splashing in the creek today," Carol said.

"You're covered in filth and you stink," Earl replied, dragging his daughter into the bathroom. He pulled back the curtain and jumped back. The snapping beast hissed at him.

"I got whipped that night," Carol said. "My rear was always chapped from whippings. I probably deserved most of them."

For her eighth birthday, Carol received the present she had been hoping for: her dad's broken watch. She immediately grabbed a screwdriver and began disassembling it on the kitchen table. Earl beamed.

Both Carol and her dad loved to tinker. Carol especially savored the time her father spent with her, huddled together over the workbench, taking apart and reassembling watches, radios, lawn mower engines, and, of course, rifles.

"It was the only real quality time we spent together," she said. "I loved sorting through a mess of gears and springs. I always wanted to understand the inner workings of things."

Carol's fascination with how things worked extended beyond the mechanical world and into the biological. As early as age six, Carol was dissecting dead cat carcasses behind the church. She used her pocketknife to slice into the cats, gutting them to see what they had been eating. Often the scrawny feral cats had empty stomachs, but occasionally she'd find partially digested mice. Next, she cut down the legs and shoulders to admire the lean, dark muscles and sinewy tendons attached like guitar strings to mottled gray bones. Finally, she spread open the chest wall, pulled back the ribs and lungs, and found the heart. Even after several days of decay, the meaty red lobes of the heart were distinctly swollen, with arteries branching from the top like a celery stalk.

"The heart is the most beautiful organ, and it always made me feel more alive to see it and touch it," Carol recalled. "When I held the heart's red flesh in my hands, I could feel my own heart beating. Seeing another animal's heart was like looking inside myself."

On weekends, Earl drove country roads, smoking heavily with the windows rolled up, hunting for woodchucks. When he saw one, he'd pull off, crouch, and shoot. Despite the suffocating cigarette smoke, Carol loved accompanying her dad on his Sunday drives, mainly to listen to the radio and to see the dead animals. Earl would examine his kill to see how far his bullet penetrated the woodchuck's skull. Carol was more interested in the animal's anatomy: How did it all fit together inside? How did life work?

Once, Earl took Carol hunting, and he shot a deer. Carol was the first to arrive beside the buck. She knelt beside him, enraptured by his moist brown eyes, so much like her own. She held her hand over the bullet wound in his chest and felt the warmth rise against her palm. Then she watched life flicker from his eyes. Yet nothing had perceptibly changed. The eyes were still brown and wet—only now they were eerily empty.

Later that evening, Earl parked at the edge of the woods. He handed a quarter to Carol and ordered his six-year-old daughter to march fifty feet, extend her arm, and hold the quarter between her thumb and index finger. Earl shouldered his favorite rifle and took

aim at the quarter. Carol saw the barrel pointed toward her, and a flash flood of adrenaline swept through her.

"Stop shaking, dammit!" Earl shouted.

Carol closed her eyes and gritted her teeth. She stood frozen in dark silence, listening for the gunshot. Finally, she heard a metallic clank, followed by the rifle's report echoing through the woods. When she opened her eyes, the quarter was gone.

2

A wave toppled Carol, and she tumbled in a froth of sand and salt-water, her body tossed like seaweed. She couldn't tell which direction was up. Then the wave flowed away, her toes felt firm ground, and she stood, sputtering and ecstatic. The ocean had grabbed her, and it would hold her for life.

When Carol was ten years old, Earl was transferred, and he moved the family to Hawaii for a year. Carol swam in the ocean nearly every day with the dark-skinned native boys. They were intrigued by the tomboy who tracked turtles and caught crabs with her bare hands. She joined their gangs and wrestled with them in the sand.

Carol flourished in both the cultural and natural diversity of the island. Porpoises and sea turtles swam in the canal near their rental apartment. Whenever a sea turtle glided past, Carol would follow it in the canal for miles, all the way out to the bay.

"They're swimming dinosaurs," she told her band of barefoot Hawaiian boys. "They're the oldest animals in the ocean."

"They're also delicious," the boys replied.

At school, Carol hung out with the native Hawaiians more than the white kids. Carol's elementary school was located in the island's affluent business-class neighborhood, and most of her fifth-grade classmates were white or Japanese. However, a handful of native Hawaiians walked barefoot to her school from their villages miles away. Carol absorbed their music, their language, and especially their knowledge of plants and animals. She started dancing and dressing like her Hawaiian friends and walking barefoot every-where. She even convinced her parents that it was customary to attend school barefoot.

"Nobody wears shoes at school. It's just the island way," she explained.

When the bell rang on the final day of class, a herd of kids thundered out of the building and down the school's steps. Earl and

Anne waited at the bottom of the steps with the other parents. The neatly dressed American and Japanese children emerged first. To Earl and Anne's surprise, they were all wearing sneakers and dress shoes. Then came a scraggly group of barefoot, disheveled, dark-skinned natives . . . and Carol.

Carol received one of the worst beatings of her childhood.

That night, bruised and banished to her bedroom, Carol listened to her parents talking through the paper-thin walls.

"What did we do wrong?" her father muttered.

"We didn't do anything wrong," replied her mother.

"I'll beat it out of her if I have to. She responds to the belt."

"That only confuses her. Maybe she'll grow out of it."

Carol opened her window, drowning out her parents with the chorus of crickets and the wash of the tides. A salty breath of wind stirred the trees. She rested her head on the sill and watched sea turtles swim silently through the canal. "Someday I'll have my own island," she dreamed. "I'll walk barefoot every day. I'll always have sand between my toes."

In 1952, Queen Elizabeth was crowned in England, the Big Bang was proposed, the United States detonated the first hydrogen bomb, and Earl Ruckdeschel was offered a promotion to manage the Kodak processing plant in Atlanta, Georgia. After only a year in Hawaii, the Ruckdeschels left island paradise for suburbia. Earl and Anne bought a brick ranch house on the northernmost edge of Atlanta. Although her house faced a well-traveled road, her backyard stretched for miles. She could walk through unbroken forest all the way to the Chattahoochee River. At age eleven, Carol was hiking four miles to the river every weekend, setting crawfish traps, tracking coons, and flipping rocks in search of salamanders.

Her parents had only one rule: be home for the family five o'clock cocktail. Every evening, Earl expected Anne and Carol to join him for a drink—usually martinis or manhattans. Her dad poured Carol her first glass of liquor when she was twelve years old. She felt the beehive tingle on her tongue and was hooked.

In the evenings, Earl polished his guns and gems. Anne knitted while watching television. Neither spent much time with Carol.

"They were traditional, conservative, and walled off," Carol said. "I got used to being by myself. I didn't know anything else, so I didn't know I was lonely. I knew from an early age that I was different. That meant being comfortable with solitude."

Not finding her place at home, she sought it in nature. In the wild, she found companionship in the creek, friendship in the forest, and a kinship with critters that ran deeper than blood.

"Out in nature is where I belong. I love it so much, and it accepts me," Carol wrote when she was fourteen.

At night, Carol slept with her window open and her pillow propped on the sill. The night air calmed and restored her, and even in suburban Atlanta she could still see the Milky Way's soupy river of stars. But as her parents' fights grew louder, she began sleeping in the basement to be closer to her menagerie of animal companions.

Her pets included turtles, salamanders, black-widow spiders, crayfish, frogs, and several snakes—all caught by hand. Once, a possum was killed on the road in front of her house, and the next day, baby possums had gathered around their mother's carcass, attempting to suckle from her withered teats. Carol scooped them up and bottle-fed them in her basement.

Carol especially liked snakes. Once, Carol was chest-deep in a pond searching for a muskrat den when she noticed a swirling ripple a few feet away. Suddenly, a snake's head poked out of the water. It opened its jaws wide, ready to strike Carol's face. Instinctively, she threw up her hand and felt the hot sting of its bite on her forearm. Fear turned to anger. With her other hand, she grabbed the snake's body and hurled it out of the water. Then she scrambled onto shore and pinned its head with a stick. She examined the snake closely. It wasn't a venomous cottonmouth, just a water snake. Blood oozed from puncture wounds on her forearm. She pinched the snake's head and lifted it to eye level.

"I oughta chop your head off. But I'm not gonna join that club," she said, as she recorded later in her journal. "Besides, you're not

worth it, you scrawny thing. If I kill you, I'd have to eat you, and you're not worth the work for such a little morsel of meat."

The snake coiled its body around her wrist and flicked its tongue at her.

"We gotta share this pond, fella." She threw him back in.

Carol skipped church every Sunday. It was all just a bunch of hocus pocus, and she couldn't buy it: some guy walking on water and raising the dead. All these grown people talking about a holy ghost. It didn't mesh with the natural world she knew.

One Sunday morning, she headed down to the river, shovel in hand, to dig up some nettles and cress. The meadow beside the river was alive with birdsong. She high-stepped through the swishing grass and gathered a potato sack full of wild greens. On her way back, she stopped abruptly in her tracks. The rank funk of rot wafted in the air. Buzzards circled overhead. She pulled back the head-high sedge: a giant snapping turtle lay on its side, dried blood staining its muzzle. Its shell was riddled with bullet holes, revealing flecks of pink flesh. A vulture had dragged the turtle's left eyeball out of its socket and was tugging at the long, stringy optic nerve.

Carol used her shovel to flip the carcass. Its skull looked astonishingly human. Beneath the flesh, she and the turtle were the same bag of bones. Someday, she would die and rot like the turtle.

She dropped her sack of greens and, flapping at flies, knelt beside the carcass. Its one remaining eye stared blankly at her. She had clanked her shovel against the bedrock reality of death. Death was not sleeping or even darkness, she realized. It was nothing. Where would she go when she died? Her body would return to the earth. And she would no longer exist. Heavenly sermons suddenly sounded a lot more appealing.

After dinner that evening, Anne washed the dishes while Earl settled in his armchair to clean a gun barrel. A cigarette hung loosely from the corner of his mouth. Carol walked into the living room with an orphaned baby possum hanging by its teeth from her pigtails.

"Take that varmint back to the basement!" Earl growled.

Carol plucked it off her braids and tucked it into her elbow.

"What happens when we die?" she asked.

"If you lived a good life, you go to heaven. If you skip church and lie to your parents, you go to hell."

She looked down at the possum in the crook of her arm. "Do animals go to heaven?"

"Only people go to heaven."

"Where do animals go?"

"They decay into the ground."

"People decay too," Carol said.

"People have souls. Our souls go to heaven when we die."

"Are you sure there's a heaven?"

"That's what faith is for. Faith makes you sure."

That night, Carol walked down to the pond. Fish dimpled the surface, scattering reflected moonlight across the water. She lay back in the dewy grass. The baby possum nibbled on her hair. Stars were dusted like freckles across the sky. Carol thought for a long time about heaven and hell and realized, for the first time in her life, that maybe her dad was wrong. Maybe there was just this one life on earth. She felt a pang in her heart. She desperately wanted her dad to be right, so that she could go to heaven and live forever. That would be a lot easier than rotting into the ground and being eaten by worms. But she could no longer pretend that she was different than other animals. She had to face a hard truth: she was a death-bound being like everything else that breathed.

She closed her eyes and let the darkness settle in. *Is this what death will look like?* she wondered. There wouldn't even be the color black. She felt utterly empty and blank, like the gaze of the turtle carcass in the meadow. She didn't want to die and become nothing. She loved being alive so much.

Then she opened her eyes and looked up again at the blackness between the stars. Her tiny speck of life was utterly insignificant in the sweep of space. Its vastness left her feeling dizzy and disoriented. But it also made her feel something else, something surprisingly close to . . . free. She was completely, utterly free to live her one and only life until she died. Death was as natural and necessary as life, and

both were far older and larger than she had imagined. Each breath connected her to the first algae and the last dinosaur. All the animals that had ever lived and died—they were all part of the same precious matter—and so was she. She belonged to it all, from the stars to the soil. She wasn't nothing. She was everything.

Carol felt solid ground return beneath her. No heaven could be more wondrous than this raw, rotting earth. She vowed to savor the stench of the dead as much as the musk of the living. They were part of the same deepening mystery.

3

Carol ate her first wild meat on a coon hunt in the north Georgia mountains when she was fourteen. She ran ahead of her dad and the other hunters, tracking their dogs at night across creeks and through the dark woods. When the dogs treed the coon, Carol was the first to arrive. She saw the glowing, banded eyes of the frightened raccoon, clinging to the topmost branch of a pine.

Behind her, the bouncing flashlights of the hunters approached. She knew what would likely come next: the men would stand around the tree and shoot at a cornered animal until its lifeless body thudded to the ground.

Carol quickly climbed up the tree. She could see the parade of flashlights getting closer. The coon inched as high as it could up the spindly pine. Carol squatted a foot below and whispered: "Hey coon. You gotta jump! It's your only chance!"

The dogs barked below them. She heard the swishing and crunching of leaves underfoot.

"Do you hear me, cooner? When you hit the ground, you can't stumble, or the dogs will be on you. Land on your feet and run. Now go!" She shook the limb until finally the raccoon released its grip, plunged thirty feet, and nearly landed on top of a baying hound. The coon rolled once and then was on its feet, running through the woods again, the dogs close behind.

The hunters arrived moments later. In the pine tree, Carol held her breath and listened.

"I thought for sure the hounds had it treed," her dad said.

"Them dogs ain't worth their feed," said one of the other hunters.

They shuffled on. Carol waited until their lights crossed the creek before climbing down.

Despite Carol's efforts, the coon did not live to see morning. When the hunters served coon the next day for lunch, she decided that the best way to honor the coon would be to eat him.

"Your flesh becomes mine," she whispered before tasting her first bite, a daily grace she would recite for the rest of her life.

Carol convinced her father to bring home one of the hunter's stray dogs, a male German shepherd mutt that Carol named Catfish. For the first time, Carol had a best friend. She and her partner in grime wandered the banks of the Chattahoochee. She caught fish and crawdads and cooked them over a campfire in an old Cherokee cave she had discovered along the bluffs. The cave became her den, a refuge where she retreated from the emptiness of her everyday life.

Caves are powerful and primeval places. They were among the earliest human shelters, and the first etchings of human art appeared deep in their bowels. Saint John received revelations in a cave, and Plato used a cave to explain reality. For Carol, the cave was home. She spent most of her teenage years camping in her cave above the river, with Catfish snuggled up beside her.

On weekends, she carried two inflatable inner tubes down to the river to float the Hooch, which was still wild and unpolluted in the 1950s. Carol watched trout spawn in the cold, clear waters. The river teemed with beavers, muskrats, and giant pike, and herons and egrets lined the banks, stalking on stilts, spearing fish.

One afternoon, Carol and Catfish got caught in a downpour. The swollen river became a thundering torrent of roaring white-water. Carol's inner tube flipped, and she fell into a rapid. Bubbles and foam engulfed her. She fought for air as the circulating water churned her repeatedly like a washing machine on spin cycle. After nearly a minute, she began to panic, flailing harder against the weight of the water.

In the frothy chaos, she tried one last desperate option: sink like a stone. Rather than fight for the surface, she went limp and let the current take her. It spun her around once more, then thrust her down to the bottom of the river, below the circulating water. The current flushed her downstream, finally spitting her out 30 yards from the rapid. Purple-lipped and foggy-headed, she swam over to an eddy along the bank. She hugged a boulder, still gasping and coughing up river. Moments later, she felt Catfish's wet tongue on her forehead.

* * *

Walking back from the river with Catfish, Carol took a shortcut through the woods along a gravel road. Along the way, they passed an old trailer with a collapsing wooden porch and rusted metal roof. The yard was littered with tires and scrap metal, and a pit bull was chained to a stake. The dog barked and lunged at Carol as she passed.

It was getting dark, and she still had several miles to go. She had already missed five o'clock drinks, and her dad would be boiling mad. Suddenly, she heard clanking metal behind her. The pit bull had ripped his stake from the soggy ground and was charging her.

Catfish dove at the pit bull before it reached Carol, and the dogs tumbled, jaws at each other's necks. Carol shouted at the dogs and tried to kick them apart. Her pants got shredded and her legs were gored. The pit bull slashed at Catfish, but Catfish pounced and momentarily pinned the pit bull, baring her gums and teeth. Carol grabbed the pit bull's chain and dragged him back down the road. He cowered under a pickup truck, licking his wounds.

Then a light clicked on inside the trailer. A shirtless, beer-bellied man wearing cut-off jean shorts and cowboy boots stomped down the wooden steps. A wad of chewing tobacco was tucked beneath his lower lip. His bloodied pit bull limped over to him, panting heavily. He grabbed a rod of steel rebar from his front yard and walked toward Carol and Catfish.

"I'm gonna beat the shit out of your dog," he said.

Carol picked up a big stick. "No you're not."

The man stopped a few feet from her. Carol stood her ground. He eyed her closely: a scrappy teenage girl, wearing tattered, blood-soaked jeans, hammer-gripping a sharp stick.

After a long silence, he dropped the rebar, spat his chew, and clunked back to his trailer.

Carol confounded the boys in high school. They didn't know whether to fight or French kiss her. She was a hard-bodied hellion who dressed ruggedly, but beneath the jeans and flannel, she was sun-kissed and sensuous. Carol had developed into a natural knockout, a drop-dead

gorgeous girl with curves and confidence. Lean and athletic, with fawn eyes and long, raven hair often braided down her back, she wore no makeup and rarely brushed her hair, yet she was radiantly beautiful.

Her reticence only added to her intrigue. Several boys had crushes on Carol, but few could break through her steely silence. Despite her confidence in the woods, she felt vulnerable and shy around people. No one had taught her how to chitchat, flirt, or gossip.

She knew that boys liked her and figured out quickly what they wanted. While playing tackle football, she felt the neighborhood boys groping for more than pigskin, and she had enjoyed getting tangled up in the surf with the Hawaiian natives.

But in high school, the social scene became more complex. Neighborhood boys became varsity lettermen with frilly-dressed girls tucked in their arms. Nevertheless, they were still intrigued by the mysterious, dark-haired nature girl who was smarter than her teachers but barely attended class. She could outdrink and outcuss even the toughest punks.

She liked the boys' attention and craved their touch. But for her, it wasn't worth painting her face and dressing like a princess. So she remained an outsider. Her classmates called her a tomboy, and in the 1950s tomboys were stigmatized and scorned, even when they were as sassy and sexy as Carol.

Two million years of evolution had hard-wired human beings—male and female alike—to explore nature, Carol reasoned. Why, then, was outdoor play still considered boy behavior?

Certainly, physiological gender differences exist between men and women. On average, women tend to be shorter and carry more body fat to aid in childbirth. They typically have fewer oxygen-carrying red blood cells and smaller hearts. Because they have far less testosterone, women tend to have less body hair, a much smaller Adam's apple, and less muscle mass.

But when it comes to endurance, women close the gap and even surpass men. On average, women can walk, run, and swim for longer periods of time than men. That's because women's smaller size makes

them more efficient, and over long distances and durations, more fat is burned, giving women a metabolic edge.

The claim that women are the weaker sex doesn't hold up—not even in prehistoric times. Our far-roaming hunter-gatherer ancestors were long-distance travelers. Even as primitive women bore, nursed, and reared children, they gathered wild foods and trekked long distances, often with multiple kids on their backs. They were just as hardy and adroit as the males, and they required a deep, intimate knowledge of the natural world for their own survival and the sustenance of their kin.

Nature, then, has never been solely the domain of men. If social norms and pressures were stripped away, nearly all girls would climb trees and scrape their knees. Nature requires a thick-skinned toughness for survival in both genders. But in the stiff, stereotyped suburbia of the 1950s, it was tougher than ever to be a tomboy.

Carol drifted through high school. She occasionally met up with a gaggle of gossipy girls to drink beer at the river bluff, but even that seemed juvenile to Carol, who had been drinking hard liquor every night with her parents since she was twelve.

She knew more than many of her teachers, and they didn't like being shown up by a scruffy slacker. "Biology was easy for me. It was like breathing," Carol recalled. "The teachers knew what the book said, but they didn't know biology. I could learn more at the river than in the classroom."

Carol skipped homework and headed for the woods, where she could learn from her favorite teacher. She recorded her observations in journals filled with exhaustive notes and exquisitely intricate sketches. She dissected birds, bats, and beavers to teach herself animal anatomy and physiology. She wasn't sure what she wanted to do with her life, but she knew for certain what she didn't want to do.

"I am not going to work at a job that I don't like until I can retire," she told her father. "I want a life outdoors."

"When are you gonna grow up? You can't make a living playing with turtles and snakes," he replied.

"I refuse to squander my life breathing stale air in an office cubicle. I need contact with the real world."

"How are you gonna put a roof over your head without income? What are you gonna do for food? Eat out of the dumpster?"

Carol felt trapped. She wanted to immerse herself in the wild, but she couldn't afford a house or land in the woods. The only way she could stay close to nature was to pare down her needs and live simply and frugally. There were two sides to every balance sheet, Carol realized.

"I knew I had to structure my life around not wanting much, so that I wouldn't require resources to support myself financially," she said. "I would have to find the resources inside myself."

Or along the road.

While hiking to the river one afternoon when she was seventeen, Carol stepped over a freshly killed squirrel carcass along the shoulder of the road. Suddenly, it occurred to her: free food! She pulled out her steel knife and sliced open the squirrel. The dark, moist tenderloin was better than anything she could buy. Instead of prepackaged, chemical-injected meat from the store, Carol could harvest all the wild meat she wanted from the side of the road.

She began collecting and tasting every animal carcass she came across: raccoon, possum, snake, bird, rabbit, turtle, even fox. Her criteria were simple: if it had a decent amount of unsmashed meat and it didn't smell completely rancid, it was good enough to eat.

With free food along the road and shelter in her cave beside the river, Carol began plotting her escape from stale, suffocating suburban life. Her exodus became even more urgent a few years later.

One night, Earl was in the basement showing off his World War II gun collection at a party. A neighbor's teenage son went over to examine a revolver that Earl had been demonstrating. Unseen, he loaded a bullet in the chamber.

"Put that down, boy!" Earl shouted, and snatched the revolver out of his hands. Then he turned and showed the gun to his friend Tom Dickey, brother of the celebrated author of *Deliverance*, James Dickey.

"This is a military .45 with a special lockout," Earl said. He explained that the lockout was a safety feature in case an enemy soldier grabbed it in close combat. Whenever the barrel was pressed against a person's chest, the gun locked up and wouldn't fire. That way, an officer's gun could not be used against him.

"How can a gun know how to lock itself?" Tom asked.

"I'll show you." Earl held the pistol against his chest and pulled the trigger. Halfway back, the trigger locked.

"The gun isn't loaded, but even if it had bullets, the trigger will lock when the gun's barrel is fully pushed in by someone's chest."

Earl demonstrated again, this time on Tom. He pressed the gun into his chest and pulled the trigger. It locked again.

"That's amazing!" said Tom.

"Now, if I pull the trigger without the barrel pushed in by someone's chest, the trigger unlocks and works just fine." He nonchalantly pointed the gun off to the side and pulled the trigger, unaware that the gun had been loaded. Earl expected to hear an empty click. Instead, a bullet exploded from the chamber. It ricocheted off Earl's table saw and struck Carol in the abdomen.

Carol felt a gust of wind blow through her. There was no pain, only a whoosh of dizziness. She steadied herself against a chair. The room was silent. Carol didn't realize she had been shot until her mom saw blood soaking through Carol's white shirt.

"Oh my God! Oh my God! Oh my God!" her mom screamed.

The room erupted in bedlam, but Carol felt strangely detached and calm. She pressed her left hand against her abdomen, concerned that her guts might spill out. Earl carried Carol out to the car and laid her in the backseat while Tom called the hospital. The paramedics met Carol at the emergency room entrance, loaded her onto a gurney, and rushed into the operating room.

The bullet had barely missed her stomach and only nicked her small intestine. "I probably could have crawled under a bush and made it," Carol said. But the surgery had split her abdomen, and she spent one long, miserable week recuperating in the hospital. "The only thing that got me through that week was the ice cream," she said.

Seven days after being shot by her father, she was tromping the wild woods again; she held no grudge but she never looked back.

After graduating from high school, she camped in her cave beside the river, testing her self-taught, self-reliant outdoor skills. She bathed in the Chattahoochee and drank from its springs. She scavenged road-killed raccoons and squirrels, then cooked the meat over campfires and shared the bones with Catfish. She fished from the river and gathered salads of violets, dandelions, chickweed, shepherd's purse, sow thistle, and watercress. There was plenty of food—even on the outskirts of the South's largest metropolis—to eat well year-round.

In the evenings, she sat atop the bluffs and scribbled in her journal. "Tonight the fireflies are truly in competition with the stars!" she wrote. "Where the bluffs meet the sky, it is impossible to tell them apart. As always, I wish for a human companion to share this with."

It was a lonely but life-changing summer: she proved that she could live on her own terms, by her own rules, without money or a steady job. In her cave beside the river, Carol made a lifelong promise to herself:

"I'll get as far away from the fighting and from expectations as I possibly can. I'll live according to my own rules. And the only way to live wild and free is to not need money. I can't allow myself to want things, because I'll have to get a job and stay locked in that way of life. I don't belong there. I belong out here."

4

But her father's words still echoed in her ears like a gunshot: "Grow up and get over turtles and snakes. You can't make money playing in the woods." So after a summer of living in a cave, Carol reluctantly enrolled at the University of Georgia (UGA) in the fall of 1959.

"I've gotta do this," she told herself. "I'll try to fit in, at least temporarily. I'll play the game for as long as I can stand it. I'll save every penny to buy my freedom in the forest."

With money she had saved washing windows, Carol bought a used jeep with a burned-out clutch stuck in a mud hole for $50. She drove it to UGA and plodded through the boring basics in freshman lecture halls. She couldn't wait to take advanced biology classes. Her intro seminars seemed like a regurgitation of ninth grade.

She felt even more alienated by the football-frenzied atmosphere of a Division I university. Most of the girls in her dorm were snobby Southern belles seeking a husband, not a degree. Worst of all was the curfew: the dorm was locked at 10 p.m. sharp, and curfew violations meant immediate expulsion.

"I wasn't used to being confined," Carol recalled. "After wandering free in the woods for most of my life, suddenly I was incarcerated every night."

Two weeks into the semester, Carol returned to Atlanta for a long weekend. Her parents had already purged the basement of Carol's critters, which infuriated her. She stormed out of the house and headed for the river. She missed the sound of murmuring water, the slap of a beaver's tail, the shriek of a red-shouldered hawk circling overhead. Her homesickness evaporated as she strolled alongside the riverbank.

The next day, she stopped at the neighborhood gas station near her parents' house, which was owned by her friend Richard Kiker, a thirty-year-old mechanic. She had spent a lot of time with him that

summer working on her jeep. A shock of tawny hair swept across his forehead. His sky-blue eyes were vast.

"Where ya headed?" he asked her.

"A quiet spot beside the river."

"Mind if I tag along?" he asked.

He told his attendant to run the register, and he hopped into the jeep with Carol. They spent the afternoon drinking beer and skipping stones from the shoals. She had never spent a day beside the river with anyone other than Catfish. She was bewildered by the ease and giddiness she felt.

They hung their bare feet off a sun-warmed boulder and talked for hours. Richard confided that he had disappointed his parents, who had hoped he would become a dentist. Instead of filling teeth, he was filling gas tanks. He also told Carol about his ex-wife and two kids, and how he was struggling with the pressures of business and family.

"I thought life would be more fun than this," he confessed. "I'm stuck."

Carol drained her beer. "Then get out of the rut. Cut a new path."

"That goes where? To dental school? To another dead-end job? I've gotta feed my family. I can't just float down the river like you."

Carol saw the buried sadness in his bottomless blue eyes.

They sat on the hood of Carol's jeep and watched the sun sink beneath the wispy braid of river. Fish rippled circles on the water.

Carol headed back to college the next morning. On her way out of town, she stopped by Richard's station to top off her tank.

"Don't break too many hearts in Athens," he told her.

"I'm not looking for love, just a piece of paper—my ticket to freedom."

The Georgia Bulldogs, led by freshman quarterback Fran Tarkenton, were hosting Alabama for the 1959 season opener at Sanford Stadium. Tarkenton had a breakout game, passing for 200 yards and two

touchdowns, and the Bulldogs defense shut down the Crimson Tide in a 17–3 rout. Athens was ecstatic. Inebriated fans flooded the streets.

Carol, meanwhile, was cloistered in her dorm room dissecting the innards of a white-footed mouse carcass she had found on campus. When the dorm supervisor knocked on the door, Carol quickly stashed the mouse platter in her desk drawer.

The supervisor was an overweight woman with round glasses resting atop puffy, red cheeks, whose allergy-clogged nostrils didn't notice the dead mouse stench. "Carol, there's a phone call for you," she said flatly.

Carol walked down the hall and picked up the phone. It was her parents, calling with tragic news: Richard Kiker had committed suicide. He had driven his car into one of the garage bays at the service station, connected one end of a garden hose to the tailpipe, ran the other end into the passenger compartment, sat down behind the steering wheel, and left it all behind.

Carol hung up the receiver and walked numbly back to her room. She sat on her bed in the dark. Her roommate was already asleep. After a long, empty silence, Carol unlatched the second-story window and climbed down. The breeze woke her roommate.

"Where are you going?" her roommate called through the open window.

"To get drunk."

At an Athens bar, Carol tossed back shots of whiskey and replayed the scenes of her friendship with Richard. She felt a cocktail of emotions: sadness, grief, loss, and a sharp pinch of guilt. Did she completely miss his cries for help? Could she have done something? Carol had hoped the river would heal him, as it had healed her. But inside, he was already drowning.

Around midnight, Carol stumbled across the empty quad, still littered with beer bottles from the afternoon's postgame revelry, and crept back to her dorm. She climbed woozily onto the first-floor window ledge, steadied herself against the building with one hand, then performed a one-armed pull-up to reach the narrow

second-story ledge outside her window. A few pebbles tumbled off the crumbling ledge. Then Carol slid the window open and stepped through.

The next morning, the dorm supervisor knocked at her door again. "You were spotted walking across the quad past curfew last night."

Carol stared at the floor.

"Start packing," she said through pursed lips. "You're expelled."

Carol believed that the price of anything is the amount of life you exchange for it. Nothing was more valuable to her than a life outdoors. She wanted to live where she could explore rugged back-country by day and see the stars at night. To get there, she realized, she would have to sacrifice a few young years. So Carol traded in her twenties working in Atlanta, hoping to scrape up enough money to buy land and a lifetime of freedom.

She tried to fit in to city life. Though she dressed differently than the well-heeled professionals around her, she noticed that they shared one thing in common: they, too, craved the wild, even in the climate-controlled confines of the city. Without untamed country to explore, city people instead pursued the undiscovered terrain of other bodies. Sex was a primitive and animalistic intrusion into an otherwise sanitized life. People were dressed-up animals disguising their animal thoughts with button-down etiquette. Without the natural world to satisfy their wild hunger, city dwellers sought it in one another, getting liquored and laid in the overpeopled urban jungle.

But neither sex nor drink could fill the gaping hole in Carol's wild heart. Lost and lonely, she spent nearly a decade scratching out a life in Atlanta, taking odd jobs to make ends meet. They didn't come easy.

"A woman can't do this kind of work," said Jim Kemph, manager of the Buckhead Radio Service Company in Atlanta. In 1959, women

didn't get their hands greasy fixing machines. How could a bronzed teenage girl know her way around a mechanic's shop?

Carol stormed out of Jim's shop, disconnected the broken radio from her jeep, and marched back in, swinging the door wide open against its hinges, the doorbell clanging loudly against the glass. She walked behind the counter past Jim and slammed the radio down on the shop's workbench. Without saying a word, she deftly removed the chassis and frayed speaker wires in less than a minute. Then she soldered the wires, reassembled the radio, and cranked up the volume to Johnny Cash's "I Walk the Line" in the parking lot outside the store. Jim hired her on the spot.

Jim was a trim, hardworking forty-four-year-old father of six children. His cinnamon-brown hair was beginning to gray after managing the repair shop on a bustling corner of Buckhead Avenue for nearly two decades. Like Carol's father, Jim was a polished conversationalist whose charisma and confidence kept the customers returning. Jim even resembled her father: tall, handsome, with a sharp, angular German nose and high cheekbones.

Jim's shop was cluttered with old televisions, dismantled record players, and antique radios. In the back corner was a metal detector used in World War II to search for land mines.

"Does it still work?" Carol asked him as the shop was closing one Friday afternoon.

"I think the coils are fried. I used it for years to search for Civil War relics around Atlanta. Then my kids arrived."

Carol tinkered with the metal detector over the weekend. She decided to test it out near the battlegrounds of the Battle of Atlanta, where General Sherman's troops killed over twelve thousand Confederates on their march to the sea.

On a moonless Saturday night, Carol swept the metal detector all around the overgrown battlefield grounds. Only the faint glow of distant streetlights shone through the forest. She waved the detector over a muddy swale and suddenly the receiver erupted with pulses. Like a hungry dog digging for a bone, she hastily shoveled away the dirt with her bare hands, unearthing a brass oval buckle with three letters engraved on it.

On Monday morning, she returned the metal detector to Jim, then casually asked, "Do you happen to know what the letters CSA stand for?"

Jim's eyes widened. "Confederate States of America." He smiled. "What have you been up to?"

Carol revived Jim's interest in Civil War relic hunting, and soon they were scouring sites together, often late at night. One evening, they went out to Stone Mountain, a sixteen-hundred-foot rock dome near Atlanta with a monumental carving of three Confederate leaders chiseled into its north face. Stone Mountain had recently been turned into an amusement park with a golf course, an aerial tram, and a giant broadcast tower atop the summit. "We defile every square inch," Carol lamented. "The Indians held Stone Mountain in such high esteem. Then we come along and take a big shit on it."

The following weekend, she and Jim explored a Civil War trench beneath an old bridge along the Chattahoochee River. Afterward, they hiked up to Carol's cave, where they drank bourbon and watched a full moon rise over the bluffs.

Jim was twenty-six years older than Carol—nearly the same age as her father—but that didn't step them from becoming closer. She continued working at the shop during the day and joining him on late-night relic hunting adventures. Soon they were traveling further afield, exploring larger battlefield sites throughout the South. Once, they journeyed together to Fort Pulaski along the Georgia coast. In 1863, the Union Army had fired the first long-distance rifled cannons at Fort Pulaski which obliterated the Confederate fort's walls from a mile away and transformed the tactics of the Civil War. Carol and Jim were determined to find some of those fort-smashing cannonballs.

Some of the shells landed in the marsh, so on a cold, starry night in early December, they borrowed scuba gear and headed for the fort. They parked Jim's station wagon behind some palmetto about a half mile away and crept in. Carol donned the scuba mask and waded into the marsh, while Jim watched from the shore. With an underwater flashlight, she plunged down to explore the soft, muddy bottom keeping an eye out for alligators.

After an hour underwater, Carol heard the oxygen tank echoing. Her skin was numb, her lips purple and swollen. She had lost sensation in her fingers and toes. Just before she turned back and headed for shore, Carol pulled back the cordgrass and noticed a rusted metal ball sunken in marsh mud. She pried it up, and found another cannonball beneath it, and then another. She unearthed six cannonballs from the marsh that night, dragging each of the large shells out of the water and heaving them onto dry land.

Jim was ecstatic. They rolled the cannonballs under the fence and loaded them in the back of the station wagon. The rear bumper nearly scraped the pavement, sagged by the weight of six hundred pounds of Civil War artillery. They couldn't completely close the back door, so Carol—still shivering in her wet clothes—climbed atop the cannonballs and held the back door shut while Jim motored down the empty two-lane road toward town.

Just before they crossed the intracoastal bridge, blue lights flashed in the rearview mirror.

"Carol, grab the tarp!" Jim shouted between clenched teeth as he pulled the station wagon to the shoulder. The police car parked directly behind him. Carol yanked a battered green tarp over both her and the cannonballs while still holding the back gate partially closed.

The officer approached the car slowly. "Keep your hands on the wheel!" he shouted at Jim, who stared blankly into the midnight darkness. The cop shone his flashlight through the back windows. Through a hole in the tarp, Carol could see the officer's breath fogging the glass.

Finally he arrived at Jim's window. Jim white-knuckled the steering wheel, jaw locked, as the cop flashed his light through the open window. He asked for Jim's license and then studied it for a long time. Finally he clicked off his flashlight.

"Mr. Kemph," the officer said, "did you know that your left taillight is out?"

"No sir. I'll get that fixed tomorrow."

He handed back Jim's license. "Have a good evening."

* * *

Back in Atlanta, Martha Kemph wondered why her husband was spending late nights and long weekends away from home. She had met Jim's new employee, the lewd jezebel who cursed and drank and wore baggy men's clothes. But she didn't suspect any mischief from her husband of nineteen years, especially with Carol, who was only three years older than their eldest daughter.

A devoted wife and devout Christian, Martha prayed for her husband every evening in her empty bedroom, after packing lunches for six children and getting them all tucked in.

One night, Jim came home late, half-drunk, with bad news: the radio store business was going under. Martha couldn't believe it. He had been working late hours and spending more time than ever at the shop.

There was only one way to stop the bank from seizing the house and the car, Jim told her: they must get a divorce.

Martha stood in stunned, horrified silence.

Jim explained his plan: once they divorced, he would deed the house to her and then declare bankruptcy. That way, at least she and the kids would have a place to live.

Martha quietly consented to a divorce, though they didn't tell their children. Martha's parents came to live with her and help raise the kids, while Jim indulged in a midlife crisis with a woman half his age.

Carol's friend Tom Dickey was also a Civil War relic hunter. He specialized in defusing artillery. In the spring of 1962, Carol and Jim brought him a hand grenade they found near the river. Tom began disassembling the grenade on his workbench in the basement.

Tom's basement was lined floor to ceiling with shelves containing mine balls, shrapnel, unexploded projectiles, artillery shells, and

other Civil War treasures dug up from Atlanta backyards, swamps in South Carolina, and Louisiana bayous.

"Don't you worry about all of the explosives you have down here?" Carol asked.

"I do fret about it some. If this house caught on fire, you'd hear the last shots fired of the Confederacy."

Tom removed the grenade plug and set it aside. He unsealed the grenade's powder chamber. Carol inched closer, buzzed with adrenaline. Jim crept out the basement door.

Tom safely emptied the gunpowder and then filled the powder chamber with water. He tossed the reassembled grenade to Carol, who gingerly caught it with her fingertips.

"You're holding history. Handle it with care."

Carol found Jim sitting in a lawn chair in Tom's backyard. His eyes were wet and pleading. "Let's get married," he said.

Carol was shell-shocked. "You're already married," she replied.

"That's a formality. Martha and I are getting a divorce."

"I don't know, Jim. You've got a family. You've got kids."

"And you've got nothing. So you've got nothing to lose."

She felt the heaviness of the grenade in her trembling hands. "All right," she whispered.

She felt no explosion of emotion, no flare of feelings. Just a wet fizzle.

Jim and Carol quietly married in a civil ceremony in north Georgia in 1962. She was twenty years old.

"It was a mistake. I was lost. I had nothing else, no direction, no idea what to do with my life," Carol recalled. "I was still trying to obey my parents and do what everyone else does: get married, have children, fit in. Only it didn't work."

Jim and Carol's marriage lasted less than a year. They moved into a public housing apartment together and continued relic hunting for a while, but already cracks were fissuring through their fragile relationship. Jim continued visiting Martha and the kids. Carol spent more time alone in the woods.

"I was going through the motions," Carol said. "There was no glue to hold us together. Deep down, we both knew there was nothing to our relationship but a few cheap thrills."

Jim and Carol divorced in 1963. Jim moved back in with Martha, and his children barely noticed his absence. He kept the radio shop afloat and rejoined his family. Carol got a divorce certificate and a few rusted cannonballs, the last shots of their confederacy.

5

"I've given normal life a fair shot, and it didn't work out," Carol wrote in her journal after the divorce. "So I've finally decided to do what I'd wanted to do all along: immerse myself in the study of nature." In 1966, she enrolled in biology classes at Georgia State University in Atlanta. Never before had she been surrounded by a community of people who cherished nature like she did.

Among them was renowned river ecologist Dr. Charles Wharton. Head of the biology department, Wharton literally wrote the textbook on Southern ecology. He was a six-foot-six, blue-eyed beanpole, with auburn hair and a warm, magnetic smile. He spoke slowly and thoughtfully, with Spanish moss hanging off his long, gentrified syllables. On the first day of Biology 101, Wharton arrived five minutes late to the lecture hall. He glided to the podium in long, smooth strides and then stood silently for several moments to scan the audience. His eyes stopped on Carol, seated in the front row.

"Human culture is built around monogamy, but our biology is not," he began. "Most animals have multiple sexual partners. Only 3 percent of species exhibit monogamous pair bonding. Monogamy" he concluded, "is not natural."

He paused, allowing his words to sink in. A few students shifted uncomfortably in their seats. Guys in the back row smirked. Carol raised her hand.

"Lots of animals mate for life," Carol said, and rattled off a list, including her two favorites, vultures and turtles.

Wharton smiled. "Most still cheat," he said. "Cheating ensures more genetic mixing and a better chance that offspring will survive."

Sex is as wild in nature as it is among humans, Wharton maintained. Goshawks fornicate ten times a day. Oystercatchers like threesomes: they form partnerships of two females and one male. Snails shoot a dart into their partners to prolong copulation. Bonobos

engage in erotic behavior, including genital rubbing, tongue kissing, and oral sex, Wharton explained.

He and Carol sparred throughout the semester, and their debates often continued after class. They began meeting regularly in his office for long conversations, then adjourned to the bar for drinks and more provocative discourse.

Like her father and her ex-husband, Charlie Wharton was a charismatic and authoritative figure with a keen intellect. He was also twenty years older than her.

Age wasn't important to Carol. It was just a number. And after her affair with Jim, she wasn't looking for entertainment anymore. Brains were what mattered most to her. "I didn't want to roll over and wonder, 'Who's this?'" she said. "I'd rather have something to talk about."

She had a lot to talk about with Charlie. For the first time in her life, Carol had met someone who shared her love for the natural world. Their heated discussions soon inflamed other passions, and the line between teacher and student began to blur.

They traveled together from the mountains to the coastal islands of Georgia conducting fieldwork. One afternoon, Charlie took Carol to a tributary of the Chattahoochee River not far from her childhood stomping grounds. For two decades, Charlie had gathered specimens from the creek. He knew it better than anyone—except Carol. She had been exploring the creek since she was in sixth grade and knew every unturned rock and eddy pool.

They hiked the creek up to Carol's cave, tucked beneath an outcropping in the bluffs, and hung their bare feet off the edge. For once, they didn't talk. They just listened, silent in each other's presence, the river chattering below.

A few years earlier, Carol had gotten drunk in the cave after relic hunting with Jim. With Charlie, it was different. Carol felt something new and surprisingly unscientific, like the heart-catching moment of seeing her first sea turtle in the Hawaiian canal. It was something mysterious, frightening, irrational, and perhaps uniquely human. Whatever it was, there was only one word for it: love.

Charlie, a forty-four-year-old bachelor, was smitten by this savvy, sexy undergrad with smoldering brown eyes who knew more about salamanders and snakes than most of his colleagues. Carol was equally fearless around tenured professors and twelve-foot alligators.

On weekends, he drove her to his cabin in the north Georgia mountains. It was at the end of a long gravel road, surrounded by virgin forests and pristine, free-flowing creeks. Carol quickly be-friended the locals living deep in the hollers. From one mountain woman named Mamie, she learned how to make soap from wood ashes, how to track a bee to its honey tree, and where to harvest wild morels, ramps, and ginseng. Carol visited her often and im-bibed her backwoods wisdom. She was dead set on learning the storehouse of skills and lore from old-timers like Mamie before they were gone.

Late one evening, Carol and Charlie were searching for sala-manders in the headwaters of the Tallulah River. Charlie knelt down in the ice-cold, ankle-deep water and proposed. Carol threw her arms around him.

"He is the one," Carol told her mom afterward.

"He's your teacher," she replied. "He's twenty years older than you."

"We'll make it work."

"You said that last time."

"I'm in love with him. He loves what I love."

"He loves one thing."

Carol and Charlie married and lived in Atlanta while they fin-ished building the mountain cabin. Carol continued working toward her biology degree, although she ended up spending most of her time cooking meals and cleaning house.

"I couldn't cook like his mom," Carol recalled. "He wanted my spaghetti sauce to taste exactly like hers."

Carol held on to her dreams of living with Charlie in the mountains—and maybe even raising a few kids who would run wild in the woods with her. She had never before considered hav-

ing a child, but with Charlie she could see a future with children for the first time.

"What do you think about having kids?" Carol asked him one afternoon, rocking in the porch swing of the half-built cabin.

"I already have hundreds of them in my lecture halls."

"I mean children of our own."

"Are you serious?"

Carol stopped the rocking porch swing with her feet. She steadied herself beside him. "It might be fun," she said.

"Aren't we already having fun?"

"Sure."

"Let's not spoil it then."

One semester before Carol was to graduate, Charlie convinced her to drop out of college so she could spend more time at home and help him with research. For the next year, she gathered specimens for his studies—while also editing his publications, grading his students' papers, washing his laundry, and ironing his shirts.

Then one brisk October morning, as the first bright leaves twirled from the trees, Carol suggested that they head to the mountain cabin for the weekend.

"I've got some writing to do. Go on without me," Charlie mumbled, nose in a book, pen in his mouth, surrounded by towers of scientific journals on his desk.

So Carol drove up to northwest Georgia alone. Autumn colors were already spilling down the slopes. During her hike up Pigeon Mountain, not far from Charlie's cabin, Carol stumbled upon a cave along its north face. She tucked her baggy jeans into black, knee-high fireman's boots and slushed through the shin-deep water gurgling from the chasm. She shone her flashlight into every crack in the limestone searching for critters. Bats stirred overhead.

Then, wedged between two jagged fins of rock, Carol spotted a salamander she had never seen before: it was rusty brown, with an olive band and a slate-black belly. It was the largest salamander she had come across—nearly seven inches long, with a spotted,

flattened tail. She plucked the salamander from the crevice and examined it more closely: it had an elongated toe on each foot, which enabled it to climb slick cave walls and rock faces. Could this be a new species?

Carol dashed down the mountain with her salamander and sped straight back to Atlanta, not even stopping to pick up a fresh coon carcass near Chatsworth. She burst into the house, eager to show Charlie.

He was with another woman.

A few days later, Carol returned to pack up her belongings, all of which fit inside a single cardboard box. He met her on the porch as she was about to leave.

"I'm sorry, Carol."

"What did I do wrong?" Her voice trembled.

"Nothing. It's just . . . I feel cramped. I guess I'm just not ready to settle down."

"Then why did you marry me?"

"I don't know." A misty drizzle pattered the leaves. He tugged on his vest. "I warned you the first day I laid eyes on you: monogamy doesn't come naturally to me." Then he turned and walked back into the house, the screen door slapping behind him.

For months, Carol felt anesthetized, like a specimen floating in formaldehyde. Her parents blamed her for a second failed marriage. Her few remaining friends and colleagues sided with the distinguished professor. Years of her life had been utterly wasted, her heart bled dry.

It turned out that Carol's salamander was indeed a new species. It was named the Pigeon Mountain salamander, and today it is on Georgia's rare and endangered list. But not even the salamander discovery could lift her spirits. Listless and vacant, she shuffled through each day and slept fitfully at night. Weeks and

months sloughed past uncalendared. The gloom was tightening its grip.

She needed to get as far away as she could. But where? The mountains were too close and still too painful. So one rainy afternoon, she hopped in her jeep and drove down the Georgia coast to the wildest spot on the map: Cumberland Island.

Cumberland was one of the biggest and most biologically rich islands in North America. It was also the most beauteous bottom jewel in a necklace of barrier islands lining the Georgia coast called the Golden Isles—so named for the amber marsh grasses flanking their shores. The immense island—over eighteen miles from tip to tip, about the size of Manhattan—was home to a greater diversity of life than a tropical rain forest.

For Carol, the sand between her toes brought back memories of her childhood on the beaches of Hawaii, tracking sea turtles and tumbling in the tide. She climbed Cumberland's towering dunes, her ears ringing with the roar of the ocean, and gazed out across the bare beach. Thousands of terns flocked along the foamy surf. Pelicans skimmed the water, their wingtips brushing the whitecaps. On the beach, she splashed saltwater on the back of her neck, then across her face. She tasted the brine and knew she was home.

The next day, Carol hiked across the entire island. She began atop the high bluffs that rim the western edge of Cumberland Island, pocked with irregular humps—Native American burial mounds that had never been excavated. Then she began a shoe-sucking slog through the marsh. To Carol, the marsh's sulfurous, rotten-egg stench was the fragrance of fecundity. Marshes are the most productive ecosystem in the world. Stewing in the marsh's oozing organic soup was a greater mass of life than anywhere else on earth.

Carol climbed out of the marshy mudbath, emptied the sloshing water from her boots, and plunged into the old-growth forest. Rainbow-colored buntings and scarlet tanagers nested in the green arms of ancient trees mottled with bubble-gum lichen. Ferns sprouted from the wet bark. Carol crossed a narrow one-lane sandy

road running north to south, a green tunnel where dappled sunlight flecked through a dense canopy of knotted, contorted live oaks draped with gray beards of Spanish moss.

Puncturing the cool, shaded forest was an oasis of light at Lake Whitney—the island's largest body of freshwater. Carol stopped to rinse her face in the lake. Dozens of alligators congregated there. She watched egrets peck at leftover flesh from the gators' open jaws. At dusk, Carol sat beside the lake, boiled a pot of beans and rice, and watched the first stars appear. Gators growled husky bellows that rolled across the water, their unblinking red eyes glowing just above the surface.

The black night swallowed the forest as Carol hiked from Lake Whitney toward the ocean. In the dark woods, every experience was heightened. Sticks in the trail were slithering snakes. An armadillo rummaging in the leaf litter sounded like a wild boar crashing toward her. Finally, the dark forest gave way to an unbroken, undulating span of dunes, carpeted with golden stalks of sea oats. Starlight flooded the sky—ancient light, thousands of years old, traveling millions of miles across the universe, bathing the beach in prehistoric candescence.

Carol walked barefoot down to the beach, the frothy surf foaming between her toes. Alone on the empty shore, she was left to face a hard truth: Charlie was gone for good. "I don't know if we ever get over the ones we love," she wrote later. "Maybe we just get past them." But she had finally stopped missing him, and once more she could feel the thrum of her heart.

She and Charlie were finished, but a new relationship had begun. The island had already started to grab hold of her. Nothing in her life had ever felt so right. On Cumberland, she felt like she had finally clicked into place. After twenty-eight years, two failed marriages, and several false starts, the island was wiping the slate clean. Twice each day, the beach—rinsed by the tides—started anew. So could she.

Birds signal territorial boundaries with their calls; bobcats with their scat; bears with clawed trees. That night, Carol—using the back of her heel—scratched her name into the wet sand. Like

the sea turtles who nested on Cumberland, Carol was imprinting herself upon the island. She had to return to the city in a few days, but she vowed to come back. She had printed that promise in the sand and sealed it by blowing a kiss to the starlit ocean. As she turned to leave, the tide filled her sand-carved letters and carried them out to sea.

6

Back in Atlanta, Carol watched thousands of mourners solemnly processing along Auburn Avenue behind the mule-drawn coffin of Martin Luther King Jr. In 1968, King was laid to rest beside Atlanta's Ebenezer Baptist Church, where he and his father had been pastors. Atlanta was a hotbed of civil rights and antiwar activism in the 1960s. The Southern Christian Leadership Conference, founded by King, was headquartered in Atlanta, "the city too busy to hate." Freedom Riders boarded buses in Atlanta, and the Student Nonviolent Coordinating Committee had organized mass sit-ins at eight lunch counters across the city that inspired a wave of direct action nationwide.

From freedom marches to the feminist movement, Carol was swept up in a rising tide of gender, racial, and cultural civil rights. She fought to include nature in that swell. In the 1960s and early '70s, Carol joined activists in Atlanta who rallied support for the Wilderness Act and Endangered Species Act, which enshrined permanent protections for wild creatures. Carol also championed campaigns to safeguard the Chattahoochee River and create wilderness in the north Georgia mountains.

But most of her nine-to-five was spent indoors beneath fluorescent lights. Carol had landed a job preparing specimens for an Atlanta museum, skinning elephants, tigers, and ostriches for exhibits. She liked working with animals—even dead ones. But after three years of tediously scraping flesh from bones in a windowless basement, she felt like she was frittering away her life.

Carol began wondering if she would ever escape Atlanta. Amid her daily drudgery, she followed one guiding principle, which kept her connected to the real world beneath the concrete and beyond the city limits: search for the source. Food didn't come from a grocery store. Water didn't come from a faucet. Ultimately, everything came from nature.

Even the seemingly mundane items in her everyday city life were derived from the natural world. Each morning, she woke up to an alarm clock, which used quartz crystals—highly compressed sand—to keep time. She brushed her teeth with toothpaste made with the same seaweed that sheltered sea turtle hatchlings. She sat on a toilet made of heated clay and wiped with toilet paper made from trees. She got dressed in clothes woven from sheep-sheared wool and drove to work in a jeep made mostly out of iron—which came from the guts of exploding stars. She filled it with oil made from dead plants and animals decaying on the ocean floor for five hundred million years. After work, she went for a hike in boots comprised of dried cow skin and the milky sap of a rubber tree and, afterward, drank river water from a glass formed by lightning striking beach sand. At the end of a long day, she rested her head on a pillow made of feathers stripped from geese.

She was no different than the caveman in her total reliance on nature. Money enabled her to hire middlemen to mine and refine natural resources for her, but it also distanced her from the source of her sustenance.

"For most of human history, we lived in direct contact with nature. Now we get resources from companies who extract them from nature for us," she wrote in her journal. "We've added a money economy between us and nature."

Carol sought to cut out the moneymaking middlemen. Outside was the natural economy that kept everyone alive. Inside was the artificial economy that separated us from real sources of things. She wanted a direct, original relationship to nature, where she used her own hands to acquire the food and shelter she needed.

In Atlanta, Carol felt like a confined animal, prowling hungrily around the perimeter of her citified cage. She had been dreaming about her escape for years. Had she grown too comfortable in the trappings of urban life? Was she too scared to fly away?

Ever since her divorce from Charlie, Carol had been living in a dilapidated, one-bedroom house. Her roommates included two tomcats, a gopher tortoise, a raven with a broken wing, two gray rat snakes, a terrarium of field mice, an aquarium of frogs and

salamanders, an injured owl, a golden pheasant, and five white leg-horn roosters.

Kids constantly knocked on Carol's door to see the animals. Finally she struck a deal with them: on Saturdays only, the kids could feed the animals and clean out cages. The kids loved petting the birds, holding the snakes, walking the dog, and chasing the chickens, and Carol enjoyed teaching them about animals—and getting a weekly break from cage cleaning.

"Kids reveal an obvious truth: natural wonder is built in to us," she wrote in her journal. "We are instinctively attracted to nature." Nature tugs on us like gravity, Carol believed. We travel long distances to stand atop mountains or stroll along seashores for reasons we can't quite put into words. Nature keeps alive a childlike wonder and enables us to see the world anew through fresh eyes.

Carol's animal house eventually prompted a visit from the land-lord, who was receiving complaints from neighbors about unusual noises and odors. The landlord had planned to evict her months prior. But then he saw what Carol's zoo was doing for the kids in their run-down neighborhood. Many of them had never seen a wild animal other than a rat. "You can keep your critters," the landlord told her. "But there's no way in hell you're getting back your deposit."

Her animal house was not much better than a zoo, Carol realized. At least she released her animals back to the wild. Still, there were cages and food bowls.

Carol hated zoos. Confining wild animals in concrete cages was a cruel expression of human pride. She saw the sadness and frustration in the animals' eyes. What was the value in gawking at miserable, tortured creatures imprisoned behind steel bars? Zoos' captive breeding programs were commendable in trying to save en-dangered species from extinction, but beyond that, she found nothing redeeming about them.

Sure, animals in the zoo had it easy: free food, no predators, and a warm place to sleep at night. Life in the wild was far less safe. Danger lurked everywhere, at every moment. Food was seasonal and unpredictable. No nest or territory was completely secure from fire, famine, or flood. Even sleep was a gamble. Birds and rabbits

rested with one eye open, shutting down half their brain for a few hours at a time.

Though wild nature wasn't safe, it was real. For millennia, animals had lived and evolved embedded in a web more intricate and delicate than humans could ever replicate. Comfort could never fully replace connection, Carol maintained. Animal and habitat were as inseparable as turtle and shell. When zoos severed this connection, they created different species. They housed artificial animals dependent on dried food, daily cleaning, and antibiotic injections.

Along the way, we humans had also cut our connection to the wild, Carol believed. Cities were zoos for people. Artificial food was manufactured for the masses. We built for ourselves climate-controlled cages and produced pharmaceuticals that helped us live longer, but what exactly were we living for? We had become zoo humans. We had stripped life of its wildness and incarcerated ourselves in picket-fenced pens that left us depressed and disconnected.

In 1969, Zoo Atlanta's resident female bobcat gave birth to two sister cubs, but one of them was sick. When her mother refused to let the sick kitten suckle, the kitten was moved to a windowless concrete cell where she was scheduled to be euthanized.

Carol knew the groundskeeper at the zoo, an old friend whom she had worked with at the museum.

"I gotta put her down tomorrow morning," he told her.

"Not if I take her with me tonight," she replied.

Carol began bottle-feeding the frail, feeble cub, whom she named Bast. Her fur was fluffy oatmeal, with flecks of honey and a dollop of stunted cottonball tail. After a few days, her mane thickened and her checkerboard spots deepened in color. Slowly, Bast gained weight and strength. She grew into her oversized paws. Carol built a forty-by-forty-foot pen in her backyard with elevated ramps, jumps, and ledges, surrounded by an eight-foot chain-link fence. She walked Bast twice a day on a leash through the pathless forest behind her house. At home, Carol crouched low, hands beneath her chin, and played pouncing games with her feline friend. They slept together on a single mattress on the floor.

Eventually, however, Bast outgrew even her backyard jungle. Carol convinced a friend to let her release Bast on his forested property south of Atlanta. Carol said her goodbyes, snuggled her one last time in her arms, and then set her free. Bast excitedly dashed about for a few minutes, but when she heard Carol's jeep engine, she chased her down the gravel driveway.

Carol couldn't sleep that night, worried that Bast was not yet acclimated to the wild. She returned the next day with food and water bowls. Bast was waiting for her at the end of the gravel driveway. She tackled Carol as soon as she stepped out of the truck and licked her face.

For several weeks, Carol drove down to feed Bast. It was a two-and-a-half-hour round-trip each day. Bast waited for her every evening. Then one night, she arrived to an empty field and a food bowl still filled.

"Bast! Here, girl!" she called. No response came from the darkening woods.

In the dusky halflight, she searched the edges of the field for tracks or scat but found none. Could she have been shot by hunters? Did a bear or cougar get her? She called again for Bast but heard only the echo of her own voice.

The sky was sprinkled with stars when she finally returned to her jeep. She started the engine and flipped on her headlights. At the forest's edge, a pair of glowing yellow eyes appeared. Bast watched her drive slowly down the gravel road, but this time she did not follow.

Carol ate her first bobcat a few months later. She spotted its carcass along a rural mountain road on a cool autumn evening, the sinking sun bathing the bare trees in tangerine twilight. Carol parked her jeep in the grass and climbed down, her boots crunching the cold gravel.

"I hope it went quickly," she said, kneeling beside the cat. As she removed the pelt around the haunches, she moistened the skin with canteen water to make the slices easier. All the while, she talked to the bobcat soothingly and reassuringly, nurse to patient, mother to child.

The cat's stunted tailbone was still in its skin, so she tugged at it with her teeth. After a half hour, she had the bobcat disassembled, laid out on the ground in cleanly dissected parts. Next, she sliced into the intestines. Warm steam hissed from the stomach, and a bilious black fluid spilled out. Carol sorted through the offal with her bare hands to find the crushed bones of a rabbit and leathery pieces of deer skin.

"You've been living high on the hog, big fella," she said.

Then she sliced away dense red meat from its shanks and placed them in a plastic bread bag. Carol ate the bobcat that evening for supper. As always, she thanked the animal before eating it. Sizzling in fat over the fire, the bobcat meat was rich, gamy, and delicious.

"We don't have a good reason not to eat cat or dog. The Indians knew that," Carol wrote in her journal. "We euthanize tens of thousands of cats and dogs each year and then dump their carcasses. We're so wasteful and ungrateful."

Carol had first discovered food stigmas at age six. Wading barefoot in a shallow creek, she saw a fish swimming upriver. She grabbed it with her bare hands and brought it to her father, who was fishing on the bank.

"Look, Dad. I caught us dinner."

He frowned. "It's a sucker fish. We can't eat that."

Later, she was told not to eat mullet. Only blacks eat mullet, her father said.

Carol was confused: why could you eat some fish and not others? There was no discernible difference in health or taste. The rules were arbitrary and absurd.

"Human stigmas around food are absolutely nuts. What difference is there between a cow and horse? Pig and dog? We eat millions of cows raised in confinement, standing in their own excrement, and ignore the abundance of wild meat all around us."

Carol rarely hunted. There was no need to spend hours hunting squirrels when freshly killed ones could be found freely around every bend in the road. Deer, possum, and coon carcasses were also plentiful along country highways. Even dead birds were morsels of nutrition.

Carol had shot her first animal—a sparrow—when she was ten years old. She had heard it rustling the leaves, scratching and pecking for grubs in the forest floor. She crept closer, sighted the bird in the crosshairs of her BB gun, and pulled the trigger. The gun popped. Four other sparrows burst from the brush and flapped away. Her sparrow tumbled and was still, shot squarely through the sternum.

"Instantly it felt wrong," Carol recalled. " 'Why did I do this?' I asked myself. Nobody taught me that feeling. It was just built-in. I think it's that way for most people—though maybe not all. I had taken life unnecessarily, and instinctively I felt remorse."

The best way to alleviate her guilt, she decided, was to make use of the bird. So she skinned it and cooked it over a campfire, whispering thanks before tasting its tender, mild, juicy flesh.

"Eating an animal is a kind of communion with nature," Carol explained. "I know it sounds trite, but I feel more connected to the web of life by honoring animals and making them a part of me. Their death is not wasted."

For Carol, dead on the road specimens—which she abbreviated D.O.R.—were especially valuable both nutritionally and scientifically. Wild meat was far tastier and healthier, free from the synthetic hormones and antibiotic injections of factory farms. Roadkill also provided free specimens for scientific study. Carol had taught herself advanced anatomy from D.O.R. specimens.

Bones especially fascinated her. There was a bone in the heart of a deer, she discovered, and many mammals—including dogs and raccoons—have a bone in their penis called a baculum. Because penis bones were like specially made keys—unique to each species—Carol used them frequently in identifying specimens. Her collection of bones, skulls, and skins was sought by universities and museums. Nearly all of her specimens were roadkill.

"I hate to hunt or trap live animals. With D.O.R.s, though, I feel great. I've got a wild specimen and I'm putting it to use."

She scraped up many gourmet feasts from street meat. She ate braised coon leg adorned with wild-harvested figs and pear slices. Dog was rich and succulent, similar to mutton, but more chewy. Armadillo was mild and—like mushrooms—absorbed whatever season-

ing was added. She often cooked and served armadillo meat straight out of the shell. Horse was tender and far better than beef. "I'd prefer horse over cow any day," she said. Hawk and owl tasted, well, like chicken. She ate a robin once that had been caught and dropped by an eagle. It was fresh, with only puncture wounds, so Carol cooked it over a fire: "It was one delicious breast bite and that's it." Woodchuck was sweet and delicious: "It doesn't get any better for an herbivore." But she preferred the stronger, gamy taste of carnivores like fox. In nearly all animals, she preferred the tender neck meat to more hunky thigh slabs. Her favorite meat was still raccoon. Second favorite was bobcat, which also had a sharp, tangy flavor. The only animal she wouldn't eat was domesticated house cat: "They're full of Friskies, and that can't be good."

Wild animals breathed fresh air, drank clean water, and ate untainted, unpolluted plants and critters. Even when they were a few days old, D.O.R. specimens tasted far better than cellophane-wrapped meat shipped from faraway feedlots. "We smugly think we're a kind people who treat animals in a more civilized way," Carol wrote in her journal, "but we've simply moved the killing floor out of sight."

For 99.9 percent of human history, food connected us to the natural world. When we changed our relationship to food, we changed our relationship to nature, Carol believed. By allowing agribusiness to feed us processed, packaged foods, we cut ourselves off at the roots. With D.O.R., Carol knew where her meat came from, and she cleaned the carcasses herself.

"There are subtle differences in the tastes of wild animals, but they all basically taste like some variant of chicken or beef. Meat is meat, really."

Carol's roadkill diet was enriched when she began working for Georgia's Natural Areas Council, a new state agency charged with identifying and protecting the wildest lands in Georgia. She was assigned to work with Sam Candler, a soft-spoken, silver-bearded heir of the Coca-Cola family. Sam didn't need the job or the money, but

he longed for new adventures and direct contact with the wild outdoors. He found both working alongside Carol. They traveled together seeking out Georgia's most unique and ecologically diverse habitats—swamps, marshes, mountain coves, wild rivers, and old-growth forests.

Carol was twenty-nine years old when she began working for the Natural Areas Council. The first Earth Day had recently been celebrated. The Clean Air Act had just been passed, and an Eastern Wilderness Act had just been introduced to designate more wilderness areas east of the Mississippi, since 99 percent of designated wilderness was out West. Carol hoped her statewide travels might help identify new wilderness areas in Georgia.

Driving rural backroads, Carol and Sam collected a trunkload of D.O.R. each day. Sam ate his first weasel, carried a raccoon baculum in his wallet because it made a great toothpick, and learned how to recognize roadkill from a quarter mile away. Tagging along with Carol and Sam for part of their travels was the acclaimed writer for *The New Yorker* John McPhee, whom they playfully nicknamed "the little Yankee bastard." McPhee sat in the backseat as they journeyed from the north Georgia mountains to the southern swamps, helping to spot—and occasionally eat—D.O.R. along the way.

Once, McPhee recalled in "Travels in Georgia," they came upon a snapping turtle hit on the road. It was still alive even though its shell was broken. Carol nudged the turtle out of the road with her foot, smearing blood across the pavement.

"I know it's bad," she said to the turtle. "We're not tormenting you. Honest we're not."

"Does it have a chance to live?" Sam asked.

"Not at all."

Moments later, the county sheriff pulled up. He eyed Carol, barefoot, wearing dungarees with a hunting knife strapped to her belt. Carol asked him to shoot the turtle.

"Surely, ma'am," he said. He drew his revolver, extended his arm, and took aim. He fired and missed twice. The shots echoed across the sun-baked asphalt. He took aim once more, holding the pistol six inches from the turtle's head. The third shot finally killed

the turtle. The sheriff blew the smoke away from the barrel of his pistol and nodded.

"That should do it," he said, tipping his hat.

Their two years of road trips were not without some tense moments. Often, Carol and Sam knocked on the doors of rural landowners and asked them to consider protecting rare wildlife habitat on their properties in exchange for tax breaks. Doors were slammed in their faces, slurs slung at them, and one farmer chased them off at gunpoint.

Back in the truck afterward, Sam muttered, "Goddamn redneck."

"What is a redneck, Sam?" McPhee asked from the backseat, notebook in hand.

"You know what a redneck is, you little Yankee bastard."

"I want to hear your definition."

"A redneck is a fat slob in a pickup truck with a rifle across the back. He hates 'niggers.' He would rather have his kids ignorant than go to school with colored children. I guess I don't like rednecks. I've known a few."

"Some of my best friends are rednecks," Carol said.

She identified more closely with the working-class southerner than the aristocratic elite. Both were equally racist and ignorant, she said, but at least rednecks got their boots muddy and earned a living by the sweat of their brows.

Redneck stereotypes had worsened recently in Georgia due to the 1970 publication of *Deliverance*, the bestselling novel by James Dickey, the brother of Carol's family friend and grenade defuser Tom Dickey. The book—and, later, the Hollywood blockbuster—followed the fictional journey of four city-dwelling, thrill-seeking weekend warriors who canoe down a wild stretch of whitewater in north Georgia. Ultimately, the conflict centers around handsome, athletic urban adventurists and rural southerners, who are darkly represented by a cross-eyed, inbred banjo player and two sinister men who sodomize a canoeist and command him to "squeal like a pig." The book reinforced stereotypes of Appalachian folk as backward, lawless, uneducated rednecks. It also inspired a new generation of

kayakers, canoeists, and whitewater rafters to explore the Chattooga River, where the movie was filmed.

"There's a lot more truth in the story than you might think," Jim Dickey told Carol over dinner with Tom one evening. He based the book on a real-life paddling trip in north Georgia. He was canoeing solo, while his friend Lewis King—the paddler upon whom the Burt Reynolds character is based—drove to a spot a few miles downstream where he could pick up Jim. King parked along a logging road and started hiking down toward the river, when suddenly two armed men appeared and demanded to know his business. They thought he was a government agent looking for their moonshine still. The men held him at gunpoint beside the river for several hours.

"Lewis was sweating bullets, praying for me to arrive before dark," Jim told Carol. Jim had flipped his canoe in one of the rapids, so he was late getting downriver. Finally he rounded a bend and spotted Lewis and the armed men just as daylight was beginning to dim. When he arrived, the shotguns disappeared, and the men even helped him carry his canoe back to the truck.

Deliverance was being filmed when Carol and Sam journeyed to the Chattooga River in 1971. They encountered no malevolent mountain men, but they met with hundreds of locals eager to protect their beloved river. Development and sewage threatened the Chattooga's pristine headwaters. In the early 1970s, rednecks and radicals joined forces, hoping to permanently protect the Chattooga as a federally designated Wild and Scenic River.

The key to the Chattooga's Wild and Scenic designation was its most famous whitewater kayaker, Governor Jimmy Carter. Carter and his son often paddled down the Chattooga, perfecting their kayak rolls at Big Shoals and Turnhole rapids. Jimmy Carter was one of the first to paddle the class-IV Bull Sluice rapid in an open canoe.

In 1972, Carter joined a whitewater rafting expedition down a harrowing stretch of the Chattooga. At Seven Foot Falls, Carter's raft guide misjudged his line, and the raft toppled into the seething rapid, spilling the governor, the guide, and two others. At the bottom of the falls, the raft folded, bucked, and straightened once more, leaving

only Rosalynn Carter still in the boat. Carter and the others swam safely to a nearby eddy. Nodding toward his wife, the waterlogged governor said, "Now you know who really steers the ship."

There was another woman behind the scenes of Carter's Chattooga legacy. Carol had documented several rare and endangered species in the Chattooga watershed and identified the river as highest priority among their Georgia Natural Areas sites. Her findings bolstered Carter's push to include the Chattooga in the federal Wild and Scenic River system. As a result, the Chattooga River today is forever protected from dams and development.

After the success of the Chattooga, Carol hoped her hometown river could also be saved. The Chattahoochee River was Georgia's lifeblood, flowing four hundred miles from Blue Ridge headwaters to the Florida panhandle, where it empties into the Gulf of Mexico. Below Atlanta's treatment plants and industrial dumps, the river became a swirling brown drainage ditch of sewage. But the northern segment was still clear-bottomed, wild, and pristine, from the mountains all the way down to the city limits.

Not for long, though. Bulldozers were already leveling the river bluff forests north of Atlanta, and a sewage line to service the city's sprawl was planned to cross the river near Carol's cliffside cave. Carol worked with grassroots activists, but they were being outpaced by development and dynamite. Something needed to happen fast.

So one morning, after filing paperwork at the Natural Areas Council headquarters in downtown Atlanta, Carol crossed the hall to the governor's office and knocked on Jimmy Carter's open door.

"Hey Jimmy!" she hollered. "You wanna shoot the Hooch with us next week?"

"You bet," he said, without even checking his calendar.

Carter was already awestruck by the brash, barefoot conservationist who moved with equal fearlessness through snake-infested swamps and the snake-infested state capitol building.

"Hers wasn't just a scientific relationship with nature, but a deeply personal one," Carter said later. "Whenever I spent time with

Carol, I was reminded of the ten-year-old boy I used to be, slogging barefoot through soft-bottomed swamps in south Georgia."

Jimmy always stopped to talk with Carol when they passed in the halls of the gold-domed capitol. They often traded stories about river adventures and trout fishing. And, as it turned out, Carol was dating a man from Carter's neck of the woods: John Pennington, an investigative journalist who, ten years earlier, had helped launch Carter's political career.

John Pennington and Jimmy Carter had a lot in common. Pennington was born one month before Carter, in the same rural Georgia county. Both grew up on farms, and their families often traded mules and other livestock. Both men attended Georgia Southwestern College in Americus. Later, Pennington served as editor of the University of Georgia newspaper, a position held previously by Jimmy Carter's cousin, Don. Don Carter, who became city editor of the *Atlanta Journal*, offered Pennington his first job as a reporter.

Pennington quickly became recognized as a scrupulous, hard-nosed investigative journalist. He covered desegregation of the first high school in Little Rock, Arkansas, and his series about corruption in Georgia prisons led to extensive state reforms.

On an overcast October evening in 1962, Pennington was crouched over a typewriter, working late on deadline, when he received a phone call from his old boss.

"Hey John. I've got something for you," said Don Carter. "My cousin Jimmy just lost the election in the fourteenth district. He's claiming election fraud."

John leaned back in his chair. "Is he just bellyaching, or does he have something to prove it?"

"According to the ballot box register, several hundred dead people voted—all for his opponent."

Pennington left that night for south Georgia and began his investigation before sunrise the next morning.

He already knew that Jimmy Carter was more than a peanut farmer. He had built a lucrative cotton warehouse, served on the county school board, and was deacon of his church. Then, on October 1, 1962, his thirty-eighth birthday, Jimmy told Rosalynn that he planned to

run for the state senate. The election was only fifteen days away. He and his family mounted an amateurish, whirlwind campaign.

His opponent was incumbent Homer Moore, who had close ties with a local boss and power broker, Congressman Joe Hurst. Hurst planned to control the election as he had for almost thirty years. He strong-armed local elections to ensure his puppets remained in office.

Homer Moore's strings were firmly attached to Hurst, and he was a shoo-in until Jimmy Carter decided to challenge him. Hurst was irate. Nobody dared challenge one of Hurst's minions, especially a south Georgia boy on Hurst's home turf. On election day, Hurst destroyed registration rolls, removed voter booths, instructed voters to strike Carter's name from the ballot, and stuffed the box with up to eight votes at a time, often folded together.

When Carter visited the polling site and witnessed Hurst's fraud, he immediately called the local newspaper in Columbus, Georgia. They sent a reporter who was already chummy with Hurst and had no intentions of writing a story about election improprieties.

Carter demanded a recount but was ignored. He traveled to the state capitol to ask for help but made little headway. Exasperated, he reached out again to the media, but no one was concerned about voting irregularities in a rural corner of the state—except John Pennington.

When Pennington arrived, just a few days after Homer Moore had been declared the winner, he discovered that there had been more votes cast than actual voters in the district. Dead people and prisoners had cast ballots in alphabetical order. Voter rolls and stubs were missing. Pennington found 102 votes that had all been cast for Moore neatly rolled in a rubber band. The ballot box itself had a gaping five-inch hole in the top that made it easy to remove ballots, and numerous witnesses attested to the fraud, saying that Hurst and his poll managers told voters who to vote for.

Pennington's exposé brought national attention to south Georgia politics. As a result of Pennington's stories, a superior court judge ordered a new election, and Carter won by a landslide. In 1962, he was sworn in to his first elected office as state senator. Ten years later, Carter became governor of Georgia.

"John Pennington probably saved my political career," Jimmy Carter told Carol.

On an April morning in 1973, Carol and Jimmy climbed into a canoe on the Chattahoochee River, just below the perimeter bridge where Carol used to catch crawfish. They paddled over rocky ledges and haystacks of rowdy, curling water.

Unlike the tense guard trailing them with an automatic weapon and scuba equipment strapped to his chest, Jimmy was perfectly at ease in the canoe. He was lean and athletic, in his forties, with a shock of wind-tossed sandy hair. A lifelong fisherman, he had spent his childhood reeling in redbellies and jack on tributaries of the Chattahoochee River in south Georgia. Carol hoped that Jimmy would cherish the Atlanta stretch of the Chattahoochee as much as his home waters downstream.

"He was such a laid-back, cool guy," Carol said. "I didn't have to try to convince him. He was already on board."

A few miles downriver, the bluffs rose steeply, casting wide shadows across the river. They banked their canoes and climbed up to an old Cherokee cave about one hundred feet above the river.

"Who owns this place?" Jimmy asked.

"A bank director. And he hasn't even slept here," said Carol.

"Have you slept here, Carol?" he asked.

"Many times. With a dog named Catfish."

They hiked back down to their canoes and paddled another mile downriver before landing beside an iron bridge, in a clear, cold eddy where Carol used to wash her hair. They stood beside the water in comfortable silence. Turtles basked on sun-warmed boulders. A blue heron stabbed its bayonet bill at minnows in the shoals.

"The river is great," Jimmy said. "I hope we can keep it this way."

A few months later, Governor Jimmy Carter signed the Metropolitan River Protection Act of 1973, which laid the groundwork for safeguarding the Chattahoochee River corridor as a national park unit. The proposed Chattahoochee National Recreation Area stalled under President Nixon but, a few years later, President Jimmy Carter

signed the bill into law himself. Carol's cave, the ancient bluffs, and forty-eight miles of river were permanently protected.

Also in 1973, John McPhee published "Travels in Georgia" in *The New Yorker*, highlighting Carol's roadkill adventures. Overnight, Carol became a national celebrity, and D.O.R. became a ubiquitous acronym.

Mademoiselle magazine named Carol Ruckdeschel one of its Women of the Year in 1974, along with Barbra Streisand, Wilma Rudolph, and Audrey Hepburn. She was invited to attend *Mademoiselle's* Women of the Year banquet in New York City but decided not to go.

"I would have been miserable trying to act what they call civilized and breathing all that smoke and pollution," she said. "Besides, they probably just wanted to look at that freak from Georgia that eats roadkill."

At the height of her popularity, Carol fled the limelight. She didn't want cameras and noise. She sought a quiet life immersed in nature.

She was still living in a run-down house in suburban Atlanta, crammed with injured animals, aquariums, and posters of scenic landscapes. It was a cheap imitation of the natural life she had imagined for herself. Returning to her cave beside the river with Jimmy Carter had reminded her of the promise she had made years earlier to live wild and free.

"The highest and best thing I can do is to find a place and know it as deeply and intimately as I know myself," she wrote in her journal.

Where was that place? She had explored the wildest pockets of Georgia, waded through its wetlands, climbed its highest peaks, paddled its thundering whitewater, and bushwhacked through its old-growth forests. But one place had stayed with her. She couldn't resist its gravitational pull. Like water tumbling headlong toward the ocean, Carol felt herself tugged downstream to the source of her wild longings from years before: Cumberland Island.

"I've gotta get out of the city. It's grinding me down," she told Sam Candler on their last trip together.

"Where will you go?"

"I don't know yet. Maybe the mountains. Maybe the coast."

"Can you buy some land?"

"Can't afford it."

"You mean *Mademoiselle* doesn't pay its Women of the Year?"

"*Mademoiselle* didn't even give me a free subscription."

Sam scratched his salt-and-pepper beard. "My family needs a caretaker to look after our property on Cumberland Island," he told her. "I don't know if it's what you're looking for. It pays even worse than the state. You'd be cleaning toilets and washing dishes."

"When do I start?"

part two

turtle island

7

Carol wiggled her toes in the warm sand. She was thirty-two and finally back on Cumberland, the largest barrier island in the East—a wild tangle of marsh, forest, and seashore. It felt like coming home. She stood atop the wild dunes at dawn, watching the shining sea lift and fall beyond the breakers. The sun's first embers warmed the horizon. Sand blew in loose swirls over the beach. The wind drizzled through the deep forest behind the dunes, suffusing its wet, green, animalic musk.

Carol wasn't the first feisty female to set foot on Cumberland Island. Women have dominated Cumberland ever since its first inhabitants settled here thirteen thousand years ago. Island women were powerful even among the native Timucuan people, whose society was matrilineal: relatives were traced through the mother's family, and women held important positions in their clan and community.

The Timucuan natives were as beautiful as their island. They stood six and a half feet tall, with copper skin and slate-black hair, and were decorated head-to-toe with jewelry and tattoos. Women's hair flowed down their backs, and they wore rawhide bikini bottoms with Spanish moss sashes that draped from shoulder to hip.

The Timucuans built their main tribal village near the present-day Dungeness dock and lived peacefully on the island for centuries, gathering nuts and berries from the forest and shellfish from the marshes. Their hunting ceremonies often involved imbibing large quantities of the "black drink," made from roasting the dark dried leaves of the island's yaupon holly. Small doses of the highly caffeinated tea provided a stimulating pick-me-up, but big batches of the bitter drink induced sweating and vomiting (its scientific species name today is *vomitoria*), which purged any physical or spiritual pollutants from the drinkers.

Much more palatable was the root beer brewed from abundant sassafras trees on the island. The sweet brew was so enjoyed

by the Timucuans that one of the island's alternate names was *missoe*, meaning "sassafras." The drink became both a blessing and a curse. When the Europeans arrived on the island in the sixteenth century, they began logging and shipping the sassafras back to Europe, where it commanded a high price as a healing tonic beverage called root beer.

In 1567, the first three Spanish missionaries to arrive were killed by the Timucuans. Eventually, the Spanish subdued the island. They also brought deadly diseases—smallpox, measles, syphilis, and influenza—that decimated the native people. Less than a decade after the Spanish arrived, the Timucuans were almost completely wiped out.

The few remaining Timucuan survivors converted to Christianity and became loyal subjects of the Spanish missions. When mainland Guale Indians revolted against the Spanish in 1597, the Timucuans sided with the Spanish and helped defeat the Guale. One of the Timucuan leaders in the battle was a female chieftain, Dona Maria Melendez. The first of many fearless women to rule the island, Dona Maria was named princess of the island for her strength and courage.

In the 1700s, the British and Spanish fought for control of the island. British general James Oglethorpe built two forts on either end of the island to defend against the mighty Spanish navy prowling the seas.

Oglethorpe befriended the Indians living along the coastal islands, among them a young boy named Toonahowi. Oglethorpe took him to England to show the royal court some of America's dark-skinned natives. During that trip, Toonahowi made friends with a teenage duke who ruled Cumberland, a scenic coastal county in northwest England. The two adolescent boys—the dark-eyed, black-haired child of the wilderness and the fair-headed, blue-eyed child of wealth—became such close friends that Toonahowi later asked the general to name the largest island back home in honor of his noble teenage pal, the duke of Cumberland. Oglethorpe obliged.

Oglethorpe secured Cumberland Island and the Georgia coast in the decisive Battle of Bloody Marsh in 1742, which occurred just north of Cumberland. Oglethorpe's outnumbered, ragtag British soldiers—most of them former prisoners and ex-convicts—prevailed over the more heavily armed Spanish. Cumberland and the Golden Isles belonged to England.

Cumberland Island's forts were deserted soon after the war, and for the next few decades the island became a refuge for pirates, criminals, and castaways. Then in 1765, Oglethorpe returned to build a hunting lodge on a scenic bluff overlooking the island's south end marshes. He named it Dungeness, after a castle in England. Oglethorpe's rustic hunting cabin was hardly a castle, but over the next century two of the island's leading ladies would build the country's most magnificent mansions on that very spot.

The first of them was Catharine "Caty" Littlefield, a petite New England debutante with ink-black hair, porcelain skin, and chocolate-brown eyes, who wore fashions that accentuated her ample bosom. Men swooned over her, smitten by her beauty, swayed by her elegance, stunned by her boldness.

It was a soldier who won her hand in 1773. Nathanael Greene married eighteen-year-old Caty, just before the colonies began their fight for independence. Though Greene was raised as a pacifist Quaker, he joined the revolution, enlisting as a militia private, the lowest station in the Continental Army. Despite not having any military experience, he quickly climbed the ranks and became George Washington's second-in-command. Washington appointed him to lead the Revolutionary War's southern campaign.

Caty Greene, pregnant with their first son, accompanied her husband in bedraggled military camps close to the front lines. With the government unable to pay for basic troop supplies, Greene personally accrued tremendous debts in order to feed, clothe, and equip his ragged soldiers. Though Greene lost every single battle he fought, he masterfully weakened the more numerous British forces through long, elusive, and tiresome retreats. Greene's ingenious tactics sapped the British of their strength and resolve even as they "won" every battle.

After the war ended, Caty was the belle of the military balls. Though she arrived on Nathanael's arm, swashbuckling officers vied for her dance card. George Washington once danced for three hours with Caty without sitting down, while Martha Washington watched enviously. Provocative and promiscuous, Caty was intimate with the most influential men of her era. She broke the rules of proper colonial women by seeing herself as more than the wife of Nathanael Greene.

She and Nathanael moved to Georgia, and after several failed attempts at growing rice on his Savannah plantation, Nathanael decided to invest in timber property on Cumberland Island. He expected hefty profits from harvesting the island's live oaks, which would help pay off his war debts. The dense, heavy live oaks from Cumberland Island were used to build the country's first war ship, *Old Ironsides*, a wooden-hulled frigate so tough that British cannonballs literally bounced off it.

But things fell apart at home before Greene could fully pursue his Cumberland Island plans. His party-loving wife grew bored on the plantation. A New England debutante, Caty was accustomed to the swirling social balls and wanton eyes of handsome men at fancy festivities. She became entangled in an affair with another handsome war hero, General "Mad Anthony" Wayne, a longtime friend of Nathanael. Anthony and Caty rode horses together, and rumors swirled that Anthony made late-night visits to her manor. There were even whispers that Caty planned to murder her husband with a butcher knife and blame it on fugitive slaves.

When Nathanael caught wind of the affair, he prepared to go after his former army comrade. But Nathanael was already weakened, broken-hearted, and overworked, burdened by heavy debts while still trying to fund his wife's lavish lifestyle.

"I tremble at my own situation, when I think of the enormous sums I owe," Nathanael wrote in his journal. "One of the payments for Cumberland Island is due, and the parties press me for payment. I seem to be doomed to a life of slavery and anxiety."

Before he could face off with Mad Anthony, Nathanael Greene collapsed of nervous strain, abetted by sunstroke, and died at age forty-four.

Almost immediately, men jockeyed to court Caty, and Mad Anthony was first in line. Caty flirted with several suitors, but she eventually settled on her children's tutor, the Yale-educated, cultivated savant Phineas Miller. They wed in 1796, and soon after, they sold her Savannah estate and moved to Cumberland Island, where they planned to start a sea island cotton plantation.

Despite her inherited debts, Caty built her dream house on the south end of Cumberland in 1803. Slaves built the grandiose thirty-room mansion using tabby, a concrete made from oyster shells left behind by over 130 centuries of Indian meals. Caty's Dungeness mansion was the largest tabby house ever constructed.

One of Phineas's college buddies from Yale was Eli Whitney, who served as a tutor and handyman on the Dungeness estate for a few years. To help their struggling plantation, Caty asked Eli to come up with a machine that separated cotton seeds from lint.

Caty and Phineas were losing money growing cotton. The tedious, time-consuming task of removing the cotton seeds by hand made it far too costly. Eli went to work on a machine that duplicated the manual process. He watched the hand movements of the slaves cleaning cotton, and after a few months of tinkering in the Dungeness workshop, Eli presented a working model of his cotton engine ("gin") to Caty, Phineas, and a few friends. He placed the machine on a mahogany table in the parlor of their mansion, dropped some fluffy cotton bolls in the hopper, and cranked the handle. Seeds came out on one side and clean white cotton fiber on the other. The audience was astonished.

But there was still a problem, Eli pointed out. After a few cranks, the machine's teeth became clogged with cotton fibers.

"Why, Mr. Whitney, you want a comb," Caty said, and handed him her hair brush.

"Madam, you have completed the cotton gin," he said.

Word of Eli's invention spread quickly. For the first time, cotton could be profitable for the South. In one hour, his machine could match the full day's labor of fifty slaves cleaning cotton by hand. Plantation owners began planting vast fields of cotton, which, in a cruel irony, ultimately required even more slave labor.

Eli and Phineas quickly formed a company to mass produce the cotton gin. Until it was patented, he closely guarded his cotton gin from outsiders. However, shy Eli had a hard time saying no to the ladies. He allowed women to peek at his new invention. One afternoon, a clever young farmer named Edward Lyon dressed up as a woman and flirted with Eli in order to get a closer look. Soon after, Lyon came out with a rival machine, and others quickly followed.

Eli and Phineas filed sixty lawsuits to protect their cotton gin patent, but they were of little use. Several models of cotton gin beat Eli to market. Though he is synonymous with the cotton gin in history books, Eli Whitney made almost no money from his invention.

Phineas and Caty still had high hopes for their sea island cotton plantation on Cumberland. But Phineas would not live to see their plans come to fruition. In 1803, less than a year after Dungeness was built, Phineas pricked his finger on a thorn and died of lockjaw a week later at age thirty-nine.

For the next twenty years, Caty managed the island plantation. She established vast orchards and gardens that provided fresh fruits and vegetables. Slaves gathered shellfish from tidal creeks. Kitchen servants made gourmet soup from loggerhead sea turtles, which were flipped upside down on the beach and butchered. She continued hosting extravagant parties, even though she was drowning in debt.

When Caty died of bilious fever at age sixty, her daughter Louisa assumed the role of island mistress. Louisa singularly supervised the island estate for the next two decades. Like her mother, Louisa continued hosting grand galas. To celebrate the end of the War of 1812, Louisa threw a sumptuous soirée at Dungeness. During the festivities, British warships—unaware that a peace treaty had been signed a few weeks earlier—dropped anchor offshore of Cumberland and commandeered the mansion. They banished Louisa and her guests to the upper floors at gunpoint.

Yet even in war, romance triumphed. As the night wore on, the young ladies looked longingly down the banisters. Finally the British sent an invitation upstairs for the women to come down and join the officers. The men were held captive, while the island ladies danced

all evening with English gentlemen in their gold-braided regimental garb. One dark-eyed belle, Ann Couper, caught the eye of British lieutenant John Fraser. The British eventually left the island and returned to England, but a year later Fraser came back and married his "pretty prisoner of Dungeness."

Louisa received another unexpected visitor from a passing ship in 1818. While tending to her orange groves, Louisa got word that a feeble, frail Light Horse Harry Lee had arrived at the Dungeness dock. A Revolutionary War hero, Light Horse Harry had helped draft the Constitution. Years later, flat broke and dying of cancer, he was sailing north toward his home in Virginia when he asked to dock at Cumberland so he could "die in the arms of the daughter of my old friend and compatriot General Greene."

Light Horse Harry was buried on Cumberland. Years later, his son, Confederate commander Robert E. Lee visited the island and solemnly placed a wreath on his father's grave.

After Louisa died in 1831, most of her land was eventually sold to Robert Stafford, whose eight-thousand-acre sea island cotton plantation on Cumberland became one of the most productive in the world. More than 350 slaves tended the cotton fields, making Stafford one of the South's largest slaveholders.

Robert Stafford lived with his mother and sister, and when both contracted yellow fever and died, Stafford's neighbor sent over a mulatto nurse slave named Zabette to help cook meals. Zabette was light-skinned, tall, and slim, with long black hair and round, chestnut eyes. She was nineteen years old when she arrived at the doorstep of the forty-six-year-old plantation owner.

Zabette helped Stafford with more than meals. She satisfied another appetite, bearing him six children. Zabette lived in separate quarters adjacent to Stafford's house, since Georgia law forbade female slaves from living under the same roof as an adult white male. Nevertheless, she spent many a night with her master.

Fearful for his reputation, Stafford was unwilling to admit the children were his. Yet he wanted to provide for them. So he

secretly ferried them north to Connecticut, where they could live free and attend school. Initially they stayed with a family friend, but eventually he built an immense house in Connecticut for his children, and Stafford's family friends became their guardians. Stafford visited the children a couple of times a year, and Zabette accompanied him as his live-in nurse. No one in the affluent New England neighborhood ever knew that Stafford and Zabette were the children's parents.

When the Civil War broke out, Zabette moved to Connecticut with the children. Stafford stubbornly refused to leave his plantation, even when Union forces overran the island in 1862. He was the only white man living on the island during the Civil War. All of Stafford's 350 former slaves had been armed by Union forces, and one evening they surrounded his house. They killed his cattle—and threatened the same for him. Stafford was rescued by Union soldiers, and after the war, a vengeful Stafford returned to Cumberland and burned down his former slaves' cabins. Today only charred chimneys remain. The twenty-three chimneys are the oldest historic structures on the island today, silent sentinels of slavery's stain.

Zabette stayed in Connecticut as long as she could, but she never fit in. Her children were better educated and more socially mobile than her, and they were embarrassed by her darker color, crude speech, and unpolished manners. Cumberland was where she belonged. Zabette returned to the island, hoping to rejoin Stafford on his plantation. When she arrived, she discovered Stafford with another mulatto woman, with whom he had fathered two daughters in Zabette's absence.

When Stafford died in 1877, he was worth over $1 million. All of it went to his children in Connecticut. He left nothing for Zabette. She moved to a squatters' field on Cumberland's north end to live the rest of her life in a dirt-floored hut. No one knows where she is buried.

Over five hundred slaves lived on Cumberland Island before the Civil War. Many of them were Gullah, a close-knit band of African people

who maintained their old traditions in the new world. The name Gullah is likely a distortion of Angola, the African country where almost half of all slaves in Georgia and South Carolina came from. After the war, many freed Gullah slaves returned to Cumberland and built shanties with rusted tin roofs on the north end of the island.

Most of them ended up working for the Cumberland Island Hotel, a resort built in the 1880s that catered to wealthy vacationers. Guests at the Cumberland Island Hotel enjoyed an orchestra and fine dining. A horse-drawn trolley carted guests out to the beach, where they were shown how to dig for sea turtle eggs in the dunes.

To maintain a steady pool of laborers, the hotel owners cleared five acres near Half Moon Bluff, which overlooked the salt marshes near Christmas Creek, and divided the land into fifty small lots, penetrated by a network of primitive sand roads. They called it the Settlement. Lots were sold to black workers at the hotel. One of them was Charlie Trimmings, son of a former slave, who built a small cabin in the Settlement for his wife and son. Trimmings worked for the hotel and cut timber to support his family.

After the hotel closed, Coca-Cola heir Howard Candler—Sam Candler's grandfather—purchased the abandoned hotel and turned it into a private thousand-acre family retreat. Howard was the son of Asa Candler, an Atlanta drugstore owner. When a rival pharmacist, Dr. John Pembleton, started selling a fizzy concoction of soda water and tonic as a headache remedy, Asa Candler bought the recipe for $2,300. He marketed Coca-Cola as a soft drink to a national audience and amassed millions.

Asa Candler tinkered with the Coca-Cola recipe, which was originally three parts coca leaf to one part kola nut. The coca leaves contained nine milligrams of cocaine per ounce, but Candler eventually replaced them with processed coca leaves that provided only trace amounts of cocaine. The cola portion of the formula—the kola nut extract—imparted a slightly bitter taste and a hefty wallop of caffeine. The U.S. government sued Asa Candler in 1911—not for lacing his beverage with cocaine, but for using caffeine, which it considered a dangerous, habit-forming drug. Candler and Coca-Cola

prevailed, and amped-up America soon became the most caffeinated country on the planet.

Howard Candler, the oldest of Asa's eleven children, was given the Coca-Cola Company as a Christmas present in 1917. He ran the company for only two years before he and his siblings sold it to a group of investors in 1919. After cashing out, he bought his one-thousand-acre oasis on Cumberland Island.

Some of the Settlement's unemployed residents found work with the Candlers, but most left the island seeking jobs on the mainland. In 1937, the few remaining Settlement dwellers constructed the First African Baptist Church from salvaged lumber and driftwood.

The unofficial mayor of the Settlement was Beulah Alberty, a plump, gray-haired African American who smoked a pipe, played poker, and distilled moonshine. She scraped up money wherever she could to fund her granddaughter's education, working first as a schoolteacher on the mainland and, later, selling coon skins and butchering island hogs. On weekends, black workers congregated at Beulah's to drop a nickel in the slot of her jukebox, toss back some gut-burning moonshine, buy a tangy barbecued pork dinner for seventy-five cents, and gamble away the rest of their earnings in five-card stud.

Part of Beulah's house was blown up after her father got in a dispute with a white landowner named Ed Fader over a liquor still on the island. Fader lit a stick of dynamite and tossed it beneath the Alberty's house, blasting apart one side of it. Beulah and her father were injured. The next day, shots were exchanged between the two families. Eventually a trial was held in superior court, but the all-white jury failed to indict Fader.

The house was eventually rebuilt, and today Beulah's house is a National Park Service visitor center. It sits directly beside the First African Baptist Church, which would soon become the island's most celebrated and controversial structure, even eclipsing the popularity of palatial mansions built by one of the world's wealthiest families, the Carnegies.

* * *

At the height of America's industrial revolution, corporate moguls built big factories in the cities and private castles along the coast. Georgia's barrier islands, with their balmy weather, hushed seclusion, and cheap land, lured the millionaires.

Several of the richest robber barons pooled their money to purchase Jekyll Island, just one mile north of Cumberland. The Rockefeller, Vanderbilt, Goodyear, Morgan, and Pulitzer families formed the country's most exclusive organization: the Jekyll Island Club. For six decades, no uninvited person ever stepped foot on Jekyll. The island was a private playground, with mansions, clubhouses, tennis courts, and swimming pools.

Other Georgia barrier islands were snatched up by auto magnate Howard Coffin and tobacco titan R.J. Reynolds. Cumberland— Georgia's largest and southernmost barrier island—was claimed by a branch of the Carnegie family.

The Carnegies had amassed a fortune in the steel industry. Andrew and his younger brother Thomas embodied the American Dream: immigrant boys who went from rags to riches, self-made men who became captains of industry.

Born to working-class parents in Scotland, Andy and Tom immigrated to the United States in 1848 and eventually landed in Pittsburgh. There they built the world's largest steel empire, Carnegie Steel, which mass-produced cheap steel that spurred the growth of the nation. They consolidated the entire steel process from start to finish: they owned the raw iron ore, railroads, and even the coal mines to fuel the steel furnaces.

Andy was the fiery CEO and commander of the operation. Tom mostly managed the books. Though they were partners, Andy ran the show. Andy never felt Tom was aggressive enough and said that he was "born tired." Tom began drinking heavily to escape the demands of his ambitious older brother.

Once Carnegie Steel had wiped out unions from every one of its factories, its iron grip on industry tightened. Carnegie Steel became

the most profitable company in the world. The Carnegies amassed personal fortunes with a real value today of $300 billion, more than the combined wealth of Bill Gates, Warren Buffett, Mark Zuckerberg, the Koch brothers, and the entire Walton family. Andrew Carnegie became the second wealthiest man in history. Only oil mogul John D. Rockefeller was richer.

The Carnegies felt their accumulation of wealth was natural and even morally correct. They defended the widening gulf between rich and poor as a good and necessary indicator of social evolution. "Great inequality, the concentration of business in the hands of a few, and the law of competition between these is not only beneficial, but essential for the future progress of the race," wrote Andy.

Andy and Tom were crusaders for Social Darwinism, a belief that the wealthy should rule and reap from the weaker members of society. Drawing from a skewed interpretation of Darwin's breakthroughs in biological evolution, Social Darwinists concocted the notion of "survival of the fittest," a phrase never used by Darwin but coined instead by British philosopher Herbert Spencer, the Carnegie brothers' favorite author and political thinker. Spencer even crossed the pond to personally visit the Carnegie brothers in Pittsburgh. Spencer preferred talking with Tom to Andy, finding Tom a more receptive audience for his ideas. It was one of the few moments in Tom's life where he bested his older brother.

Social Darwinists applied the "survival of the fittest" ideology to economics, class, and race. They believed the rich and powerful were more fit and better adapted to the social and economic climate. Therefore it was natural and proper for the strong to thrive at the expense of the weak. They opposed social welfare programs, safety regulations, or laws restricting child labor. Such actions would only coddle the weak and the unfit.

The Carnegies believed it was naturally and morally right for wealth to be concentrated at the top of a competitive capitalist society. As Andy put it, "Millionaires are the bees that make the most honey and contribute most to the hive even after they have gorged themselves full."

At the dawn of the Gilded Age, Social Darwinism seemed especially attractive. The Carnegie steel factories fueled America's meteoric rise from Civil War ashes to the world's wealthiest nation. Robber barons were reaping unprecedented profits. To Tom and Andy, the world was an industrial utopia of idealized steelworkers engaged in noble toil. Powerful blast furnaces perpetually ran fast and full, overseen by two knights in black steel armor.

But there was a dark side to the Carnegies' fairy tale. Social Darwinism validated the exploitation of workers, including children, who were paid pennies a day for long hours of backbreaking labor. Sweatshops were common, urban slums festered, and most of America was impoverished. Void of any social protections, the age of robber barons led to labor insurrections and social violence in the late nineteenth and early twentieth centuries.

Social Darwinism was later used to support eugenics, which sought to weed out the undesirable genes of supposedly inferior races through forced sterilization. Hundreds of thousands of Americans were sterilized—especially blacks, the working poor, and people with disabilities, and eugenic euthanasia programs were implemented in mental hospitals.

Tom and Andy Carnegie had helped erect those pillars of Social Darwinism. However, Andy eventually began to question some of its central tenets. He ultimately ended up giving away 90 percent of his wealth to build twenty-eight hundred libraries around the world. Did the lives of his underpaid steelworkers and his ruthless pursuit of personal wealth weigh on the conscience of the man who had grown up in poverty? "Maybe with the giving away of his money," says Andrew Carnegie's biographer Joseph Wall, "he would justify what he had done to get that money."

Tom Carnegie had no such misgivings or philanthropic leanings. Instead of a legacy of libraries, Tom eyed a private island off the Georgia coast as a vacation home for his family. The Carnegies had been snubbed by the Jekyll Island Club to the north, and Tom wanted an island of his own anyway. In 1882, Tom Carnegie purchased twelve thousand acres of Cumberland, including Dungeness and all of Stafford's property, for $75,000, as a gift to his wife, Lucy.

Lucy, the daughter of a wealthy Pittsburgh coal tycoon, had been enchanted by Cumberland Island ever since she was a nine-year-old girl attending boarding school in nearby Fernandina Beach, Florida, a few miles from the island's southern tip. At one time, Lucy included Andrew Carnegie among her suitors, but she settled on his younger brother. She and Tom had nine children together—six sons and three daughters.

Lucy's first act as empress of the island was to raze the ruins of Caty's old Dungeness manor and build an even larger sandcastle overlooking the south end salt marshes. Then in 1886, one year after the new Dungeness mansion was built, Thomas Carnegie died of pneumonia at age forty-three. Alcoholism and stress from his strained relationship with Andy contributed to his illness and early death. Lucy Carnegie—like Caty and Louisa before her—became the widowed matriarch of Cumberland Island.

For the next thirty years, Lucy was queen of Cumberland. In her towering fifty-nine-room mansion, she hosted exquisite dinner parties and lavish galas that were attended by industry chiefs, politicans, and celebrities. Guests in elegant topcoats and evening gowns sipped mint juleps on the veranda and waltzed the night away in Gatsby-esque grandeur. In the smoke-filled parlor, cocky young heirs in silk-collared tuxedos loosened their ascots and wagered staggering sums in poker.

Dinners were always formal. Waiters stood behind the chair of each guest at an enormous round dining room table. Gourmet dinners were served on gleaming dishes trimmed in fourteen-carat gold. Picnics were only slightly less ceremonious. Servants carried trays of hot food from the mansion out to gazebos with white gingerbread trim, where long tables were covered with white satin cloths and set with silver. Occasionally the family picnicked on the beach, where they fished, swam, rode horses, and roped sea turtles to small wagons for races.

The mansion was surrounded by marble patios, fountains, greenhouses, statues, and rose gardens framed by arched hedges.

The immaculately manicured Dungeness lawn hosted croquet tournaments and horseback races. Lucy's family and friends also enjoyed a golf course, tennis courts, a skeet shooting range, and a marble-floored pool house, where high diving boards and parallel rings were suspended above the seventy-five-foot-long heated pool. Mischevious Carnegie heirs secretly greased the second ring, then bet unsuspecting guests that they couldn't make it across the pool.

"Of course they'd always bite. And then they'd fall, right smack in the water," recollected Nancy Copp, Lucy's great-granddaughter.

The pool house was also where some of the most serious boozing took place. "The Carnegies liked to drink," recalled Polly Stein Carnegie, the wife of one of Lucy's grandsons. Rarely were they seen without a cocktail in hand. From time to time, Carnegie boys drove the boat twenty miles to Jacksonville and spent the night carousing, and occasionally they ended up in jail. One Carnegie heir regularly instructed a servant to set up a card table in the middle of the woods and pour him shots until he passed out.

"There was an underlying sadness in some of the Carnegie clan, exiled to a remote island with a powerful matriarchal figure in charge, leaving them with nothing to do but hunt and fish, drink too much, and chase after what women could provide," recalled Lucy's great-grandson James "Pebble" Rockefeller Jr.

Over three hundred employees labored daily to keep the Carnegies happy, including cooks, laundresses, chambermaids, and butlers, all of whom were white. Blacks worked outside the mansion. Most of the stable cleaning, road maintenance, farming, buggy driving, and lawn mowing was done by Robert Stafford's former slaves.

Lucy bought a 119-foot yacht, which she named *Dungeness*, and in 1884 she became the first female member of the New York Yacht Club. She proudly wore a commodore hat held in place with a diamond-studded hairpin and cruised from the Bahamas to Maine with family and friends. A crew of seventeen drove it daily to the mainland for supplies. They also hired trains to deliver food and clothes from New York down to south Georgia.

Lucy and her family initially used Cumberland as a winter retreat, traveling back north to their Pittsburgh manor for most of the

year. But Lucy eventually moved to the island full-time, and as she got older she hoped her nine children would follow. To encourage them, she made an incredible offer: when her children married, she would build each one a mansion on the island. Four of them took her up on it.

Lucy built Stafford Mansion on Robert Stafford's former cotton plantation for her eldest son, Bill, an avid golfer who installed an eighteen-hole course in the old cotton fields. Wild Bill also liked gambling and fast cars. His claim to fame was being able to jump flat-footed into a barrel and then jump back out, a feat that earned him thousands in wagers. Bill drank heavily and married a prostitute, which got him banished from the island by Lucy. He lived for a while on a boat moored to the dock in St. Marys, the mainland town across from Cumberland. After his wife died, he built a small house along the waterfront, which had the reputation of being a brothel. Wild Bill lived out his days sipping bourbon from the dock and gazing longingly at Cumberland in the distance.

Lucy built the Cottage, a twenty-nine-room house at the end of Dungeness' west lawn, for her fourth son, Morris. As a child, Morris was cleaning his rifle when the gun accidentally fired. The bullet only grazed his head, but his siblings joked that it triggered his liberal leanings. Morris read Karl Marx and other socialist writers. For fun, he left socialist tabloids on the tables of the ultraconservative Racquet and Tennis Club in New York. Morris also helped persuade Uncle Andy to establish his charitable library foundation.

Plum Orchard Mansion was constructed for Lucy's fifth son, George. It was the largest and grandest of her children's mansions and the farthest from Dungeness—nearly nine miles north, on a bend of the Brickhill River. It would later become the most controversial, too.

The fourth mansion, Greyfield, was built for her first daughter, Retta. The three-story manor boasted wide porches overlooking saltwater marshes and the Intracoastal Waterway. Retta's daughter, Lucy Ferguson, turned the grand house into the opulent Greyfield Inn.

As Lucy's health diminished, she feared her island empire would crumble after she died. So she drew up a will that strictly

forbade the sale of any mansions or land on her island estate until all of her children had died. In the winter of 1916, Lucy passed away in her sleep.

Lucy had been the glue that held her family together. In the decades after her death, the family's cohesiveness weakened and its money began to run dry. None of her children ever held jobs. Some heirs squandered their riches. Others lost money in sour business deals. Dungeness was boarded up, and eventually other mansions were shuttered, too.

By the 1950s, many of the Carnegie children and grandchildren wanted to cash in on their island property. Though Lucy's will prevented the sale of their lands, they logged several parts of the island for quick cash, and then hatched a plan to strip-mine the island for titanium. It technically would not require the sale of any property, only the leasing of mineral rights. However, extracting the titanium would require extensive forest clearcutting, leaving behind deep gashes and a flattened, denuded wasteland.

In 1955, the Carnegie heirs sought bids from several companies. The highest bidder was Glidden, a corporation that promised $4.25 million in royalties to the Carnegies. Over seven thousand acres—roughly half of the island—was slated to be mined and cleared.

Nearly everyone in the Carnegie family was ready to sign on the dotted line—except one significant holdout, Nancy "Big Nanny" Carnegie Rockefeller. Her family called her "a fly in the ointment" for standing in the way of the mining plans. But Nancy knew that Lucy would not have approved of strip-mining Cumberland. The proposal violated both Lucy's will and the spirit of the island.

"I had to stop it," Nancy said. "Mining the island would have desecrated it."

Big Nanny sued her own family, and the case went all the way to the Georgia Supreme Court. She prevailed, and in 1957 the strip-mining plans were scrapped.

* * *

When the last of Lucy's nine children died in 1962, several Carnegie heirs immediately sold their lands to developers, including Hilton Head investor Charles Fraser. He was a brash, balding, potbellied man who planned to build a gated community of expensive homes on Cumberland. Fraser bulldozed property boundaries across the island—which later became the North and South Cut Roads—and cleared an airport runway to accommodate corporate jets. He constructed his cedar-sided real estate headquarters on the south end at a spot he dubbed Sea Camp. His blueprints outlined plans for dredging Lake Whitney, establishing a marina, building tiki bars along the beach, clearing a new golf course, and transporting visitors to the island on aerial gondolas.

He brought down his ninety-foot yacht from Hilton Head so he and his cohorts would have comfortable quarters during the construction of the resort. In the late 1960s, he began meeting with other Carnegie heirs, hoping to purchase the remaining island properties. Swaths of clearcuts were already razed, and smoke was belching from Fraser's earth-moving machines. It appeared nothing could stand in his way.

Except another gritty island woman.

Retta Wright, Lucy Carnegie's granddaughter and heir to Plum Orchard mansion, wasn't going to let the island be destroyed by developers. She realized that the last hope for protecting the island was the National Park Service. It had been eyeing Cumberland since 1955, when it had announced plans to create a network of national seashores, since only 6 percent of shoreline along the Atlantic coast was protected. National Seashores were national parks focused on protecting beach resources and recreation. The National Park Service recommended sixteen sites along the Atlantic for national seashore status: Cumberland Island was ranked second, just behind Cape Cod, as most impressive and most urgent. Environmental groups rallied behind the Cumberland Island park proposal, especially when they learned of Fraser's plans for the island.

While other Carneiges were sipping wine with Fraser, Retta invited President John F. Kennedy's Secretary of Interior, Stewart

Udall, to tour the island. He liked what he saw, and he began working on a national seashore bill for Cumberland Island. Meanwhile, Retta implored her family to consider selling to the National Park Service instead of Fraser. Initially, the rest of the family resisted the idea of a national park. They found it distasteful that big government might open their vacation playground to the general public.

But they were growing increasingly hostile toward Fraser, especially after a Carnegie heir married one of Fraser's junior executives. The wedding was held at Plum Orchard mansion, and Fraser arrived at the reception carrying a large suitcase of maps. To the Carnegies' horror, he unrolled his blueprints while the newlyweds danced, and he touted his eco-sensitive development plans in between toasts. The Carnegies' disdain for the obnoxious, new-money developer soon soured into outright revulsion. They decided not to sell any more land to Fraser and joined Retta in negotiations with the National Park Service.

The National Park Service offered island families a sweetheart deal: not only would it pay them millions for selling their land, but the families would also get to continue living on their land for the rest of their lives (or for a set number of years). Each of the twenty-one landowners who sold their property to the National Park Service received special rights to live, drive, and recreate within the national park. The National Park Service would maintain their roads, haul off their trash, and build docks for their use. They could lease their vacation properties. The National Park Service would also keep their estates private and ensure they could frolic separately from the unwashed masses. It was the best of all possible worlds: receive millions, guarantee the upkeep and protection of the island, and continue to live there for decades to come.

Nearly all of the Carnegies sold to the National Park Service. Retta's family generously sold their land for significantly less than market value, and they donated Plum Orchard mansion outright. Other Carnegie families were not as altruistic. They sought top dollar for their lands and secured lifetime rights for unborn grandchildren.

After the Carnegies turned on Fraser, he grudgingly signed over his lands to the park. He used the money from the sale to build a deluxe development on Florida's Amelia Island, just south of Cumberland. But he remained bitter about how the Carnegies had vilified him. He pointed out that, despite their professed love for Cumberland Island, the Carnegies had clearcut large portions of Cumberland and tried to strip-mine the island. "The Carnegies on Cumberland are among the most selfish families in America," Fraser said decades later, still bruised by their rejection. They deserved no credit for saving Cumberland, he argued. It was only Lucy's trust and the Georgia Supreme Court that kept them from raping the island for timber and titanium.

There was one other unsung hero in the national seashore saga—and this time it wasn't an island woman, but a rural county clerk named Edwin "Fats" Godley.

In order for the national seashore bill to be signed into law, Congress needed the support of the local Camden County board of commissioners, and time was running out. The five-person board was divided: two supported the national seashore, two were on the fence, and one boisterous commissioner was loudly opposed to it. He was dead-set on a bridge connecting Cumberland to the mainland. "No bridge, no deal," he told Representative Bill Stuckey, who was championing the national seashore bill in Congress.

"That session of Congress had just about ended," Stuckey recalled. "Either the bill went through or you could kiss it goodbye."

So Congressman Stuckey arranged to meet with the commissioners over dinner and drinks. He also extended an invitation to the county clerk, Fats Godley. During the five-course meal, the congressman guffawed with the commissioners and swapped hunting stories while dining on straight-from-the-net seafood. Then, just before dessert, the congressman excused himself to the restroom. On cue, Fats Godley invited the commissioner opposed to the bill over to the bar in the adjoining room. There he bought the commissioner several vodka shots. Within a few minutes, the wobbly commissioner could barely keep his head off the bar. Meanwhile,

Congressman Stuckey had returned to pitch the seashore bill to the two undecided commissioners.

By the end of the evening, the Camden County board was behind the national seashore bill, and the bridge was kept out of the legislation.

Cumberland Island National Seashore was officially established on October 23, 1972, though land acquisitions continued for the next decade. The thirty-six-thousand-acre barrier island became the country's largest and most biologically rich national seashore.

One Carnegie heir never sold to the National Park Service: Lucy Ferguson, heir to the Greyfield estate. Lucy initially opposed the legislation creating the national seashore, and her political influence nearly prevented it from being enacted. She despised the National Park Service almost as much as poachers, whom she regularly chased off with a shotgun. Both were uninvited intruders upon her island. She believed the Carnegies had been better island stewards than the National Park Service could ever be. When she overheard a junior park employee lecturing to visitors about her island, she chimed in, "You tell 'em, goldfish. You've been around the bowl."

Lucy viewed the entire island as her own, including the animals. She laid claim to the entire population of cattle and hogs that freely roamed the island. Also hers were the sea turtles—and their eggs, which she liked to use in her cakes. Even the humans were part of her island empire. "She thought she owned just about everything that walked on Cumberland," one of her cousins quipped.

A wisp of a woman, Lucy was barely five feet if she stood on her toes, and she weighed only eighty pounds. Yet Lucy was the toughest, bossiest, and meanest in Cumberland's long history of matriarchs. She was a strict authoritarian who demanded complete control of her island domain. According to island lore, she once shot at an airplane that flew too low across her island, though she didn't come close to hitting it. She even ordered around the park rangers, whom she called Smokey Bears.

"With a little point of her finger, sort of like the Red Queen in *Alice in Wonderland*, she could command that something get done," explained her oldest daughter, Retta.

Lucy and her husband, Robert, had four children, whom she raised on Cumberland. Lucy taught them how to hunt deer, swim in the ocean, dig clams, and ride horses. On the mainland, Lucy built a horse track for racing thoroughbreds. Lucy had been a champion equestrian as a young girl, and she brought her horses over to the island. During World War II, when the U.S. Army patrolled the beach on horseback watching for German U-boats, Lucy sometimes wandered over to their barracks and taunted the officers, "Why don't you boys bring your horses to the beach and see how fast they are?" Lucy's steed usually won.

When family money began to run out, she supported the plans to strip-mine Cumberland. She even sued her family in a separate effort to break Lucy's trust. When the state supreme court squashed the strip-mining deal, Lucy came up with a new plan: she decided to turn her mansion into an upscale bed and breakfast. The Greyfield Inn brought wealthy tourists to the island, where they played badminton on the shore and sipped martinis on the gabled porch at sunset.

Lucy ran Greyfield Inn with an iron fist. The first sight of her jeep rolling past the north gate at Greyfield caused the staff to issue a special alert. She conducted unannounced bra checks, running her hands up the backs of female employees. She refused to buy a dishwasher for the inn because she thought it engendered laziness. She fired employees without explanation—including her son Ricky and her granddaughter Gogo.

Of utmost importance to Lucy was defending her island from intruders. She wanted to keep her family utopia untouched by outsiders. She armed her property manager, J. B. Peeples, and instructed him to chase off any poachers who set foot on Cumberland. J. B. drank a lot, and he had cut off the fingers of his right hand in a table saw accident. That didn't stop him from smoking. He held a cigarette between his nubs and smoked it to the very end.

One sweltering, bug-slapping night, J. B. heard a boat motoring up the tidal creek behind the abandoned Dungeness mansion. He stamped out his cigarette, cocked his gun, and crouched behind a tree. Two men with rifles crept up the bank. J. B. stepped out and shone a spotlight in their faces.

"Get the hell off this island or I'll blow your goddamn head off!" he shouted.

The men took off running back to their boat. J. B. recognized one of them as A. L. Hickox, a man Lucy had arrested for poaching a few weeks earlier. He pursued them and demanded that they stop. When they didn't, he shot Hickox in the back. The wounded poacher limped back to the boat and escaped.

The doctor who treated Hickox on the mainland confirmed that he had been hit in the back with buckshot pellets. But Hickox claimed that he had accidentally shot himself.

A few weeks later, on June 24, 1959, the grandiose Dungeness mansion caught fire. The blaze was spotted just a few hours after sunset. It had started on the third floor of the abandoned estate. Fed by the tinder-dry pine paneling, peeling wallpaper, and rotting curtains, the fire swallowed the fifty-nine-room manor.

Carnegies were having cocktails on the veranda at Plum Orchard Mansion when they smelled smoke. Suddenly, one of Lucy's employees raced up the drive, shouting, "Dungeness is on fire!" They dashed down to Dungeness and stood helpless beside the burning mansion. They watched the floors crumble and the family hearth collapse, and they could hear the furniture's pine resin exploding. With no water or firefighting equipment, all they could do was try to keep the fire from spreading. Palm trees beside the mansion were on fire, so they cut them down. Boats lined the Cumberland Sound to gawk. The arsonist was also allegedly there that evening, watching his handiwork from the shadows.

The fire burned all night. The bright orange glow could be seen from the town of Brunswick thirty miles north. By morning, the ruins still smoldered. Only a charred shell of the three-story castle still stood, its roofless ruins pointing jagged brick fingers to the sky.

With no energy source inside the vacant mansion and no lightning storms nearby, authorities ruled it a clear-cut case of arson. A. L. Hickox, J. B.'s victim, was the obvious suspect, but the proof had gone up in flames with the mansion. The sheriff determined that there was insufficient evidence to arrest Hickox. He was never charged.

Though they differed in their political views, Lucy and Carol were remarkably similar in both personality and appearance. Like Carol, Lucy had high cheekbones, chocolate-brown eyes, dark hair, and a radiant, olive complexion from a life outdoors. Both wore old, discarded clothes from thrift stores and carried a bandana and buck knife wherever they went.

Lucy and Carol were misunderstood loners who found refuge in nature. They saw and experienced the world differently, and one reason may have been deafness. Carol had lost much of her hearing in her right ear after the shooting range accident with her dad. Lucy was nearly deaf, a legacy of having scarlet fever when she was thirteen. But Lucy could still hear well enough to become adept at selective listening, especially with National Park Service personnel. She often feigned deafness when she didn't like what was being said, a trait Carol instantly admired.

They both felt a close kinship with animals. Lucy raised thirty Dalmatians, dozens of chickens and peacocks, and a pet deer. She traveled the world and brought back exotic animals. Ostriches laid eggs on the porch of the Greyfield mansion, and kangaroos bounded across the freshly mowed lawns. Sicilian donkeys roamed the island with a herd of fifty Hereford cows.

Like Carol, Lucy even had a fondness for vultures. Lucy once rescued a baby black vulture from the mainland and raised it on the island. It perched on Lucy's shoulder and ate only the choice-grade beef that she hand-fed it.

Both Lucy and Carol were expert naturalists who spent their days wandering the woods and mucking deep into the marshes.

They were the only two women who lived full-time on Cumberland. Though forty years apart, Lucy and Carol were eccentric, bareback-riding, gun-wielding women who felt a deep affinity for the wild. The elder Carnegie matriarch and the penniless young naturalist shared an abiding passion for the island—but they would soon clash sharply over how to save it.

8

When Carol arrived on the island in the summer of 1973, Sam Candler gave her an aerial tour of the island in his single-engine Cessna. Carol marveled at the lemon-colored marshes between Cumberland and Little Cumberland, threaded by brown ribbons of tidal creeks. Christmas Creek snaked across the north end, splintering Little Cumberland from the main island like a hangnail.

Cumberland was a sliver of sensuous beauty, shaped like a conch shell. It was three miles wide at its midriff, though its girth narrowed to less than a half mile at its southern waistband. Most of the Cumberland's interior was cloaked in thick forest, scarred only by the Candler compound and four Carnegie mansions.

The plane yawed in the sea wind. Sunlight glinted off Lake Whitney, the freshwater heart of Cumberland and home to most of the island's alligators. Sam banked left and glided low over the wide, blond strip of beach. Cumberland's soft, cream-colored sand was 150 million years of weathered Appalachian quartz and granite that had washed downriver into the ocean, where waves had sculpted sandbars into barrier islands. Cumberland—like all barrier islands—acts as a shock-absorbing shield, sheltering the mainland from the full force of storms and tides.

As they flew south, crumbling slave chimneys appeared through the trees, near an overgrown meadow and landing strip for the Carnegie planes near Stafford mansion. Just past Stafford, the Greyfield Inn came into view. The gabled manor and its sprawling green lawns were nestled against the western edge of the island, with a dock jutting into the sound. One mile south of Greyfield, Charles Fraser's abandoned real estate office had been turned into Sea Camp, the National Park Service headquarters, where rangers met passengers disembarking from the ferry. Near the southern end of the island, Sam's plane swooped over the charred, crumbling

ruins of Dungeness, which overlooked a vast expanse of tidal creeks all the way out to the pelican-dotted jetty.

The developed beaches of Florida loomed to the south. North of Cumberland were resort beaches stretching all the way to Savannah. And on the mainland across from Cumberland were marinas, factories, and the belching smokestacks of paper mills. Even from the air, Cumberland was an oasis, a place apart.

Woolly mammoths, sloths, giant tortoises, and saber-toothed tigers once roamed the island after migrating from the mainland during the last Ice Age. After the glaciers melted, many animals—including deer, coyote, bobcat, and armadillo—swam over. Today, Cumberland has the greatest biological diversity of any barrier island. It was designated a national park in 1972, six months before Carol arrived.

Sam banked the plane north toward home and put the entire island under his wing. He spiraled down, nearly skimming the pine tops, and landed on a bumpy grass airstrip near the Candler compound. He swung open the plane door to utter silence. Two horses grazed on the edge of the runway. One looked up to watch people emerge from the giant painted bird, then returned to munching grass.

Climbing out of the plane with Carol was her boyfriend, John Pennington. Two decades of hard-nosed investigative journalism had worn him down. He was ready to chuck it all and follow his girlfriend to a remote island, where they would work as hired help for a wealthy family. An award-winning writer for the South's largest and most prestigious newspaper was now folding linens and changing lightbulbs.

John was broad-shouldered, robust, and chiseled, with dark skin, a sharp nose, and a gray-flecked beard. Carol especially loved the light that danced in his hazel eyes—a warm, flickering flame that threw sparks when he laughed. He had a deep, mellifluous voice that was gentle and reassuring, and he radiated an aura of intellect and authority.

John had recently left his wife and three children. Soon after, he began pursuing Carol. He was sixteen years older than Carol and

was enchanted by her boldness, beauty, and brilliance. They had been dating only a few months in Atlanta when Carol was offered the custodian job for Sam Candler's family on Cumberland Island. Before she left, John asked if he could join her. They were both looking to escape, he said. They should do it together.

John had other reasons for following Carol to Cumberland. He was burned out, his marriage had fallen apart, and he needed a fresh start. Amid the island's isolation and inspiration, he hoped to pen the next great American novel. He lugged a battered old Royal typewriter to the island and began pecking at the keys.

"Island life promised few temptations for the pocketbook. I left my newspaper job in Atlanta and paid the price in lost income to get away from the contrived environment of the city," John wrote in a story about Cumberland for *National Geographic.* "I wanted to feel the touch of a clean breeze, the wet kiss of the rain in a natural setting, to hear the ocean's roar instead of the freeway's, the trumpeting call of the pileated woodpecker instead of the jackhammer's clatter. I wanted to calm some discordant notes and reattune myself to nature's rhythms."

As they drove from the airstrip to the Candler property, they passed the Settlement, the cluster of collapsing, abandoned shanties where the African American freedmen and hotel servants had once lived. At the edge of the Settlement was the First African Baptist Church—now a sagging one-room structure with white clapboard and a rusted tin roof.

Then Sam toured them around the Candler property: the old two-story hotel where the family dined; several modern chateaus where Sam's brothers and sisters vacationed; a one-room cabin where a Gullah fisherman named Jesse Bailey lived; the house of African American couple George and Audrey Merrow, African American handyman and cook; and a dingy, decrepit cottage where John and Carol would be staying. The hired help were the only year-round residents on the compound. The Candlers visited their vacation retreat a few times each season.

Sam, Carol, and John stood on a cedar bridge spanning a tidal creek and watched for the gator that lived in an algae-covered pond. Carol tossed an acorn into the pond, rippling the surface.

"There's something you should know about my family," Sam said. "They're somewhat traditional. They're not comfortable with an unmarried man and woman living under their roof."

Carol kicked at the bridge pilings. "We're not leaving. We just got here."

Sam scratched the back of his neck and wiped beaded sweat from his brow. "Maybe you could imply that you and John are planning to get married."

"There's a church just down the road," John said.

"I'm not getting engaged," replied Carol.

"Just play along," Sam said. "For a while, at least."

"Come here, missus," said John, wrapping his arm around her waist. The light in his eyes twinkled. In the pond, the alligator rose to the surface, its snout covered in lime moss, its corrugated spine barely dimpling the water.

"Call me that again and you're gator bait," Carol said.

Carol put in her hours polishing silverware for the rich and famous, while John drove the Candler boat back and forth to the mainland, hauling groceries and supplies. George mowed the lawns and tinkered with engines, and his wife, Audrey, cooked meals for the families. The Candlers sat around a long, wooden table and rang a dinner bell when they were ready to be served. Audrey appeared through the swinging door with shrimp cocktail, shucked oysters, and wine-braised pork tenderloin.

Audrey was a plump, ponderous woman and a deeply devout born-again Christian. "Cumberland is the Lord talkin' to himself," Audrey told Carol. "And my, how he do carry on. Ain't it all so praiseful?"

It soon became Audrey's singular mission to save Carol from her sinful, godless ways. Once, when Carol went out to the beach to gather mussels, she found an empty glass bottle planted squarely in the middle of the mussel flats. In the bottle was a note scrawled in Audrey's handwriting that read: "Give your heart to Jesus and be saved."

"Do you know anything about this message in a bottle?" Carol asked when she returned to the mansion.

Audrey grinned. "That was God's handiwork, not mine."

Carol didn't have much use for religion. It was a comforting fiction that people invented to avoid facing death. The biblical command to "be fruitful and multiply, fill the earth and subdue it" was one reason the planet was such a mess, she reckoned. Jesus seemed like a stand-up guy, though John the Baptist inspired her more ("the guy wandered the wilds living on locusts and wild honey!"). She was impressed by Jesus' forty-day sojourn in the wilderness, and she liked his speeches about poverty and living simply. But she didn't buy his water-walking miracles or his heavenly gibberish. Jesus was a good man—maybe the best of men—but still a death-bound mortal like the rest of us.

"Why do the sleepy-eyed masses flock to church every week to recite the same worn-out prayers?" Carol wrote in her journal. "Most of them are afraid of dying. They want absolute reassurances of an afterlife to shield them from the hard realities of life and death."

Still, she was intrigued by Audrey's unswerving faith in a heavenly hereafter. She had never met someone so unshakably certain.

"What's heaven gonna be like, Audrey?" Carol asked while washing dishes together one evening. They worked side by side in the clammy kitchen, the windows wet with condensation. Carol lathered and rinsed the dishes while Audrey dried and stacked.

"Aww, honey, in heaven, there's no misery, no work. God will wipe away every tear."

"What exactly does this heaven look like?" Carol asked.

"Why, it'll look just like this, sugar, but everything gonna be good. Once you got your ticket to heaven, this world don't matter no more."

Carol turned off the water and leaned against the sink. "So you're just waiting around so you can die and go to heaven? We're already living in paradise. Heaven is right here if we open our eyes to it."

Audrey swung her towel over her shoulder. "That's easy for a pretty white girl like you to say. This life ain't no heaven for me."

* * *

The pretty white girl made a meager $25 a week working for the Candlers. John was paid more and worked less, but Carol didn't care. She would have worked for free to live on Cumberland, and she didn't need much money to get by.

She had to feed herself, though. So Carol plowed a garden using the Candlers' tiller and planted okra, tomatoes, peppers, eggplant, pole beans, creasy greens, and collards. In the cooler months she grew radishes and arugula. She fertilized her garden with seaweed that had washed onto the beach. She also raised chickens and kept a hive of bees.

The island's white-tailed deer and wild hogs were plentiful, and she gathered wild chanterelles and salad greens from the lush maritime forest. But the most abundant island resource—tidal creeks teeming with shrimp, crabs, and fish—remained elusive. She tossed a fishing line from the Candler dock with little success. She hung crab traps from the pier that caught nothing but grass and mud. She found a drift net on the beach and cast it in the creek for hours, but she came up empty every time.

Carol was practicing casting the net off the Candler dock one evening when she heard a voice behind her: "Yo arm broke?" It was Jesse Bailey, the reclusive resident fisherman. He lived alone in a small cabin by the creek, and he rarely spoke to anyone except his mangy, flea-riddled mutt, Jessico. Jesse was responsible for gathering fresh fish and shrimp each day for the Candler family.

"Throw that net wide," he told her. "Put some muscle behind it."

Carol tried again, but dragged in only a tangled, dripping net.

"Don't aim it. Throw it." Jesse showed her how to hold the net like a bullfighter's cape, arm extended and parallel to the ground. From his hands, the net swirled out like a windblown blossom over the water.

Imitating Jesse, she threw the cast net again. It spread wide and sank to the bottom. Then she pulled the drawstring toward

her and yanked hard. The net came up jumping with mullet, sea trout, and flounder.

"Hot diggety!" Carol shouted, amazed by her catch flapping about on the dock.

"You can admire 'em later," Jesse said. "Get yo net back in the water while the tide's right."

Jesse had spent his entire adult life on Cumberland Island. The fifty-six-year-old fisherman was the king of Christmas Creek, a serpentine tidal sluice coiling through the north end's saltwater marshes. It lived up to its name: Christmas Creek offered abundant gifts of fish and shellfish, and Jesse knew its maze of meandering tributaries like the lines on his palm.

Carol began joining Jesse on explorations of the creek and its marshes. At low tide, she met Jesse before dawn at the Candler dock, where his rusted motorboat was tied to a barnacled pier. Jesse climbed in first, followed by Jessico, who curled beside the boat's bucket stove, still warm with glowing coals from the previous night. Jesse stirred the embers with a cedar stick until a small flame leaped.

"Make yo self useful," Jesse said to Carol. "Grab them nets."

She heaved the cast nets into the boat and climbed in. Jesse tugged the rip cord several times until the engine finally sputtered to life, spewing puffs of dark smoke.

"I is too hungover to chitchat witcha," he said, arcing the boat away from the dock. He held a cigarette between tobacco-stained fingers. Jesse's weathered face was ringed with white stubble. His clothes—a worn denim jacket, threadbare khaki pants stuffed into gum boots, a faded hat—were all smeared with marsh mud.

They headed into a small tributary, where curtains of cordgrass closed in quickly. Jesse cut the motor and drifted into a tidal pool ringed by oyster beds. He guided the boat over to the beds and chunked oysters into the boat. Then he rolled up his sleeves and climbed into the prow on his knees, plunged his bare arms over the side, and searched the silty creek bottom for clams. Like a blind man, he gathered them by touch, pulling black bivalves out of the sludge.

He talked to the clams, cajoling them sweetly with feminine names, counting them by twos as they clanked the bottom of the boat.

"Never clean out a clam bed," Jesse told Carol. "Only take a few. Remember, we just passin' thru."

Jesse poled upstream and tossed his cast net. Moments later, he dumped its catch of flopping mullet and white-bellied sea trout in the boat, atop the clams and oysters. He pushed the writhing fish into a pile with his foot. Carol enjoyed the sounds of the water lapping lazily against the skiff and the easy silence passing between her and Jesse.

Weighed down by the bounty, the boat worked hard against the ebb current on its way back to the Candler dock. Jesse tied up the boat while Carol loaded the catch into burlap sacks and hauled them ashore. As they shucked oysters together on the dock, Carol asked if they could venture out into the sound the next day.

"My boat can't make it that far," Jesse said.

"Why don't we take the Candler boat?"

"Can't. Ol' man Candler says I is a drunk."

Jesse's drinking had indeed worsened. He constantly reeked of stale whiskey, and increasingly he skipped fishing trips to sleep off his hangover. The Candlers threatened to fire him if he didn't remove all the liquor from his cabin by the end of the month.

"Here's the deal, Bailey," Carol said. "I'll keep your liquor for you and dole it out each morning. One glass only—enough to keep you buzzed but not wobbly. In exchange, you keep me in seafood."

There was a long silence. Carol started to wonder if he had heard her. He shucked one oyster, then another. Finally, he said: "I can live wit' dat. I ain't gonna clean them fish, though. I catch 'em. You clean 'em."

Every morning, Jesse showed up at Carol's cottage at first light, awaiting his daily splash of liquor. John was usually still asleep, so Carol sat on the porch and drank holly tea while Jesse sipped his bourbon. Jesse didn't talk much at first, but it wasn't because he was scared or shy. He was Gullah and spoke with a distinct dialect—a long, lilting creole with a slow, tidal cadence.

"Folks say I talk funny. So I don't say much, cept to folks who wanna listen," he told Carol.

Carol doled out two drinks on Jesse's fifty-seventh birthday. She started cutting his matted gray hair and washing his clothes. During his haircuts, he began telling Carol about his Gullah heritage.

"Most Gullah is ashamed. Can't get no job talkin' Gullah. Folks can't unduhstand what we's sayin. It don't bother me none, tho. I is proud a be Gullah."

Jesse was born in one of the world's last remaining traditional Gullah communities, just thirty miles north of Cumberland. For centuries, Gullah lived mostly in small farming and fishing communities, often on isolated islands. In one-room praise houses, they danced ring shouts to improvised African drumbeats, stomping and clapping in a circle (American jazz and blues likely grew out of the Gullah ring shout). Gullah women wore head wraps and wove baskets from the marshes' sweetgrass, and they enjoyed a rich cuisine based primarily on rice.

In the seventeenth and eighteenth centuries, rice fields blanketed most of the Georgia and South Carolina coast. American colonists had discovered that rice would grow well in coastal Georgia's moist, semitropical climate, but they didn't know how to grow it. So they purchased Gullah slaves from the traditional rice-growing region of Africa.

Gullahs were the largest group of slaves imported to the Deep South. They were also the only group of slaves to retain most of their traditional African culture. One major reason, ironically, was disease. When the Gullah arrived on slave ships in the seventeenth century, they brought with them malaria and yellow fever, which thrived on the swampy coastal islands and especially around waterlogged rice plantations. The Gullah slaves had already developed resistance to these tropical diseases, but their white masters were extremely vulnerable. Fearful plantation owners moved away from the rice fields and left their farms altogether during the rainy summer months when disease was rampant. The plantations were often run by trusted Gullah overseers. By the early 1700s, there were

more Gullahs than whites in Georgia and South Carolina. European visitor Samuel Dyssli remarked in 1737 that the Southern coast "looks more like a negro country than like a country settled by white people."

The Gullahs also benefited from geographical isolation, living on remote sea islands accessible only by boat. When the islands' rice economy collapsed after the Civil War due to competition with larger rice plantations farther west in Louisiana, Arkansas, and Texas, most white farmers abandoned the islands entirely. The Gullah were left behind in areas of meager commercial importance and of little interest to the outside world, enabling them to maintain their own independent communities and traditions.

As a result, Gullah have been among the most fiercely resistant fighters in American history. Gullah have led mutinies and fomented insurrections. Many Gullah were able to escape slavery entirely by fleeing to Spanish-controlled Florida, which in the eighteenth century was a vast tropical jungle. Gullahs established their own free settlements in the Florida wilderness and built friendly relations with refugee Indians hiding out in the swamps. In time, the two groups came to view themselves as parts of the same loosely organized tribe—the Seminoles.

Seminole comes from the Spanish word *cimarron*, meaning "runaway," and it applied equally to the Gullah and the Indians. Both had fled from American colonialism, and for nearly a century, the biracial alliance of renegades lived free in the Florida wilds. Nearly a quarter of Seminoles were Gullah, and they became known as the Black Seminoles. The Black Seminoles flourished and reared several generations of children in freedom along with the Indians.

In the early 1800s, the Seminole Wars erupted when American armies advanced into Florida. Gullahs and Indians fought side-by-side to stop the American advance, but eventually they were driven south into the more remote Everglades. There they continued resisting American forces through full-scale guerilla warfare, fleeing deeper into the wetlands' cover.

After thirty years and thousands of American casualties, the Army finally captured most of the Seminoles by 1842, though a small band of holdouts never surrendered and remained ensconced in the Everglades.

American generals didn't know what to do with the Black Seminoles: return these fugitive slaves to their owners or relocate them to reservations? Fearing the rebellious Gullahs might incite more insurrections back on the plantations, the military marched them west to Oklahoma.

Not surprisingly, the Black Seminoles did not stay put on the reservation. Some escaped south across Texas to the deserts of Mexico, where they established another free settlement. Heavily armed bands of Texas Rangers rode into Mexico to destroy the settlement, but the Gullahs defeated them. Later, a handful of Black Seminoles were invited by the U.S. Cavalry to join the army. Three of them won Congressional Medals of Honor—America's highest military decoration.

But many remained resistant to American rule. Today, there are still small Black Seminole communities scattered across North America and the West Indies. They live on Andros Island in the Bahamas; in rural Seminole County, Oklahoma, where they are still official members of the Seminole Indian Nation; and in the dusty desert town of Nacimiento in northern Mexico. Elders in these far-flung communities still speak Gullah.

The largest traditional Gullah community was located on Georgia's Sapelo Island, where Jesse Bailey was born in 1916. No bridges connected Sapelo to the mainland. An hour-long boat ride through narrow, gator-infested tidal creeks was the only way to reach the island. Jesse's family grew bountiful gardens in the fertile black soil, hunted and trapped wildlife, and fished the fecund waters. At an early age, Jesse learned how to cast for shrimp, trap crabs, and gather shellfish from the marshes.

Then in 1934, tobacco titan R. J. Reynolds Jr., purchased over half of Sapelo Island. The Gullah were forcibly concentrated into a 434-acre tract called Hog Hammock on the island's south end.

Many Gullahs began leaving the island for education and jobs, and others sold their land to developers. Today, only forty-one Gullah remain on Sapelo.

Jesse was one of the last to leave. When he was eighteen, he fell in love with a girl, and she with him. But their families said they were too young and forbade them to marry. Heartbroken, Jesse struck out on his own. He served in World War II and worked in a yacht yard before eventually landing a job gathering fish and bait for the Candlers. The spell of Cumberland came over him, and Christmas Creek became his new mistress.

Jesse's girl from Sapelo eventually married another. Jesse occasionally cavorted with a Candler maid, but the island became his abiding love. On his adopted Cumberland homeland, he was one of the last traditional Gullah in coastal Georgia, a holdout living alone on ancestral island soil, fishing the tidal creeks, telling stories in his native tongue, walking in the footsteps of his forebears.

"Know bout Hush Yo Mouth?" Jesse asked Carol one afternoon as they hiked along the edge of the marsh gathering mussels. He led her through shoe-sucking mud and lime-green walls of cordgrass to a hidden island in the marsh called Hush Your Mouth. At high tide, the mini-island in the marsh was surrounded by a moat of tidal creeks. At low tide, Jesse and Carol could cross the creeks in one leap without getting their boots wet.

"Lotsa folks hid out here," Jesse said. For centuries, the one-acre island had been a refuge for fugitives and outlaws. Pirates menaced the Georgia coast in the seventeenth and eighteenth centuries and frequently holed up on Cumberland. Blackbeard was rumored to have buried his treasure somewhere along the Georgia coast. Buccaneers, squatters, and lawless bands of backwoodsmen escaped to tiny, tucked-away hammock islands like Hush Your Mouth. During the Civil War, fugitive Gullah slaves from Cumberland Island plantations sheltered temporarily on Hush Your Mouth, and after the war they formed freedmen settlements nearby. Thick palmetto shielded

the island's rim, and a canopy of pond pine and live oak screened Hush Your Mouth's shaded interior, reducing access and visibility from the outside.

Carol and Jesse spent the afternoon on Hush Your Mouth, watching a storm roll in across the marsh. A line of thunderheads gathered over the water, staining the sky black. Lightning danced between the swollen anvils of cloud: first a warm glow in one, then a blinding flash in another. They sat front row center for the entire show, until a thick curtain of cloud descended after the final act.

"I'm glad such simple things make me happy," she told Jesse.

Rain whipped sideways across the windswept marsh as they hiked toward home. Amid the pattering of the rain, they heard a horse whinnying. Ahead, a ragged mare was stuck chest-deep in the marsh mud. Her tawny skin sagged loosely over her bony frame. Maggots were already feasting on her rump. Blood pooled beneath her eyes.

"Dat mud done got her in its grip," Jesse said. "She ain't gonna budge."

Carol ran back to the Candler garage and grabbed a shovel and some two-by-fours, along with rope from Jesse's boat. She placed a platform of boards around the horse and began digging around her legs. The horse slurped water from rain puddles and tried to nibble at nearby clumps of marshgrass.

"She can't eat no mo'," Jesse said. "Look at 'em teeth. They is worn down to nubs."

The cold rain lashed down, and the horse's skin shook violently. After an hour of digging, Carol could reach down to the horse's hocks but still couldn't free her legs. So she looped the rope around the horse's ribs and wrapped the other end around a nearby cedar tree as a fulcrum. Carol dug her heels in deep and pulled on the rope. The horse swung her head feebly from side to side and moaned.

The rain drizzled on. Carol, covered head-to-toe in marsh mud, her hands rope-burned and flayed, took a break to wring out the water from her flannel. Then she dug in deeper and pulled until her hamstrings quivered. Finally, she heard the mud begin to gurgle and hiss. The horse's hooves slurped out. Jesse joined her in pulling, and the listless horse lurched out of the mud and onto her

side. She lay heaving and twitching. Carol tried to coax her onto her feet, but the horse was too tired. Her tongue lolled, and she sputtered blood. The rain had finally stopped, and the darkening marsh was still and silent.

"It's late," Jesse said. "You done all you could. We'll come back tomorrah to check on her."

The next morning, Carol woke before sunrise and dashed out to the marsh. She brought another rope and a sack of feed. Stars still clung to the blushing sky as Carol slopped along the rim of the marsh.

She saw the silhouette of the horse ahead, lying on her side. Carol walked closer and saw something move. She dropped her feed sack and ran toward her.

The horse was dead. Vultures roosted atop the carcass and had already begun plucking at its flesh. She shooed them away and knelt beside the horse. "I should have stayed," she whispered, her eyes bright and burning. "You didn't deserve to die alone." Then she unsheathed her knife and slowly cleaved slabs of leathery horseflesh. The vultures watched from the trees.

9

When Carol returned home, John was in his bathrobe pouring a vodka and Coke. A clean sheet of paper hung limply from his typewriter.

"I thought you were driving the boat this morning," she said.

"Just finishing up this chapter."

"Buddy will blow a gasket if you're late."

John shrugged. Carol sliced a hunk of horse meat into the skillet, along with a couple of eggs from her hens.

"They've got George and Audrey on bells," he mumbled. "They're too lazy to get up from the table. They gotta ring a goddamn bell so their black servant can lift a fork to their mouth."

"Easy, John." He had been drinking heavily since he started writing his novel.

"I'll drive their boat and buy their groceries, but I'm not gonna be their slave. If they ring a bell at me, I'm gone."

"They only put the blacks on bells."

He tossed back the rest of his drink. "I'm a writer, not some peasant."

"I don't like it either. But we gotta do something to earn our keep. I can wipe their ass during the day if it buys me nights on the beach."

Every evening since she had arrived, Carol had been observing loggerhead sea turtles crawling ashore to nest. She walked along the water's edge until she came across the V-shaped tractor-tire tread of turtle crawls. On moonless nights, she nearly stumbled over giant sea turtles lumbering up the beach.

With their rear flippers, turtles scooped out flask-shaped holes deep in the dunes. Once they finished digging, Carol huddled behind

the turtles like a quarterback and counted the eggs as they dropped from her cloacas. The turtles rocked back and forth, grunting and heaving, as over a hundred eggs dropped one by one coating Carol's bare hands in a viscous ooze. Because sea turtles drink saltwater, they shed excess salt through tears, which dripped from the corners of the nesting turtles' eyes. Carol's eyes were wet, too. She was awestruck by the ancient turtles, matriarchs of mother ocean, elders emerging from the coal-dark water like shadows of the earth's past.

Two months later, the impregnated dunes spilled their secrets. Beneath the stirring sand, one hundred hatchlings broke through their shells, climbed out of the nest, and scampered to the sea. After witnessing her first turtle nest hatch, Carol wrote in her journal: "It was nothing short of soul stirring—the prehistoric turtles, the wild beach, the transparent darkness, the wind, the primeval pounding surf. There was a feeling of being especially close to the undefinable Source."

Even as a child, Carol had been especially fascinated with turtles. She once had watched a turtle in her backyard thaw and return to life after freezing. Turtles' blood acts like antifreeze, allowing them to tolerate extremely cold temperatures. They also can thrive in the hottest, driest deserts. Turtles have spread across every continent except Antarctica and have colonized nearly every ecosystem from mountaintop to ocean floor. Sea turtles can collapse their lungs, enabling them to dive a half-mile deep into the dark ocean. They've even been to outer space. Turtles orbited the moon before astronauts: in 1968, the Soviet Union launched an unmanned spacecraft carrying a pair of tortoises, who returned safely to earth after a week in space.

Turtles are one of the oldest animal species still on the planet, dating back 230 million years. They are survivors, enduring the eons with unswerving, steadfast stamina. Their longevity is due largely to their shells. No other animal has built such a bony box around itself. It formed over millions of years as turtles' ribs widened and fused together. Turtles can't be detached from their shells, just as we can't be separated from our spine. Their shells also have nerves

and veins embedded in them, so if the shells are injured, the turtles bleed and feel pain.

Large birds can scoop up turtles in their beaks, lift them in the air, and then drop them on rocks to break open their shells. The only human known to be killed by a turtle was the Greek tragedian Aeschylus, whose bald head was mistaken for a rock by an eagle flying overhead.

All turtles, tortoises, and terrapins have shells. Tortoises live only on dry land, turtles live mostly in water, and terrapins live in brackish marshes. Sea turtles are among the few turtles who can't fully retract their head inside their flattened shells, which are streamlined for swimming through the water.

Sea turtles also have flippers instead of feet, and they're much larger than other turtles. All seven species of sea turtles are endangered, and five of them nest on Cumberland Island. *Leatherbacks* are the largest, and they have a peculiar third eye—a sensitive, signal-receiving pink splotch on their forehead—that may act as a compass in their ocean navigations. *Kemp's ridleys* are the smallest and most endangered. *Hawksbill* turtles have shells that change colors—from amber to chocolate—depending on water temperature. Tortoiseshell—harvested primarily from hawksbill sea turtles—was one of the most popularly traded items in the world for most of human history. It was used to make elegant jewelry, combs, brushes, and ornaments until it was banned in 1973 by the Endangered Species Act. *Green* sea turtles are one of the ocean's largest vegetarians. *Loggerheads* are the most common turtle to nest on Cumberland and make the longest migrations across the Atlantic.

Loggerhead sea turtles are so named for their broad, block-like head, which is covered in thick mahogany scales with canary yellow borders. The world's largest loggerhead nesting ground is the Southeastern United States, home to over twenty-five thousand nests each summer, more than half of all loggerhead nests worldwide.

At first, Carol watched the nesting sea turtles from a distance. But her scientific curiosity soon got the best of her. Before long, she was counting eggs, measuring shell lengths, and flagging the buried nests so she could watch them hatch a few months later.

She stayed all night on the beach with the turtles. She slept only a couple of hours, between sunrise and 8 A.M., when she had to report for work at the Candler compound. Usually she crashed in the dunes just before dawn and let the sun wake her. When she opened her eyes after the black-and-white night, she was swallowed up in color: the sapphire sky, the golden sea oats along the dunes, the clouds hanging like pink fluffs of cotton candy above the water. The island iridescence invigorated her every morning, helping her slog through the day's housekeeping and maintenance, so she could do it all over again the next night.

Carol soon joined the island's turtle tagging project, one of the first in the country, which the University of Georgia had launched in the late 1960s. Her friend Rebecca Bell, who worked for the university and lived on Little Cumberland Island, taught Carol how to staple the metal identification tags into nesting turtles' front flippers. Later, Cumberland was the first place to use satellite tags, which enabled researchers to follow sea turtles after they left the beach. Turtles tagged on Cumberland were found feeding along the coasts of Africa, South America, and northern Europe.

Research on Cumberland also showed that sea turtles return to nest on the same beaches where they were born. Biologists used genetics and tagging to confirm that turtles who hatched on Cumberland traveled across the Atlantic, and then thirty years later swam back to their birthplace to nest. It was an astounding—and puzzling—discovery of one of nature's longest and most remarkable migrations: a creature returning to a pinpoint target after three decades at sea. How could turtles find their way back to their home beaches from thousands of miles away? Was it millions of years of patterned instinct, or was it observational clues that they followed? How did their grape-sized brain guide them back to the exact beach where they had hatched thirty years earlier?

Carol published her first scientific paper on sea turtle migration patterns in the mid-1970s. She believed that the turtles likely used a variety of tools, including scent markings on the beach, underwater topography, positions of the sun and stars, and motions of the currents and tides. However, Carol suspected that the earth's magnetic

field was their primary map, and the iron compounds in the turtles' brains were their compass needles.

Carol was deeply intrigued by the turtle navigational mystery, but she also worried about the impacts of tagging. To tag a turtle, Carol grabbed the rim of the turtle's shell and flipped her onto her back. It was no easy feat: a 120-pound woman hoisting a 300-pound turtle upside down. The turtles snapped their razor-sharp jaws, flailing and groaning. Quickly, Carol stapled metal tags into the turtle's cartilaginous front flippers. Then she rolled the turtle back onto her belly. Turtles often flung sand at her as they crawled away.

"I could tell a tagged turtle just by reaching for her flipper," Carol said. "If she had been tagged before, she jumped as soon as I touched her. Untagged turtles didn't jump. That taught me two things: turtles feel pain, and turtles remember."

Did the turtles remember Carol when they crawled ashore to nest? She certainly remembered them. Hundreds of turtles nested on Cumberland, and by the end of her first summer she could identify dozens of them on sight, even before checking their flipper tags. One of them was the giant loggerhead turtle that Carol later rode bareback. The easiest to recognize was an old female loggerhead whose left rear flipper had been chewed off by sharks. Carol named her Stumpy. Stumpy's one-flipper tracks in the sand were unmistakable, and she nested seven times in Carol's first summer.

Stumpy couldn't dig her nests very easily with only one rear flipper, so Carol helped her scoop out sand. She also vigilantly guarded Stumpy's nests, shooting scavenging hogs in the dunes nearly every night. Two months later, on a still, sticky midsummer evening, Carol noticed dimples in the sand above one of the nests. The bubbling beach erupted into a boil of hatchlings clambering out of their shells and flapping toward the surface.

Amid the mosh pit madness, the first gritty, gooey hatchlings climbed onto the beach and scrambled down the dunes. Carol chased away ghost crabs scuttling toward an easy feast: over one hundred morsels of turtle meat scraping their way out of a hole. They groped and stumbled over each other, leaving ribbons of sand trails as they made their mad dash to the sea.

Night herons dive-bombed the hatchling parade, grabbing a beakful of fast food. Other hatchlings got stuck in rutted vehicle tracks, where ghost crabs gobbled them up. A raccoon waited at the bottom of the dunes, picking off hatchlings as they skittered past. Emptied hatchling husks were strewn across the sand.

Only a trickle of turtles made it to the ocean, where each sliding pane of water lifted them from the beach like a spatula lifting cookies off a tray. Stalking the surf were hungry crabs, fish, and sharks. But these hundred hatchlings had a shot at life, and they were ready to take their chances in the wild waters.

Carol walked back to the nest. A lone hatchling remained buried in the clutter of broken shells. It raised a front flipper helplessly, mired in goo and sand. In the dunes, the raccoon skulked closer, and the antennae eyes of a ghost crab watched her.

Carol was a practical, matter-of-fact scientist who understood the hard laws of nature. Crabs and coons had to eat, too. But sea turtles were on the brink of extinction. So she scooped up the hatchling and carried her down to the ocean's edge.

"You're on your own from here," she said. Carol set the hatchling onto the wet sand. The baby turtle flapped frantically as the tide washed beneath her and carried her out to sea.

Thanks to satellite tagging technology and genetics, biologists can track turtles on their nine-thousand-mile migrations, and they can chart and even re-create a turtle's journey from hatchling to adulthood across the open ocean, like the one made by Carol's rescued hatchling. Her journey began on Cumberland Island. At the ocean's edge, the hatchling dipped her snout into the wet sand and imprinted the scene on her brain, recording the magnetic energy of wind and wave converging there.

Then the water swept beneath her, and she gasped for air amid the choppy surf. The tides spun her sideways and knocked her upside down. Panicked, she thrashed her flippers and breathed the last of the oxygen in her lungs. Her pebble-sized heart pounded harder. Acid flooded her arteries. Her body went limp. She started to drown.

As she sank, the undertow swept her out beyond the big waves. It was calmer out here—and deeper. Drawn to light, the hatchling instinctively and desperately swam toward the moonlit water above her. She popped to the surface and gulped in the air. For a moment, she rested in the embrace of the ocean, bobbing and rocking in the gentle waves beyond the surf.

Her brothers and sisters were nowhere to be found. Hatchlings face tough odds: only one in ten thousand reaches maturity. Most don't make it off the beach. Out of the hundreds of nests laid each summer on Cumberland, perhaps one or two hatchlings will survive.

The hatchling was alone and adrift on the ocean, dodging jaws in the dark waters below. She had no teeth, and her shell had not hardened. A bird's shadow passed overhead. She could not float on the exposed surface much longer. She glanced back at the beach where she was born. Then she dove and began a three-day, nonstop swim.

Underwater, she was built for speed. Her shell was smooth and streamlined. Her blunted rear flippers acted as rudders, while her long front flippers were her oars. Her body—the weight of a triple-A battery—would be powered by these hinged water wings on a journey crossing one-third of the planet.

Animal migrations are magnificent for many reasons: the steep odds, the amazing feats of precise navigation, and the animals' unwavering focus. All animal migrations seem driven by an instinctive sense of something we humans find admirable: a larger purpose. Migrating animals are undeterred by blazing heat or blinding blizzards. Flocks stick together and work together, following primordial pathways, driven by a common cellular memory.

Monarch butterflies migrate three thousand miles from Canada to Mexico to overwinter. Humpback whales travel four thousand miles from the Arctic to Hawaii to feed and breed in warm, turquoise waters. Over two million wildebeest cross the Serengeti plains of Africa on their eighteen-hundred-mile spring migration. Sandhill cranes fly five thousand miles from Texas to Russia. The arctic tern holds the overall record for the longest animal migration, flying

forty-four thousand miles round-trip from pole to pole each year, breeding in Greenland and wintering in Antarctica.

Sea turtles, unlike most other migrating animals, travel solo. They don't flock along flyways or gather in groups. They captain their own ships across thousands of miles of open ocean.

Traveling one mile per hour, the lone hatchling swam stealthily through kelp forests and sparkling coral reefs. Danger lurked everywhere: prowling the wild waters were reef sharks and hammerheads, giant tuna and marlin, electric eels and toothed fish.

After nearly seventy miles of nonstop swimming, the hatchling was flagging and fatigued. Her flippers hung beneath her, limp and listless. She had only a few caloric fumes left to burn in her tiny tank.

Then a current caught her. The hatchling had reached the Gulf Stream, a spinning ocean gyre that circulated clockwise from the Caribbean to Europe. The five-mile-an-hour current propelled her eastward on a blue highway across the vast Atlantic.

The next day, a thunderstorm roiled the ocean. Groans of thunder echoed underwater. Afterward, the storm's sweepings stretched for miles, where it it had churned up clouds of microscopic plants called phytoplankton. The hatchling followed the trail of debris and flotsam, filling her empty belly with the storm-stirred green goodness. Without phytoplankton, the ocean would be a vast water desert. Phytoplankton produces half of all the planet's oxygen—more than all of the world's rain forests and trees combined. The one-celled photosynthetic plankton coating the ocean are the lungs of the planet.

Every five minutes, the hatchling pricked the ocean's satin surface to take a quick breath. Sea turtles are the most ancient marine creatures that still have to breathe air.

She crossed underwater mountains taller than the Rockies and passed over plains and trenches where sunlight never reached. Swimming mouths were everywhere in the ocean, and for two weeks the hatchling dodged them.

Finally, after flapping seven hundred miles from Cumberland, she arrived in the Sargasso Sea, smack in the heart of the Bermuda

Triangle. Over ten million tons of seaweed floated in its tranquil waters. The hatchling nestled beneath one of the seaweed mats, gorging on plankton and small shrimp, and slept safely in the floating grass bed.

The Sargasso Sea is an ocean eddy stretching two million square miles. It's the only sea without shores. In the Sargasso Sea, the water is clear and blue, winds are calm, and it rarely rains. An ocean oasis for tiny turtles, the Sargasso Sea is the still eye of the Atlantic, surrounded by swirling ocean currents that feed the seaweed sanctuary.

Sargassum—a species of brown seaweed—can live for hundreds of years. Some of the sargassum floating there today might have been seen by Columbus. Sailing the ocean blue in 1492, Columbus was the first European to describe the Sargasso Sea. Ever the optimist, Columbus took the seaweed as a sign that he was close to shore, though he was still hundreds of miles from landfall. Meanwhile, his crew feared becoming entangled in the sargassum. For centuries, sailors dreaded passage through the "sea of lost ships." Ships had often vanished without a trace in the Sargasso Sea: derelict vessels were found shipshape but deserted, and slave ships were discovered with nothing but skeletons aboard. The ships weren't swallowed by sargassum, however. They were stalled by the sea's deadly doldrums. Ships found themselves becalmed for weeks in windless waters.

The Sargasso Sea was every sailor's worst nightmare—and every sea turtle's dream. The hatchling haven harbored thousands of turtles who floated and fed in the sargassum thickets and slept in rafts of seaweed, sheltered from the open ocean.

Over the next decade, the hatchling grew until her shell was hard as a shield, her head tough as a helmet. She began foraging beyond the sargassum jungle in search of her favorite food: jellyfish. Masses of moon jellies, medusas, and lion's manes floated up from the abyss. She joined other fledgling turtles in devouring the tentacled, translucent treats. She was now ten years old and the size of a Frisbee. To tiger sharks patrolling the sargassum, she looked like a dinner plate floating on a platter of golden seaweed.

There were other dangers, too. Barges began to rumble through the Sargasso Sea with towering mounds of seaweed piled on their decks. The barges gathered sargassum using mechanical rakes skimming the surface, and harvesters sold the seaweed at $50 a ton for biofuels, fertilizers, and cattle fodder. The sargassum refuge was disappearing to feed cows.

After ten years, it was time for the juvenile turtle to venture out of the shrinking seaweed sanctuary. She swam out to the gyrating Gulf Stream current and began a four-thousand-mile journey farther eastward to soak in the bath-warm waters off the western coast of Africa. Unlike her swim to the Sargasso Sea as a defenseless, delectable dinner-to-go, now she was built like an armored tank.

The turtle carried on her back the weight of her species, which had dwindled to less than 2 percent of its original population since Columbus first set sail. They had persisted through ice ages, million-year droughts, and meteor-induced mass extinctions. Now, the sea turtle hoped to survive the greatest threat her species had ever faced—us. She would need some help from an old friend back home.

10

Carol was becoming feral. She ate wild-caught critters, sometimes raw. She trained her body to rely on only one meal a day, staying lean and mean like the other predators stalking the island. She bathed in the surf. Her body was adapting to sleeping in short snatches, just like animals. The exhaustion toughened her resolve. "Overextend your will to strengthen it," she wrote in her journal.

On Cumberland, she lived through all five senses. She and the island were melting into each other. "It's almost like you become the weather out here," she noted. Thunder rattled her bones. Heat drained the sap from her veins. Rain washed her clean.

Carol memorized and sketched every species of plant and animal on Cumberland. "We no longer know the names of things," she said. "When we don't know the names, we cannot mourn their loss."

She began dissecting every dead sea turtle that washed ashore to figure out why they were dying. She soon preferred the fetid funk of carcasses to the pungent perfume and cologne of the wealthy islanders. Citified living smothered our natural instincts, Carol believed. Only contact with the wild could uncover them. It couldn't happen in a day hike. It required deep immersion in wilderness, where senses are sharpened and instincts honed.

"When I look at a human, I see an animal," Carol wrote. "I see our disguised animal thoughts and instincts simmering beneath modernity, seeping to the surface."

Carol didn't think we should abandon civilization and become hunter-gatherers. She sought a border life that combined the vitality of wilderness with the technological growth of modern society. The ideal human being straddled the frontier between wild and civilized, an amalgam of the best of both worlds.

But the balance had tilted lopsidedly toward civilization and away from wilderness. Pollution coated the planet, and people crowded out animals and ecosystems. Less than 1 percent of the

globe was still supposedly protected for nature, and it was disappearing fast.

Carol knew she couldn't save even 1 percent of the world. But maybe she could save a wild island and the hundreds of turtles who nested there.

On a starry summer night in 1974, Carol walked along the surf's edge at low tide, searching for turtle tracks, while John trailed behind her. It was his first time patrolling with Carol.

"I'm getting eaten alive," he said, slapping the back of his neck. Mosquitoes hummed in his ears and sand flies nibbled at his ankles. He scratched his forearms until they bled.

"You shouldn't have worn shorts and a T-shirt," Carol replied. She wore a long-sleeve flannel shirt with a wire notebook stuffed into the chest pocket, a bandana around her neck, and a floppy, wide-brimmed hat with a pencil slotted through a notch in the brim. Tucked into her firefighter's boots were baggy, mud-smeared jeans with a knife and watch hanging from the belt loops. Most of her clothes were shades of brown, green, and gray—her favorite color—which blended with the muted tones of the forest and beach.

Her outfit of salvaged men's clothes was often ridiculed, especially by the fashionable island families who vacationed on Cumberland, but long-sleeve shirts and rugged pants were the most practical attire for life on a barrier island. Sand flies swarmed the seashore, especially at night. The forest was infested with ticks carrying Lyme disease. Mosquitoes bred in the marshes, and fire ants fed in the open fields. Cumberland was home to venomous cottonmouth moccasins and diamondback rattlesnakes, the largest and deadliest rattlers in North America. Alligators slid through the sloughs. This wasn't Cancún or Daytona, where beachgoers with bare skin, board shorts, and bikinis stretched for miles. This was a wilderness island, where exposed flesh was chewed, chawed, and chomped.

John doused his bare arms and legs with bug spray, but it offered little relief. Carol pulled a poncho from her backpack. "Wear this. You'll get sweaty but at least you won't get eaten up." Then she gathered wax myrtle from the dunes and slathered his face with oil

from its crushed leaves—a natural insect repellent once used by the native Timucuans.

A blueberry moon ripened on the horizon. The wind was still, the ocean taut and glossy. Across the beach, ghost crabs scuttled sideways and vanished into burrows, their stalked periscope eyes poking up from the sand. Rotted skeletons of stranded turtles littered the beach. Vultures had already picked at many of the fresh carcasses. Others were bleached and bone dry.

"Why are there so many dead turtles?" John asked.

"Don't know yet, but I've got a hunch, " Carol said. It was a murder mystery that she would spend the next four decades trying to solve. Carol conducted a necropsy—an animal autopsy and dissection to determine the cause of death—on each of the ninety dead sea turtles that first summer.

The necropsies were already revealing some tantalizing clues. Carol straddled one of the putrefying turtle carcasses and lifted its smashed skull. Sharks usually went for the flippers, not the hard cranium, she explained. And there was no ripped flesh to indicate a boat strike. She suspected that the turtle took a blow to the head from a blunt object, like a sledgehammer.

"Who would bash in the brains of a harmless sea turtle?"

Carol nodded to the orange lights of shrimp trawlers moored just offshore. They were so close that Carol could hear the shrimpers' conversations.

Farther up the beach, Carol spotted the glowing eyes of a hog digging in the dunes, its cheeks swollen with turtle eggs. Domesticated hogs, set loose by island families, had overrun Cumberland and were ravaging sea turtle nests. Pork filled Carol's freezer, but she didn't shoot hogs just for their meat. Carol wanted them off the island. She reached for the gun tucked into her jeans.

"Don't shoot it," John said.

"That dang hog is gobbling up mouthfuls of endangered species."

Twenty yards downwind, Carol clicked a bullet into the barrel of her revolver and aimed.

"You're tinkering with evolution."

"I'm restoring it," Carol said. Humans brought hogs to the island only a few decades ago, she explained. Turtles have nested on Cumberland for millennia—and they swam a long way to get here.

John swatted at sand gnats swarming his ears. "Maybe turtles are meant to go extinct."

"Not on my watch."

Carol steadied her pistol and squeezed the trigger. The hog snorted, rolled down the dunes, and landed in a clump of sea oats. Blood leaked from its toothed snout. Carol dragged the hog by its hind legs out onto the beach and cleaved a hunk of pork belly. "We'll have bacon for breakfast," she said.

Fireflies flickered through the trees like camera bulbs flashing in a crowded stadium. John pulled a bottle of whiskey from his backpack as they trekked up to Long Point, the northernmost tip of Cumberland Island, where a turtle had nested at the bottom of the dunes. Carol used a cockle shell to dig another nest higher in the dunes, where it wouldn't get inundated by the tides. She filled the new nest with eggs in the exact same order they were deposited, since the gender of sea turtle hatchlings was determined by temperature—warmer eggs closer to the surface resulted in females, while cooler temperatures deeper in the nest produced males—or, as Carol put it, "hot mamas and cool dudes."

"First you shoot a hungry hog. Now you're digging nests for the turtles," John said. "I know your intentions are good. But I don't think you should be playing God."

"Look around," she replied. Dozens of dead sea turtle carcasses were strewn along the island. Thousands more littered the Southern coast. And those were just the few that actually washed ashore. "It's a turtle holocaust out here, and no one seems to care."

Around midnight, they came upon a dead leatherback—the world's largest sea turtle, weighing over a ton, with a twelve-foot wingspan. It would have filled a pickup truck, with its flippers hanging over the sides and touching the ground.

This was Carol's first leatherback sighting—and also a first for the island. No one had ever seen a leatherback, dead or alive,

on Cumberland. She knelt beside its hulking carcass and stroked its thick, lustrous pelt. She strummed her fingers along its ridged back. Its unwrinkled skin was loose and movable, like an elephant's. Carol used her steel knife to carve open the flat-bottomed shell, slicing through ivory-colored muscle and brown ribbons of fat.

John, bone-tired and mosquito-tormented, grew weary of watching. "I'm heading home," he said.

"It's not even a hair past midnight," Carol replied.

"Why don't you come back with me?" John said. "You've been on the beach every night since we arrived. The turtles can spare you for a few hours."

"This is my first leatherback. Come on, John. Stick around till dawn."

"No more damn turtles. You care more about them than me."

Later that evening, Carol checked the nests of Stumpy, the one-flippered sea turtle. One of her nests hatched just before dawn, and Carol described it in a letter to her parents: "Sand trails spider-webbed out from the nest as the hatchlings scampered toward the surf. Maybe it was the effects of chronic sleep-deprivation, but standing atop the dune watching the tiny turtles swim in the mother ocean for the first time, it felt—there's no other word for it—holy. What a way to spend a Sunday morning! Just think: some people have to go in a big building and bow down to some tortured idol to find the same satisfaction. I get miracles every day. Ain't I lucky?"

Carol had been writing her parents every week. She sent them animal bones and shells, along with updates about her island life. The letters became a weekly combination of field notes and diary. She found it a lot easier to communicate with her parents on paper.

In the same letter, she confessed that things weren't going well with John. He had worked a desk job all his life and wasn't used to long hours of manual labor, even if it mostly consisted of driving a boat to the mainland to get groceries.

He had other regrets. John had left behind a wife and three children in Atlanta, and the guilt began to weigh heavily on him. Did

he make a mistake abandoning all that he loved to work a crappy custodian job on Cumberland Island? "John was literally being eaten alive by guilt," said his close friend Robert Coram, a colleague from his days at the newspaper. A few years later, it turned out, John was diagnosed with colon cancer.

The great American novel wasn't materializing, either. Even on a remote wilderness island, he was too distracted. John got caught up in island social gatherings and stayed out late cavorting with some of the younger Carnegies and Rockefellers, especially since Carol spent every evening on the beach. When he actually sat down to write, he stared at the blank paper in the typewriter, banged at the keys for a few minutes, and then drank himself into rage or stupor.

John's depression-fueled drinking had made him increasingly volatile. The light was fading from his once-sparkling eyes. Carol loved the man he used to be. But she didn't trust the drunk that he had become. She wasn't going to let another guy drag her down again.

Carol wrote to her parents: "He complains of writer's block. It's more accurately called a hangover. He's been drinking heavily, especially at night, and it usually leads to tantrums. He is extremely possessive of my time and jealous of my work, and his drunken rampages are only getting worse."

Her parents wrote back a week later: "Please try to work things out with John. He clearly loves you, perhaps overly so. He's hard working, handsome, and loves the outdoors almost as much as you. Think of the stability he could provide to your uncertain future. Think of how much fun you could have together sharing your adventures, rather than going it alone."

Carol fired back a quick one-line response: "I learned long ago never to rely on anyone for my happiness."

The beach was her nightly escape. Every evening, she fled into the arms of the ocean. Sea turtles became her closest companions, and she immersed herself in their night life. She was a midwife for the hundreds of turtle mothers who entrusted their offspring to the island.

Carol fiercely guarded her nests and didn't back down from a fight, especially when it came to turtles. Sea turtle populations

had declined by 98 percent in the past five centuries. She believed wholeheartedly that saving sea turtles was the key to saving the human race.

"If sea turtles go extinct, we'll go down with them," she said. "Turtles are the ocean's pulse. When the turtles are gone, the ocean will flatline—and so will we."

The ocean covers most of the planet, produces most of our oxygen, provides most of our food, and absorbs most of our pollution, she explained. When the ocean can't support sea turtles, it won't support us either.

Already, humans are starting to feel the sting. Plummeting sea turtle populations have led to massive blooms of their main meal: jellyfish. When sea turtles once numbered in the hundreds of millions, they controlled the population of their favorite food. With sea turtles on the brink of extinction, jellies now swarm the seas. Jellyfish plagues are closing beaches around the world and filling the void left in our overfished oceans.

As long as humans have wandered the planet, turtles have nourished and protected us. Giant sea turtle shells were used as shields by ancient hunters. Their abundant eggs fed many coastal cultures, and fishing communities from Africa to Asia relied on turtle meat as their main source of protein.

In nearly every civilization, turtles were considered sacred, appearing in cave drawings, Egyptian petroglyphs, and Native American totems. Mayans saw the earth as a giant turtle afloat in a circular sea. Hindus believe a sea turtle carries the entire universe on its back.

Many cultures worldwide have arrived at similar turtle-centered origin stories. In each version, the world begins covered in water. Only a few animals inhabit the flooded earth, and one of them is a sea turtle, the only animal that can swim down to the bottom and retrieve mud. The turtle dries the mud on its back, providing the first solid earth. More mud is added until it forms Turtle Island. The turtle eventually bears the weight of the entire world on its shell. Many indigenous cultures still refer to the earth as Turtle Island.

For centuries, sea turtles have aided people, especially those lost at sea. Japanese fishermen etched markings on the shells of turtles

crawling ashore to nest, so that marked turtles could guide them back home. Sea turtles were even credited with the success of the European colonization of America: because sea turtles can live for years without eating, thousands were stored alive in the holds of explorers' ships in the sixteenth and seventeenth centuries. The turtle meat sustained them on their long voyages to the new world.

The Seri people in the Gulf of California still sing the sea turtles home to their nesting beaches. Dr. Jeff Seminoff, a marine biologist at the National Marine Fisheries Service, was skeptical of the singing ceremonies until he accompanied two elder Seri fishermen in the late 1990s: "It was a gray, windy day on the water, and our boats nearly capsized. I was wondering what the hell we were doing out there. Then the two elders start singing. It was a low, steady, guttural chant. Instantly, the rain stopped, the wind calmed, and the clouds parted. And—I'm not kidding you—turtles started surfacing around our boats. I was astonished. But the Seri were just matter of fact about it: 'This is how we sing in the turtles.' As a scientist, I couldn't explain it. But there they were."

Turtles may have even altered the course of science and history in 1835, when Charles Darwin landed in the Galápagos Islands and met the world's largest living species of turtle, the Galápagos giant tortoise, which weighs nearly nine hundred pounds. Most intriguing to Darwin were the tortoises' shells. Turtles from each island had slightly different shells, an observation that helped him formulate his theory of evolution.

Today, the turtle is one of the most ancient animals on the planet. It is an unexpected evolutionary star. Instead of taking center stage, it has watched stoically from the sidelines. It hid in the shadows as dinosaurs dominated the planet, settling for durability over dominance. When the lights went out on the dinosaurs, the turtle pensively pondered the furry mammals that stepped forward to shine and, later, the hairless hominids that swarmed across the savanna.

For 230 million years, the humble turtle has plodded onward, enduring drought, volcanic eruptions, million-year glaciations, and meteor impacts. It survived at least three mass extinction events that wiped out 95 percent of the species that ever lived on earth. T-rex

and the saber-toothed tiger were far stronger and faster, but in the evolutionary race, the slow and steady turtle won.

Turtles aren't quite as sluggish as Aesop's famous fable made them out to be. A softshell turtle can outrun a human on flat land, and sea turtles can swim up to thirty-five miles per hour. But turtles have definitely earned their long-lived reputation. The oldest turtle known to science, Adwaita, lived 255 years. He was born in 1750 in India and, like Gandhi, he was a vegetarian. Adwaita ate the same meal for all ninety-three thousand days of his life—a plentiful mix of lettuce, carrots, wheat, and salt that fueled his stout 550-pound frame. A lifelong bachelor, Adwaita died in 2006 after his shell cracked and infected wounds developed.

Jonathan, a 180-year-old turtle, is the oldest known turtle alive today and the oldest land animal on the planet. He resides in a preserve on the British colonial island of St. Helena, and despite his age, he continues to mate regularly with three younger females.

In 2012, a pair of giant turtles at an Austrian zoo broke up after 115 years together, marking the end of the world's longest known animal partnership. And in 2013, a pet turtle in a cardboard box was discovered after being accidentally locked in a storage closet for 31 years. It had survived by eating insects and drinking drips of condensation.

No other animals consistently live as long as turtles. They are one of the creatures closest to immortality. Don't be fooled by their wrinkles and slow pace: turtles don't really die of old age. Turtles' organs do not break down over time, and older turtles are actually more fertile than juveniles. Turtles even have the power to stop the ticking of their personal clock. Their heart isn't exclusively stimulated by nerves, so it doesn't need to beat constantly, and they can turn it on and off at will. Deep-diving turtles can slow their heartbeat to conserve oxygen: nine minutes can elapse between beats.

Turtles may be able to stop their hearts and live for centuries, but they can't avoid shrimp trawls, longlines, drift nets, dredges, pollution, disease, oil spills, boat propellers, garbage patches, ocean acidification, dead zones, and beachfront development. On land, crime syndicates sell turtles as food, medicine, pets, and collector's

items on a global black market, where some endangered turtles fetch as much as $60,000. Half of the world's three hundred species of turtles are headed for extinction—including all seven species of sea turtles. The turtles' supreme longevity hasn't spared them from becoming the most endangered reptile on the planet.

Near the end of the summer in 1974, Carol was crouched in the dunes watching a turtle nest near Long Point. It was a cool, breezy September evening around midnight when she saw bright lights moving across the water. Two motorboats bounced along Christmas Creek and landed on Cumberland. When the fishermen's spotlights flashed across the beach like strobes, the turtle aborted her nest, dribbling eggs behind her as she scampered back to the sea.

Fuming mad, Carol marched up the beach toward the pack of fishermen, who were unloading coolers and lawn chairs. A radio garbled a football game's play-by-play from their brightly lit beachfront encampment. Carol stood in the shadows.

"Howdy, fellas!" she shouted. One startled angler fell out of his lawn chair. The radio cut off. A scruffy-bearded man wearing a blaze-orange cap and camouflage jacket walked toward her, drawing on a cigarette. A crowd gathered behind their camo-clad leader.

"It's awfully dark and dangerous for a purty gal like you to be out here alone," he said.

"I'm sorry, guys, but you can't fish here," Carol said. "The beach is closed at night for turtle nesting."

There was a long silence. Carol stood her ground. The fisherman crushed his cigarette on the beach and blew the last puffs of smoke in her face. "Little lady, I've been fishing here since I was a boy. My granddaddy brought me here, long before there was any law telling me where I can and cannot fish."

Carol's pulse raced. "I like to fish, too. But this beach is protected at night. There's plenty of fine fishing back in the creeks."

The fishermen snickered and crowded closer. Their spokesman tugged on his cap. "No tree hugger is gonna chase me off, especially one with tits."

The anglers erupted in guffaws and catcalls. Carol casually pulled back the flaps of her unzipped jacket by resting her hands on her hips, revealing the nickelplated .45 pistol tucked in her belt.

"Now listen, fellas, I don't want any trouble."

The chew-spitting fisherman stumbled backward over his cooler. The others hurriedly packed up their tackle and loaded up the boats.

The next morning, Sam Candler stopped in to visit Carol, who was changing the oil in the Candler boat.

"Word has spread across the island: there's a pistol-packin' mama patrolling the beach." He grinned. "Any idea who they're talking about?"

11

Despite Carol's sleepless summer of all-night turtle patrols, feral hogs had destroyed nearly all of the island's sea turtle nests. Formerly domesticated pigs released for sport hunting had overrun the island, digging up nests and devouring turtle eggs. To guard the few remaining nests, Carol shot fifty hogs on the beach in one weekend.

Lucy found out and was furious. All of the island hogs belonged to her, Lucy claimed. But Carol continued shooting hogs. An old, crotchety Carnegie heir wasn't going to stop Carol from hunting feral swine, especially to protect primordial sea turtles.

Lucy had other reasons for not liking Carol. She was an island newcomer and outspoken outsider who didn't play by the rules. She didn't obey Lucy's commands or bow down to Carnegie prestige. Carol thought endangered animals deserved the same rights and protections as people. She was even promoting the idea of a federal wilderness designation on Cumberland Island, a level of environmental protection greater than that provided by the national park.

Worst of all, though, was Carol's party foul: she had brought a black man, Jesse Bailey, to the Greyfield Christmas festivities one year. Jesse was Carol's best friend, and she didn't think anyone would mind him tagging along. But Lucy didn't like "Negroes" at her private parties. For months afterward, Lucy fumed that Carrion Carol shot all of her hogs, ate ticks, and "kissed Niggermen right in the mouth."

"I have shot some hogs, and I do smash ticks between my teeth. It's the fastest and easiest way to kill them," Carol admitted. "But the only black man I have kissed is Jesse, and only on the cheek. I suppose kissing a black guy was the most shocking thing she could think of, so she gave it a run."

Lucy and Carol crossed paths one evening at twilight. Carol was riding a wild horse bareback, racing as fast as she could back home to beat the darkness. The first stars were already burning through

the dusky sky. Flying through the forest, she saw headlights in the sandy road ahead and slowed her horse to a trot. She stopped beside an idling jeep. It was Lucy.

Carol could see jealousy flicker in the old woman's eyes. All her life, Lucy loved to race horses, but now that she was in her late seventies, she could no longer ride. Carol hopped down from the stallion.

"You shot my hogs," Lucy said.

"They're eating your turtle nests."

Lucy leered sideways at Carol. "You some kind of turtle hugger?"

"Turtles have just as much of a right to be here as us. Maybe more. They're the true island matriarchs."

Lucy glared. "Why are you on my island anyway?"

"It feeds me."

"Well don't feed on my hogs. I'm an old woman, but I'm not getting moldy yet. I'm still full of piss and vinegar."

Lucy got out of the jeep to examine Carol's horse. She stroked his withers. "I heard about the fishermen you chased off a while back."

"You're not the only woman here who can handle a gun," Carol said.

"I don't tolerate poachers on my island."

"I'm on the beach every night. They won't come ashore on my watch."

Lucy nodded. "Stop by and see me some time. I won't bite."

Carol began visiting the elder island empress every week with a notepad and tape recorder, collecting Lucy's aging warehouse of knowledge about the island's natural history. Lucy knew where the alligators denned and bald eagles nested. She had observed the last pocket gophers on the island and the first armadillos to arrive. Carol scribbled down every detail.

"I wish my kids had turned out like you," Lucy said one afternoon. "None of them give a damn about the natural world."

Islands are constantly in motion. So was Carol. She worked all day cleaning house for the Candlers and tracked turtles all night on the

beach. Carol was propping her eyes open with toothpicks to stay awake. She drank strong home-brewed tea made from island yaupon holly leaves, ate gingersnaps, and snuck in ten-minute naps between turtle crawls.

One moonless night, while waiting for a turtle to finish nesting, Carol curled up beside the turtle and fell asleep. She dreamed that she was back in her cave beside the river, her dog beside her, warmed by a crackling campfire. Then, to her horror, she looked deeper into the flames and saw the burning skeletons of feral cats.

Suddenly, something bumped her. She opened her eyes and forgot completely where she was. All she saw was a large moving animal right next to her face. She sprang to her feet, fists cocked in fighting position, heart pounding. A hot, tingling flash of adrenaline coursed through her veins as she prepared to defend herself against . . . a nesting sea turtle. She unclenched her fists as her hazy-headed awareness slowly returned.

When the first flush of dawn tinted the horizon, Carol hoped to squeeze in a few hours of shut-eye. That's when she noticed a small dead turtle on the beach: it was a Kemp's ridley.

"Shucks," Carol mumbled.

Kemp's ridleys were especially rare sea turtles. Until the 1960s, scientists weren't sure they were a separate species because they had never actually seen a ridley nest. For decades, they had searched the globe for nests and come up empty.

Unbeknownst to science, ridley nesting grounds had already been discovered. In 1947, a young pilot named Andres Herrera was flying over a deserted stretch of beach in northeast Mexico when he was awestruck by a stunning sight: forty thousand sea turtles crawling ashore on a single stretch of coastline. Ridleys blanketed the beach. Waves of turtles climbed out of the ocean and over each other, throwing sand and digging in a frisky, feverish nesting frenzy. Herrera could have walked the entire beach on the backs of ridleys and never stepped foot on the sand. Herrera filmed the scene, showed it to family and friends, and then shelved it.

For thirteen years, the film collected dust while biologists continued to scour the world's shores for ridley nests. Finally, Archie

Carr, the father of sea turtle biology, heard rumors about the footage. He teamed up with another turtle biologist to track down the film, and their sleuthing eventually led them to Herrera. Archie teared up like a sea turtle as he watched the faded, flickering, black-and-white footage, scratched and shaky, panning across a Mexican beach completely covered in ridleys. Archie had spent two decades searching for a single nest, and here were tens of thousands of them crammed into a few miracle miles.

The ridleys' simultaneous mass nesting was called an *arribada*—arrival in Spanish. Other sea turtle species nest at night across several months in multiple locations, but nearly all Kemp's ridley females nest on the same day on a single Mexican beach. They travel thousands of miles from as far north as Canada to converge on the same beach on the same day. No one knows how they communicate the timing of their mass nesting migration.

Like a flash mob, they storm the beach without warning. Predators are even more surprised by their daylight arrival: fewer coyotes, feral dogs, jackals, and bears are active on the beach during the hot, dry day, and they fill their bellies quickly, allowing most ridleys to nest unmolested.

But soon after scientists discovered the ridley nesting beaches, locals found them, too, and began digging up the ridley eggs to eat and sell. Turtle eggs are used like Viagra in Latin America. Men drop eggs in their beers and chug them, believing that turtle eggs enhance their virility. Even more ridleys died in the nets of bottom-dragging shrimp trawlers. The ridley population crashed, and by the late twentieth century only three hundred ridleys came ashore.

Carol dissected the dead ridley at dawn, skipping her two hours of sleep between sunrise and work. She couldn't miss an opportunity to look inside the world's most endangered sea turtle and search for clues to its ongoing massacre. She found one: bloody lungs, which indicated that this sea turtle went into oxygen-starved shock just before death.

Afterward, Carol returned to her cottage and collapsed on the threadbare mattress. She was wrung out from long days of work and

sleepless nights on the beach. Her head felt like a can of spray paint turned upside down, the little ball slowly sinking. "I can't keep this up much longer," she whispered to herself. She closed her eyes. In the soggy summer heat, the bedsheets stuck to her sweat-damp skin.

Moments later, she heard commotion down at the Candler dock. Carol wiped away a puddle of spittle drooling from the corner of her mouth, dragged herself onto her feet, and groggily opened the door. Across the yard was the governor of Georgia.

Jimmy Carter was staying with the Candlers for the weekend. He often brought Rosalynn and his family to Cumberland, and he wrote in his autobiography that Cumberland Island was his favorite place to reconnect with what really mattered.

At the dock, Jesse was casting a net for shrimp, and Jimmy asked if he could try a cast.

"Sho," Jesse said, handing him the net.

Jimmy bunched the weighted edge in his left hand, twisted back, and flung it like a Frisbee out into the creek. The net slapped the water and sank toward the muddy bottom. Jimmy tugged the net and pulled in a catch of minnows, mullet, and a few plump brown shrimp.

"Not bad fo a guvnuh," Jesse said. "But you pulled the line fore the net reach the bottom. Dats where the good stuff is at."

Later that afternoon, Carol and Jimmy strolled along the marsh. Carol plucked a stalk of sweetgrass and twiddled it between her teeth. Jimmy paused and looked out across the marsh.

"I'm planning to run for president," he told her.

Jimmy confided that he was nervous about his chances. He was a peanut farmer from Plains, Georgia, population six hundred. He had never held a national office. He didn't have the finance machinery of the other candidates. "Worst of all, I don't know how to compromise on any principle I believe is right," he said. "When it comes to principles, I'm as stubborn as a south Georgia turtle."

"That's what will make you a great president," Carol said.

Word spread quickly about Jimmy Carter's candidacy. When Jesse heard the news, he laughed. "Jimmy run for president? He'll win. He know how to talk to people. But I can show him somethin about throwin that net."

* * *

Six Candler families used the compound for vacations, including Buddy, Sam's older brother. Buddy was domineering and browbeat the hired hands. He screamed at Jesse for being late with his oysters and tongue-lashed Audrey for serving lukewarm meals. He even laid into John for using the wrong rope to tie up the boat.

"These richies are so goddamn spoiled and used to getting their way," John said.

"Not all of them. Sam's a good guy," Carol replied.

"I don't know how he puts up with these goons. They show up, get drunk, shoot up the place, and then leave."

"That's the best part," said Carol. "They never stay for more than a few days. The rest of the time, we have it all to ourselves."

Sam Candler visited the island most often. Unlike the others, he was quiet, intelligent, and sensitive. He cared deeply about the island, his property, and the people who looked after it. He loaned money to Jesse, and he gave extra vacation time to George and Audrey so they could visit family on the mainland. And he shared Carol's passion for protecting the wild.

Once, Sam and Carol hiked together to observe the endangered wood storks nesting in a grove of trees near Lake Whitney. Sam looked through the binoculars at their featherless ash heads, white bodies, and long, hooked bills. Carol nodded toward the reptilian eyes watching them from the lake. "The wood storks wouldn't be nesting here without the gators," she said, explaining how the gators ate coons and other predators that tried to raid the wood storks' nests.

"Gators guarding bird nests. Who woulda thunk it?" Sam said.

Gators protected sea turtles, too, Carol told him. With healthy numbers of alligators behind the dunes, there were fewer coons, hogs, and other nest scavengers.

Carol and Sam walked along the lake's tangled bank, where shards of coon bones were scattered along the water's edge. Unlucky coons chancing a drink had been chomped by gators waiting silently below the surface.

"How are things with you and John?" Sam asked on the way back home.

"Lousy."

"Don't let my family find out."

"What do you mean?"

"They still think you and John are engaged."

His brother Buddy was already looking for a reason to fire Carol. Her rooster had been waking him up early every morning, and he'd finally had enough. At sunrise, he marched over to Carol's chicken coop with his shotgun. Carol returned from the beach just as Buddy was taking aim.

"What are you doing?" she shouted.

"I'm gonna shoot your goddamn rooster."

"You're not gonna touch him," Carol said, standing between the chickens and the barrel of Buddy's shotgun.

Buddy lowered his gun and scowled. "You get rid of that rooster, or I'll get rid of you."

Carol made new discoveries on nearly every island hike. She followed vultures to hidden alligator dens. She observed a white snail in the dunes that had not been seen for over a century, and she found a new island species of millipede in the still-smoldering duff of a wildfire.

She studied everything from the tiny to the titanic. She kept jars of roaches and kissing bugs on her kitchen table to observe their reproductive habits, and she published a paper on the whales of Georgia based on her dissections of dead carcasses that had washed ashore.

In 1978, Carol discovered a new island species of sundew, a carnivorous plant, and one summer afternoon, she invited John to see it. They bushwhacked through tick-infested palmetto and arrived at the edge of a small pond.

"Where is it?" John asked.

"You're standing on it," she said.

Carol bent down to photograph the plant. The viscous fluid on the sundew's leaves shimmered like diamonds in the filtered sunlight of the forest. "Insects think it's nectar. Really it's a trap," Carol explained.

They watched a fruit fly circle the sundew and land on one of its sparkling drops. The fly's legs stuck to the glistening glue. It tried to squirm free from the gooey grasp as the sundew's pink tendrils slowly wrapped its body, stinging it with digestive enzymes that dissolved the bug alive.

Afterward, John and Carol hiked out together to Terrapin Point, an open spread of mudflats along the island's western rim, and watched the sun sink into the marsh.

"What's happening with us? I left everything to come here with you," John said.

"I never asked you to do that. I never asked you for anything."

"That's the problem. You think you don't need anyone."

"I don't."

A clapper rail rattled its lonely call across the marsh.

"This isn't some fling," John replied. "I'm looking for someone to share my life with."

An aching blue silence swallowed the sky. Carol watched a line of pelicans sail across it. "I can't be that person for you," she said.

John bit his lip. "You're like that goddamn sundew! You're a man trap! You lure guys in and eat them alive."

John stormed back to the cottage, and eventually Carol followed. She had nowhere else to go. And if the Candlers found out they weren't together, they'd both get sacked. So she moved all of her belongings—a desk, a mattress, a microscope, and several shelves of books—to the rear room of their cottage, and she came and went through the back door.

She walled herself off emotionally, too. She stopped talking to John, and her silence only amplified his anger, which occasionally fomented into full-blown fury. The tirades were heard by the Candler family, who began asking questions.

John drank heavily for the next few months. He and Jesse liquored up at the Candler dock and went fishing together. He abandoned his novel completely. "I'm just so damn lonesome," he confided to his friend Robert Coram.

Soon after his breakup with Carol, John began dating a young girl working at one of the Carnegie mansions on Cumberland. She

spent weekends with John, and Carol heard them through the thin cottage walls.

Her name was Lum. She was twenty-six years old and had lived on a sailboat for a year before throwing anchor on Cumberland to work at the Greyfield Inn. After a few months, she left her job at the inn and moved in with John.

To escape the noisy cottage, Carol began spending even more time in the wild. She climbed high into trees to watch ospreys nest and waded deep into swampy burrows to count gator eggs. She necropsied every dead sea turtle that washed ashore and befriended the vultures feasting on their carcasses.

She found another new friend unexpectedly one afternoon while examining a dead otter. She lifted the carcass, and wedged beneath it was a baby otter, still clutching his dead mother's teat. Carol could feel his heart pounding. She stroked his throat with her finger. Then she scooped up the infant otter and carried him in her shirt pocket. The whiskered ball of charcoal gray fur licked her hand with his smooth pink tongue.

She named the otter Gator and bottle-fed him for several months. During the day, Gator splashed in an outdoor bathtub and a shallow pond Carol built for him. Carol had to teach the otter pup how to swim. He clung tightly to Carol's braids and screamed at first. But after a few days, Gator was rolling and splashing in the water, chirping and grunting playfully. At night, Gator curled up at the foot of Carol's mattress.

Gator followed Carol everywhere. On land, Gator resembled a dachshund, with his short legs and long, tubular body. He especially loved trips to the creek, where Carol gathered mullet for him. Carol hoped that Gator would eventually swim away on his own. But he always followed Carol back home, bounding behind her, tail held high.

Carol made new human friends, too. Louie and Betty McKee, a wealthy couple from Jacksonville, built a vacation house on the north end of Cumberland Island. When they came over to the island on weekends, Carol often joined them for drinks and fiddle music on their front porch.

She also began hanging out with Gogo Ferguson, the raven-haired Carnegie heiress who helped her grandmother Lucy Ferguson run the Greyfield Inn on the island's south end. Gogo was disarmingly beautiful, with olive skin, a petite, chiseled frame, and flashing eyes like Carol.

Gogo's real name was Janet. She had earned her nickname as a baby when her first words were not *ga-ga* but *go-go*. She was born in 1951 and lived in Massachusetts most of her life, but beginning at age four, when her parents divorced, she and her two brothers got shipped down to Cumberland for the summers to stay with Grandma Lucy at Greyfield.

"We'd go looking for turtles at night," Gogo recalled. "Back then before the park was here we were allowed to, I think, in the '60s we had dirt bikes, motorcyles . . . It was like *The Lord of the Flies*. We had the run of the island."

While her parents were having cocktails at Greyfield, Gogo and her cousins frolicked on the beach and motored from mansion to mansion. Gogo especially enjoyed swinging the big bell for dinner at Plum Orchard mansion and swimming in its indoor pool. At Dungeness, they played games of "murder mansion" in the spooky, abandoned manor.

Gogo attended boarding school in New England and majored in art at Southeastern Massachusetts University. After college, she wasn't sure what she wanted to do with her life. She bounced around and traveled, and she worked for a year making candy sculptures for a confectionery shop. Then, at age twenty-eight, Gogo came back to the island to help Lucy manage the Greyfield Inn, one of the most exclusive bed and breakfasts in the country and the only commercial establishment on Cumberland Island. Rooms at the inn boast emerald velvet Chesterfield couches, wing chairs, four-poster beds, and sturdy clawfoot tubs. Guests spend the day hiking, reading, bicycling, kayaking, fishing, relaxing on the beach, and going on naturalist-led vehicle tours of the island. In the evenings, they gather in the dining room, feasting on fresh seafood, oatmeal molasses bread, and mocha torte.

"When my dad opened the inn it was black tie," Gogo recalled. "It was very formal. I remember women always in long skirts, evening skirts or evening dresses. . . . I loved that." In the late 1970s, when Gogo first managed the inn with Lucy, men still wore sport coat and tie to dinner.

"My grandmother was my inspiration and teacher as a child," says Gogo. But later on, as manager of Greyfield, Gogo found that her grandmother had strong opinions about how the inn, and the island, should be managed. "It was her home and if she wanted people up at 6:30, she wanted 'em up at 6:30. She could care less whether it was an inn. It was her home and we were not allowed to change any of the bedspreads. " Committed to the inn, Gogo worked long hard hours for her imperious grandmother.

Both Gogo and Carol were young women mending broken hearts and trying to find their place in the world. Both had married and divorced at a young age. They even resembled each other: both were slim, strong, dark-haired, and as beautiful as the island that they loved. Though Gogo now denies it, Carol remembers that she and Gogo hiked together to Lake Whitney to watch the gators, strolled the beach collecting seashells, and waded knee-deep in the mudflats near Hush Your Mouth in search of delectable bivalves.

Carol persuaded Gogo to join her on the island's volunteer fire crew, where they wrestled with heavy hoses and learned how to cut firebreaks. Gogo and Carol took flying lessons together—along with Gogo's brother and others. Carol got woozy on their maiden voyages, but soon the sickness subsided, and she relished soaring over the island with the pilot instructor. Below them, the island came into view: a green forested gem sparkling with the sunflash of lake and tidal creek. They marveled at the vastness and vulnerability of Cumberland. Its emerald forest, marshy labyrinths, and yellow ribbon of beach seemed even more precious from the air.

Both women hoped to protect the island, though they had different ideas about how it should be accomplished. Gogo and her family supported the park, but they also placed a high value on their private stewardship of Cumberland. Carol felt public management and stronger wilderness protections were best for the island.

Though Gogo denies it, she and Carol strolled the beach to-
gether one afternoon talking about men, marriage, and mistakes.
Carol confided in Gogo about her troubles with John. (Gogo denies
that this took place.)

"He is a mess right now," Carol said. "I'm not going to let him
pull me down the drain with him."

Gogo, Carol recalled, suggested that perhaps she was just scared
of having real feelings for anyone.

"No guy is worth it," Carol said. "I have more important things
to do than get caught up in emotional drama."

Gogo was having relationship issues of her own. She had fallen
for a handsome park ranger, but Lucy disapproved of the relation-
ship. According to Carol, Lucy asked the Park Service to transfer
him from the island.

Gogo left Greyfield for a two-month vacation in Scotland, but
when she returned, Lucy had replaced her as manager of the inn. "I
was just devastated," Gogo said.

So she left the island and moved to D.C. Ben Fuller, an art
dealer she had met at the Greyfield Inn, asked her to work in his
gallery. He was fond of wearing a double-breasted suit with his long
hair tied back in ponytail. After six weeks together, they married. Ben
ended up embarrassing Gogo and her family by using the Carnegie
name to sell his paintings. Gogo had a daughter with him, but they
divorced a year later.

"It was a mistake, but we have an incredible child and so it
wasn't that much of a mistake," Gogo said.

Gogo still returned to Cumberland for vacations, and she met
up with Carol for long walks and talks. On their hikes together,
Carol often pointed out bones and skeletons of island wildlife:
the rib of a rattlesnake, the femur of a bobcat, the vertebra of an
alligator.

Like her grandmother, Gogo had always been interested in
animal bones. But Gogo's interest was less scientific and more artistic.
She saw a bare beauty in the curve of a horse skull or the shell of
an armadillo. Gogo eventually decided to make jewelry out of her
Cumberland collections. She later opened a shop in Martha's Vine-

yard, where she spent part of the year, and fashioned pendants and earrings out of bone and shell mixed with turquoise, jade, and onyx and cast in silver and gold. Her jewelry was earthy and elegant, raw and refined, and it soon dangled from the ears and wrists of high-end clients such as Goldie Hawn and Carly Simon.

In the summer of 1978, Carol stopped by one of Louie McKee's parties before heading out to the beach. Louie had connected his radio to a car battery and was blasting Johnny Cash tunes. A group of Greyfield gals were already drunk and singing loudly. Carol tossed back a tumbler of gin and joined them. They used spoons as pretend microphones and sang "Ring of Fire" until their throats hurt.

Louie watched Carol singing from the porch steps while his wife cavorted with the fiddle player. John and Lum were at the party, too, tangled up together on the porch swing. Just before Carol left for the beach, John sauntered over.

"Howdy stranger," he said. "I wanted to let you know: Lum and I are getting married."

Carol caught her breath and tried to smile. "That's great, John. I'm really happy for you."

"We're gonna leave the Candlers. I'm done working like a slave."

"Jesse will miss you," Carol said. "I will, too."

He smiled at her one last time. The light in his eyes had returned and, inside, she felt a flicker of the lost feelings she once had for him. But the man she had loved was long gone—and so was the woman who had once fallen for him. All she could do was walk away.

That night, she found herself alone once again on a dark beach. The wash of the tides soothed her sadness.

The turtles crawled ashore in record numbers that night: she tagged ten turtles and marked as many nests. Just before sunrise, Carol waded into the ocean and rinsed off her forearms, caked in guts and goo. Ten yards away, a pod of dolphins arced across the water. Sleek and silver, they talked to each other with whistles, clicks,

and buzzes that sounded like zippers ripping open. Carol felt a light vibration in her chest as one dolphin rolled past her. Its wet, unblinking eyes met hers.

Carol watched the sun climb out of the ocean before returning home. The glowing apricot painted the clouds with streaks of salmon and lilac. It was a soft, tender sky that hurt her heart. Fatigue had peeled back her skin, and every sensation touched a raw nerve. Her knees felt weak, and she longed for someone to lean against.

When Carol arrived back at the compound, Buddy Candler's truck was parked in front of her cottage. Buddy sat in the front seat, engine idling, and rolled down the window halfway.

"You lied to us," he said.

"I'm sorry, Buddy. It wasn't my idea."

"Pack up and get out. You've got two weeks." Then he grinned from behind the glass. "Don't forget your chickens."

He revved his engine and spun off, kicking up a cloud of dust and sand. Carol tasted the grit between her teeth.

p a r t t h r e e

shot through the heart

12

Just as foxes have dens and birds have nests, the human animal is deeply attached to home turf. Home is hardwired into us. Our hunter-gatherer ancestors had home ranges that they knew as intimately as their own bodies. They knew where water flowed out of the ground, when trees' fruits ripened, and which plants provided medicines. Human survival—then and now—depends on our connection to our habitat. Home is the geography of life.

Home is not just shelter, nor is it simply the scenic backdrop to our lives. Places shape people. *Home* comes from the Sanskrit word *aham*, meaning self. Where we are determines who we are. It's why we take pride in our hometowns and root for the home team.

Humans long to belong. Home is where we mesh, where we fit into place. It's a refuge where we feel centered and connected to a larger community, where relationships root, where bonds deepen.

Modern humans are homeless and homesick, Carol believed. We didn't know our neighbors, whether human or animal. We didn't know where our food and water came from.

We had boxed ourselves in: we lived in climate-controlled boxes, drove fossil-fueled boxes, and worked in skyscraping stacks of boxes so we could buy boxes of food from big-box stores. But our home wasn't a box; it was a sphere. Our lonely blue marble was the only planet we had. Our extended human family shared its home planet with our animal relatives. They were our contemporaries, Carol said. Saving wildlife was saving ourselves. We were all in this together.

To protect endangered species, the first step taken is to safeguard its critical habitat, the territory essential to its survival. Humans have critical habitat, too, Carol believed, whether a neighborhood park, backyard creek, or tree that we climbed as kids. We must go home again, she maintained, and protect the places that sustain us.

Carol's critical habitat was Cumberland Island. Like the magnet in a sea turtle's brain guiding her back to her birth beach, Carol had been called home to Cumberland. A homing instinct deep inside her had drawn her there.

Then suddenly the Candlers had given Carol the heave-ho. She had two weeks to pack up and leave her island home. But Carol wasn't leaving without a fight. She knew carpentry and mechanics better than most men, and she worked cheap. Surely one of the other wealthy island families could use an extra set of hands, she reckoned. But they all turned her down, politely insinuating that they didn't want a female custodian, especially one who ate horse.

She was thirty-six years old and stuck. Finally she had found where she fit, only to be told that she didn't belong. She considered every possible option. Move to the mainland and buy a boat? Look for work on another nearby island? Get hired on with the National Park Service?

Then she remembered the vow she had made in her cave beside the river years ago: she would live on her own terms in an honest and original relationship with the natural world. She didn't need a job, she realized. She needed land.

With property of her own, she could scrape up everything else. She could gather shrimp from the creeks, hunt hogs, and grow a garden. The island had plenty of freshwater springs and abundant wood for fuel and shelter. The only thing missing was the land. And no one knew land better than her new friend Louie McKee.

Louie was a surveyor who had mapped every parcel of Cumberland and owned several properties on the island. He had made a fortune in Florida real estate and was a prominent figure in Jacksonville business circles. When he learned about the National Park Service plans for Cumberland, he shrewdly purchased 126 acres, subdivided them, and sold them a year later, netting 1,400-percent profits. He kept one property for himself. Louie built a two-bedroom house on Cumberland Island's Half Moon Bluff as a weekend vacation cottage. It was surrounded by live oaks draped in Spanish moss, and it overlooked a tributary of Christmas Creek and the north end's amber marshes.

Carol drove down to Louie's house in her rusted jeep—now over twenty years since she first pulled it out of a mud hole and fixed it up in her dad's garage. Louie was drinking a scotch on the front porch, looking out across the marsh at high tide.

"Still riding that hunk of junk?" he said.

"It beats walking—though not by much."

He offered Carol a drink. Louie was fifty years old, fair-complected, and freckled, with a slight paunch and reddish-brown hair graying at the temples. Carol joined Louie on the porch and watched the twilight stars rise out of the marsh. Inside the house, his wife Betty was being entertained by Ebby Johns, a wiry country boy who played a mean fiddle. Ebby used to work for Louie's surveying business, but these days he spent more time with Betty. Music and laughter trickled out of the open window onto the dark porch.

"The Candlers are kicking me to the curb," Carol said. "I have to be out by next weekend."

"You can stay here if you want."

"I don't think Betty would like that."

He glanced back at the window. "Betty and I have an understanding."

There was a long silence. Carol felt her throat catch.

"Do you think there's any island property still available?" she asked him.

"None that you can afford."

"I guess I'm out of luck, then." Carol felt the island slipping away from her. She tossed back the rest of her scotch and shook the ice against the glass. Louie poured them both another drink.

"You might be able to buy the old Trimmings house in the Settlement."

"It's about to collapse," Carol said. "A sneeze would knock it over."

"If you can keep it propped up for another year, the Park Service will buy it from you."

Carol sat up straight in her chair.

"Do you know who owns it?"

"I can find out."

He slipped his hand around hers. In the tar-black Cumberland night, Carol saw the lightning flash of Louie's smile.

The next morning, Carol and Louie boated off the island and found the deed at the county courthouse. The original owner of the half-acre lot was Charlie Trimmings, a former slave who had built the shack in 1895 from boards that washed up on the beach. Now, the dilapidated house and property belonged to his grandchildren—seven brothers and sisters living in Brunswick, Georgia, about an hour north of Cumberland. Carol drove up to Brunswick that afternoon. She tracked down the address of the eldest male, Ike Trimmings, who lived in a small vinyl-sided house near the paper mill. His wife answered the door.

"What you want?" she asked, hands on her hips.

"I was hoping to speak to Ike."

"Why a white girl want to talk to my husband for?"

Just then, Ike walked around the side of the house.

"It's all right, Esse," he said, smiling. "I'm Ike. Most of my kin still call me Bubba."

"Howdy, Bubba. I'm Carol Ruckdeschel. Good to meet you." They shook hands. Esse eyed Carol from the porch.

Bubba worked at the paper mill in Brunswick six days a week. He was in his forties, thickly built, and slightly hunched from decades of factory work, but his broad face and toothy grin radiated warmth.

"So, Miss Carol, how can I help you today?"

She breathed deeply. She felt the heft of the first thirty-six years of her life teetering on the edge of some new counterweight.

"I was wondering if your family would have any interest in selling your house on Cumberland Island."

"That old shack?" Esse shouted from the porch. "Why would a white woman want that old shack? There must be gold buried there or somethin'."

"No gold that I know of," Carol said. "But the island is priceless to me. I've been working as a custodian there, and I'd like to have a place of my own."

"Custodian, eh? Cleanin' up after the rich folks?"

Carol told him about washing windows and hauling garbage for the Candlers, living with the other black caretakers, and doling out liquor to her best friend Jesse every morning. She described Jesse's wisdom, humor, and grace, and how she had learned to cast a shrimp net from his johnboat. Bubba nodded his head and smiled.

"Miss Carol, if you were black, you could be my sister."

"Listen, Bubba. I've been scraping by my whole life, working like a dog and saving up to put a roof over my head. Your house is the only one on the island that I can ever afford."

"That shanty ain't worth the nickel in my pocket," Esse hollered. "I'm tellin' ya, there must be gold under that house, Bubba." Esse stared straight at Carol, her eyes searching Carol's for a glimmer of doubt. Carol didn't flinch.

"I'll talk it over with the rest of the family," Bubba said.

Esse was right. It wasn't exactly gold, but that house held hidden treasure. The National Park Service was planning to buy the Trimmings shack and every other property on Cumberland. As part of the purchase deal, it would offer each of those homeowners the opportunity to live there—within a federally protected national park—for the rest of their lives.

Only a handful of Cumberland insiders knew about the National Park Service's deals. Certainly Bubba and his family were unaware of the potential for selling their house to the park and receiving lifetime rights. But Esse suspected something, and she wasn't going to rest until she figured out Carol's hidden motives.

Carol didn't rest either. She slept fitfully, fearing the worst. The Trimmings house was her last hope. All she could do was wait.

Since Carol didn't have a telephone, she gave Louie's phone number to Bubba. Every day for the next week, she stopped by Louie's to borrow a tool or drop off some greens from the garden, hoping for a phone call. In the meantime, they sat on the porch or strolled down to the bluff, hanging their bare feet off the dock and watching

mink swim the creek. Louie was a bright ray in her increasingly gloomy outlook.

Other than their tastes in music and alcohol, Carol and Louie had little in common, though. At heart, Louie was a city guy. Though he enjoyed fishing on Cumberland, he was an urbanite who preferred the comforts and conviviality of Jacksonville's social scene. But he had taken a keen interest in the wilder, younger woman visiting him. While Ebby and Betty were hootin' and hollerin' to fiddle music, Louie and Carol began wandering off into the woods together. They soon became romantically entangled, though Carol didn't see anything long-term developing with Louie. Louie was a welcome distraction from her worries, and, conveniently, he was also a helpful handyman with real estate know-how.

On her last day, Carol still hadn't heard from the Trimmings family. She took a long walk on the beach to consider her options. She was prepared to move back to her animal house in Atlanta if things didn't work out with the Trimmings' property. She was considering Louie's offer of staying with him for a while, too. He only came to the island for a few days at a time. She would have the place to herself while he was in Jacksonville.

Carol splashed a handful of seawater across her face and then headed back to the Candler compound to collect her belongings. Everything she owned—mostly clothes, books, and field notes—filled three boxes. She had already dug up her vegetable garden and relocated her beehive. Carol was sharpening her knives against a whetstone, preparing to butcher her chickens, when she heard Louie's truck drive up. He rolled down the window and smiled.

"Bubba called. His family wants to meet with you tomorrow."

Carol wore her only nice clothes—a black, loose-fitting dress and a plain white blouse she had picked up at the Salvation Army thrift store. Bubba waved from the porch and welcomed her in. All of Bubba's sisters were gathered in the living room, talking and laughing. One of the women eased out of her chair and walked up to Carol.

"Howdy, ma'am. I'm Frances."

"Nobody call her Frances since she was sixteen!" Bubba laughed. "Everyone just call her Sister."

Bubba led Sister and Carol into the kitchen for a drink. On the counter was a chocolate cake that Esse had baked for Carol. The hardness in Esse's eyes had vanished. Carol thanked her with a hug.

"I still wouldn't sell it to you," she whispered.

Bubba ushered Carol back into the living room, and everyone grew quiet.

"Miss Carol, we all talked it through, and we gonna sell you that property."

Carol shook hands with Bubba.

For the first time in her life, Carol had a place to call home.

In the fall of 1978, Carol bought a wobbly shack on one-third of an acre for $36,000. Carol had saved every penny from working in Atlanta, but she was still several thousand dollars short. So her dad loaned her the money. It was also a kind of penance for his stern parenting. "I know it wasn't always easy for you," he told her. "I'm glad you finally found what you were looking for. At least you can't get into any trouble out there."

"I can get into trouble anywhere," Carol smirked.

After the legal ink dried, Carol felt pangs of guilt about the Trimmings deal. She stayed in touch with Bubba and Esse—and with the animated elder sister, Frances. But still.

"It was devious," Carol told her parents after signing the papers. "I feel really bad about it."

Despite her misgivings, she was finally free. "I'm here! This is mine!" she shouted when she opened the door to her shack for the first time in 1978. She didn't have to worry about making money or pleasing a boss. She could live off the land. She could live by her own rules.

"Now I'm safe," she wrote in a letter to her parents. "Nobody can run me off. Now I can concentrate on a place without having to worry about supporting myself. I can always go to the mainland and work for a week, enough to buy beans and a sack of corn."

For the rest of her life, Carol would live mostly outside the money economy, acquiring most of her food and resources directly from the island. Age thirty-six was the last time Carol worked for someone else.

"I wasn't ever going back to cleaning toilets for the Candlers. I had my foot on solid land," she said. "I was finally starting my life."

Carol didn't move in to the Trimmings cabin right away. For the next year, while she rebuilt the cabin, she lived in the old storage shed across the yard. Her shed wasn't much better than her leaning, sagging cabin. The shed was just boards and a screen that creaked and groaned with every puff of wind. She installed a woodstove and slept on a mattress on the floor.

Carol did have electricity, thanks to developer Charles Fraser. While planning to build his development on Cumberland, Fraser convinced the local utility company to install underground electric lines along the entire island. When his resort plans folded, the underground electricity infrastructure was left behind for the handful of remaining residents. Carol's only electrical appliances were a small refrigerator and freezer that she used to store scavenged meat and animal carcasses.

Already Carol had begun collecting driftwood that washed in from the ocean. Some of the planks were from centuries-old hulls of shipwrecked boats covered in oakum. Piece by piece, she hauled planks from the beach to her house, dragging them behind her jeep.

For Louie, the cabin construction was a great excuse to spend more time with Carol. He and Betty had finally divorced. It was an amicable parting, and Betty and Ebby continued coming to the island for fiddle-playing festivities. Louie looked forward to building a new life with Carol. Together they replaced the joists, repaired the chimney, and patched the roof.

Even in carpentry, Carol went against the grain. She purposely installed the exterior wood backwards to provide a tighter seal and a more weathered look. She attached her roof screws along the ridges so they wouldn't leak. She salvaged doors, windows, and roof

tin from collapsed and abandoned island structures. She hoped to use the dead pine tree beside her shed for interior woodwork, but the vultures were roosting in it, so she couldn't bring herself to cut it down.

While she rebuilt her cabin, she ate dead-on-the-road armadillo and dead-on-the-beach porpoise. Jesse brought her mullet. She cast crab traps and shrimp nets off the Half Moon Bluff dock. She mucked barefoot out into the mudflats to harvest clams, and she stripped off her trousers and waded half-naked into tidal creeks to fish. And she happily shot hogs on the beach that were raiding turtle nests.

Carol had switched to morning turtle patrols rather than staying up all night. But she was still short on time. So she began waking at 3 A.M. every morning. She monitored turtles before twilight, hunted and gathered food around sunrise, hiked the island during the day, worked on her cabin in the afternoon, and went to sleep around sunset. If Louie was around, he joined her for an evening drink. Though infatuated with Carol, he usually returned to his house at night. He didn't like to sleep on the floor of the shed, and he sure as hell wasn't waking up at 3 A.M.

Carol had other bed buddies instead. Gator the otter still slept with her each night. She had also acquired an old tomcat named Spider who crawled under the mosquito net to sleep beside her each evening. One midsummer night, Spider and Gator had just curled into the crook of her legs when Carol heard the thin drum of rain on the tin roof. She loved drifting off to sleep in a summer shower.

But the patter of rain grew louder. Lightning flashed and splintered across the sky. Thunder shook the shed walls. Winds heaved limbs and ripped leaves from the trees.

Then Carol heard a *crrrraaaack* outside the shed, and she suddenly remembered the dead pine tree just outside her window.

She waited for the tree to fall on her. It was probably better not to see it coming, she figured. So she laid stiff as a board, bracing for the impact. Spider's fur bristled. Gator shivered beside her. Carol squinted her eyes closed and held her breath.

The jarring thud from the crash rattled the shack's frame, and the top of the pine landed inches from her head. The wind had snapped the pine tree like a matchstick, but it hadn't broken at the base. It had split ten feet up. Even then, the top of the tree had scraped the corner of the shed. Had the tree snapped at the base, or even a foot lower, Carol, Gator, and Spider would have been crushed.

By 1979, Cumberland Island National Seashore had officially opened to the public. Backpackers had begun hiking the trails, and a few made it all the way to the north end of the island. Louie didn't like the idea of dirty strangers roaming near his house—or Carol's. Alone in the backwoods, she might be easy prey for a deranged camper. So, as a housewarming gift, Louie gave Carol a sawed-off twelve-gauge shotgun to keep beside her at night. Carol thought it was unnecessary, especially since she already had a pistol, but she took the shotgun to make Louie happy.

"I promise I'll never shoot it unless I'm serious," she told him.

Carol frantically worked on her cabin, hoping to complete as much renovation as possible before the National Park Service offered to buy it, so she could receive the highest possible appraisal. Louie helped on the weekends, and he even hauled discarded wood over to the island from an abandoned house in Jacksonville. But he usually went fishing while Carol worked. Louie's air-conditioned house was just a half mile from Carol's place, and she often met him there in the evenings. He always had her drink poured when she arrived, and usually he was on his second or third.

Once Carol finished renovating her cabin, she decided to build a garage and chicken coop on her property. She also converted the shed into her lab. Carol was still running electrical conduit to the lab when the National Park Service trucks pulled up to appraise the property and make an offer.

Louie had three decades of experience with deeds and contracts, so he helped Carol draft her rights agreement. Her contract with the National Park Service was the only one that included chickens.

"I was afraid the park wouldn't let me keep my hens and roosters, so I made sure they were included in the deal," Carol explained.

Before selling to the National Park Service, Louie also suggested that he and Carol give each other partial ownership in their respective properties.

"That way, if one of us dies, the other can make sure the land is protected and not misused," Louie explained. Carol agreed. She had become mistrustful of the National Park Service after learning of its proposal to develop large parts of the island and run vehicle tours all over it. She was already crafting plans to stop them.

But first she had to secure her spot on the island. In 1979, Carol sold her property to the National Park Service for $45,000—by far the lowest price of any park acquisition—along with the right to keep a flock of chickens and the right to live on the island for the rest of her life.

Of the twenty-one lifetime rights holders, sixteen were Carnegie and Candler families, two were longtime north end families, two were attorneys (the Carnegie attorney Thornton Morris and the county attorney Grover Henderson), and one was a reclusive, dirt-poor naturalist. Carol lived on Cumberland year-round; the others mostly vacationed there.

In her journal that evening, she wrote: "I'm home. No place like it."

Carol was eager to meet more of her neighbors—the alligator at Ashley Pond, the pair of peregrine falcons on the south beach, the gopher tortoise burrowing near Terrapin Point, and the snow-white deer grazing in the dune meadows.

Her home had human neighbors, too. The old Trimmings house was part of the Settlement, the collection of former African American dwellings clustered on the north end. Nearly all the other houses had already collapsed, but Grover Henderson had managed to acquire Beulah Alberty's old house just a stone's throw away from Carol's cabin. And across the yard was the one-room First African Baptist Church. Louie lived just down the road at Half Moon Bluff, which continued

to be a popular party spot on the weekends. The Greyfield gang and other island folk came up to the north end for drinking and dancing, and the revelry lasted late into the evenings.

Carol loved the boisterous bluegrass, but after a while the parties got old. She preferred to wander the wild dunes with nesting turtles than to drink cheap beer and listen to repetitious chatter.

"It's the same conversations with the same people, night after night," Carol wrote in her journal. "Partying is all the island people ever do, so after a while, there isn't much to talk about other than the previous night's party."

Things with Louie were also starting to wear thin. They quarreled frequently, and after a few drinks Louie became abusive. Carol wrote her parents on February 14, 1979: "Unhappy Valentine's Day. Louie got a little far in his cups Sunday night. It resulted in Louie and I having a slight altercation." A few weeks later, she wrote her parents again: "Things are okay here, I guess. Louie has settled down a little. I don't feel a physical threat now, anyway."

But the abuse worsened, and for the first time in her life Carol knew real fear. "When you're afraid, it's a whole new ballgame," she wrote. "Every day, I live with the fact that there is someone out there determined to hurt me."

She wanted out of the relationship but was afraid that a confrontation would provoke even more rage. So she tried to just let things dissolve. She stopped attending the fiddle parties. She spent her weekends in the woods and swamps searching for gators, and she resumed sleeping on the beach with the sea turtles.

On clear, moonless evenings, Carol sometimes saw the lights of Rebecca Bell's truck on Little Cumberland Island to the north. Rebecca had taught Carol how to tag turtles years earlier, and they had remained friends. In the middle of the night, in between turtle patrols, Rebecca and Carol flashed their red-filtered lights at each other across Christmas Creek (red-filtered light does not disrupt turtle nesting). After a while, they invested in a citizen's band (CB) radio—a walkie-talkie attached to a signal-transmitting radio. For Carol, who lived without a phone or television, the CB radio was a lifeline. She relished her evening chats with Rebecca.

"Howdy, girl. Any nests on your little spit of sand?" Carol said, pressing the transmit button.

"Just two false crawls. It's been lonely," Rebecca's garbled voice sputtered back. "How are things with Louie?"

"Like flat soda," Carol said. "The fizz is gone."

"Sorry to hear that."

"It was fun while it lasted."

A few weeks later, Carol got a call from Rebecca, inviting her to a national sea turtle conference in D.C.

"I can't afford it," Carol replied.

"The conference is already paid for, and we have a free place to stay in D.C. All we need is gas money."

Carol wanted to get away from the island. She had been avoiding Louie, who continued to lash out. During his outbursts, she smelled stale alcohol on his hot breath. His explosive temper, fueled by binge drinking, had swallowed the gentle, soft-spoken man she once knew.

"The relationship with Louie has run its course," she wrote in a letter to her friend Anne LaBastille. "There was never anything long-term about it. We had some good times together, but it wasn't going anywhere."

However, Louie continued stalking her. Carol realized that she needed to put some physical distance between them so things could calm down. The turtle conference in D.C. was the perfect excuse.

Jesse drove Carol over to Little Cumberland in his johnboat to meet up with Rebecca.

"I'z worried about you," he said on the way over, a cigarette drooping from his lips.

"I'm worried too, Jess."

"Maybe you should go talk to Louie."

"I've tried. He just gets more worked up. There's no easy way out of this."

Carol climbed out of the boat and handed Jesse her outgoing mail, which included her letter to Anne LaBastille, her weekly note

to her parents, and a scathing letter to the National Park Service about its development plans. Jesse added her letters to the Candlers' mailbag, which was delivered by boat to the mainland post office each week. She also asked Jesse to feed her animals while she was away.

Carol looked back across the creek at Cumberland Island. For the first time, leaving the island was filled not with remorse but relief.

Carol's windows-down, radio-blaring road trip with Rebecca was a much-needed girl getaway. They belted out tunes and traded island gossip. It was 1979, and tensions in Iran had caused a spike in oil prices. Carol spent most of her money on gas and had little left for food. Near Richmond, she spotted a dead woodchuck on the side of the interstate and made Rebecca pull to the shoulder.

"Free food! And look, only its skull is crushed. The rest is good eating!" Carol said, scraping the carcass into a cooler. "Do you think the folks we're staying with will mind if I skin it in their backyard?"

The conference was held at a posh hotel in downtown D.C. Carol got gussied up for the event, wearing a men's khaki button-up shirt and a clean pair of jeans. At the conference, she was instantly enthralled: never before had she been surrounded by so many like-minded turtle geeks.

Yet Carol was an anomaly even among the turtle experts. Most were older men with university positions. Carol's high school education and lack of formal training was frowned upon, especially when she questioned one professor over his conclusion that sea turtles appeared to be shrinking in size.

"Are you measuring the turtles with calipers or tape?" she asked.

"Does it matter?"

"Sure it does. Some folks measure with a flexible tape. Others use calipers and measure the straight-line width. The results differ by several centimeters or more."

The professor scratched his head and winced. "And who are you, madam?"

Later, she even challenged the feds. A top scientist with the National Marine Fisheries Service claimed that trawling by shrimpers had little effect on sea turtles.

"Baloney!" Carol said. "Trawling is the number-one turtle killer."

"Do you have evidence for such a hypothesis?" he retorted.

"I've got the necropsies of hundreds of dead loggerheads that continue to wash ashore in record numbers." Whispers rippled through the crowd.

Carol stayed late at the hotel bar, sparring with various scientists over their turtle research. She may have lacked PhD pedigree, but she had gutted more turtles than any of the leading researchers.

After a few drinks, the white-haired professors started to enjoy the saucy spitfire who had crashed their party. And after years of wrestling with ideas alone on an island, Carol was thrilled to trade barbs with some of the country's sharpest scientific minds.

Rebecca nudged Carol and glanced at her watch. "We gotta get going." They were about to leave when Carol overheard a bald guy next to her talking about salamander sex.

"Salamanders don't need males to reproduce," Carol interjected. She described how some all-female populations of salamanders on Cumberland Island can reproduce by humping each other.

"They're just producing clones," the bald professor replied. To survive long-term, salamanders still need the genetic mixing of sex with males. "That's why nearly every animal hierarchy is led by an alpha male."

"But females still have the upper hand sexually," Carol said. She described how female scorpions devour their male partners after sex. Female fireflies, praying mantises, and spiders are sexual cannibals, too. "Men can beat their chests all they want, but ultimately, women call the shots."

Speechless, the bald man grinned and reached for his whiskey. His name was Bob Shoop, a herpetologist from the University of Rhode Island, and he had spent the past twenty years studying salamanders and becoming one of the world's leading researchers, only

to have a drunk woman at a bar go toe-to-toe with him. He was tall, sturdily built, bald, and rosy-cheeked, with riveting ocean-blue eyes. Unlike the other stiffs dressed in starched shirts and bow ties, Bob wore jeans and a blazer. His lips were floppy and loose, stretched out by his sunny, spacious smile.

"A female's eggs are the limiting resource," Carol continued. "We produce one egg once a month. Males produce millions of sperm every day. If all the men on earth died tonight, the species could continue on frozen sperm. If the women disappear, it's extinction."

The crowded bar was getting louder. Bob scooted his bar stool closer to hers. "I guess that's why we males ram our heads together and have pissing contests all the time."

"That's right," Carol said. "How much convincing does it take for a male to give up his sperm? Zero. I could ask you for your sperm right now and you'd probably give it to me."

Bob felt his cheeks flush.

"Women, on the other hand, need a lot more convincing," Carol continued, "because our eggs don't come as easily, and we're only fertile for a few days a month."

"It would be a whole lot easier if women just announced when they were in heat each month," Bob said. "We can't smell your phero-mones like tomcats."

Carol wanted to keep scrapping with him, but Rebecca was tugging at her to leave. Bob scrawled his phone number on a napkin and handed it to her.

"Could I call you some time?" he asked.

"I don't have a phone."

"That's the best rejection I've ever received."

"No, it's true. Here's my mailing address . . . write me."

On the way home that evening, Rebecca's car sputtered to a stop on the shoulder of Interstate 95, leaving them stranded along the coun-try's busiest freeway. The elderly retired professor with whom they were staying couldn't drive at night, and neither Carol nor Rebecca knew anyone else in D.C.

"Wait a second!" Carol shouted, pulling a napkin from her pocket.

Carol walked to a pay phone and called Bob. He hopped in the university van and rescued Carol and Rebecca from the side of the interstate, and then brought them back to the conference center where he and his grad students were staying. Carol and Rebecca couldn't afford a room at the swanky hotel, so Bob gave them his bed while he slept on the floor. He was a perfect gentleman.

But that's not what his grad students were thinking. They had been hanging out on the hotel roof drinking that night. They couldn't believe their eyes when they saw their esteemed professor drive away in the university van after midnight and then return with two attractive younger women, whom he escorted to his room.

Carol came back to Cumberland with renewed energy for her sea turtle research. She'd been gone only a few days, but over a dozen turtle carcasses had washed ashore while she was away. On the beach, Carol chased away the vultures, who had descended on the turtle graveyard.

One by one, Carol began carving into the turtles, bloated by the midsummer heat. After a weekend in an air-conditioned hotel, the island sun felt like sandpaper on her skin. Sweat stung her eyes. She felt like she was breathing through a damp dishrag.

As she sliced open carcasses, Carol read the story of each turtle. Fissures and rifts in the bone told tales. From the tangle of intestines she unraveled the turtle's life and death. Most of the carcasses had bloody fluid in their stomach, soggy lungs, and foam in their trachea—evidence of drowning. Sea turtles must surface for air, but when trapped in a shrimpers' trawl net they go into oxygen-deprived shock and die.

What was even more intriguing were the turtles who had apparently died of shark attacks or boat propeller strikes. When Carol examined their caracasses more closely, she discovered the same evidence of drowning. Most of the turtles hit by boats or attacked by sharks were already dead, she realized. They were floating lifelessly

in the ocean after drowning in trawl nets. Shrimpers' trawls were killing a lot more turtles than anyone wanted to know.

Carol was scooping shrimp out of the dead turtles' stomachs when Louie drove up in his truck. He braked hard, skidding in the wet sand. He stood over her, arms folded, flat-footed, his shadow swallowing the sun's light.

"We need to talk," he said.

"There's nothing left to say."

He glared hard at her with wet, red-rimmed eyes. His mouth was a stubborn line. Then he kicked the beach, spraying her with sand. Carol wiped her face with a bandana as he stormed back to his truck, revved the engine, and roared away.

Louie continued to host weekend bashes at the bluff while Carol immersed herself in her turtle work, which was suddenly attracting national attention. Her data showed that more endangered sea turtles were dying than ever before. Reporters regularly came to the island to interview Carol. When Patti Hagan, an editor from *The New Yorker*, asked to visit in the fall of 1979, Carol worried that her cockroach-infested cabin would be unsuitable for a well-heeled Manhattan writer. So she reluctantly asked Louie if Patti could stay at his air-conditioned house. He agreed.

They all had drinks together on Louie's front porch. Patti and Carol talked turtles and island politics late into the night while Louie sat quietly in the shadows knocking back vodka tonics.

Around midnight, Carol stood up to leave. It was dark, and Carol had to walk a half mile back to her cabin, so she said good night.

"I'll walk you home," Louie offered. He could barely lift himself out of his chair.

They walked in silence through the forest. Ragged clouds hid a sickle moon overhead. Then Louie said, "I read your letter."

Carol's throat tightened. "What letter?"

"You told that Anne woman that our relationship had run its course."

"You're reading my mail? What the hell, Louie?"

"You're done with me, huh. Is that how you feel?"

Carol swallowed hard. "We had some good times together, but now it's time to move on."

Suddenly, out of nowhere, Louie punched Carol in the eye. In the dark, she never saw it coming. He knocked her flat and momentarily unconscious.

She awoke to the taste of metallic blood trickling from her nose. Louie stood over her. *Get up, Carol,* she told herself. *Get up and get the hell out of here.*

Which way to run? She wanted to head for home, but Louie's house was closer, and Patti was there.

Louie turned his back for a moment. Now was her chance. She wobbled to her feet, steadied herself, then broke for Louie's house.

Between twisted oaks, she ran through the black night, one eye wide open, the other swollen shut. Behind her, she heard the snap of twigs beneath his footfall. *Don't look back, don't look back,* she told herself.

"Carol! We need to talk!" he shouted.

Her jackhammer heart pounded harder. In the soot-black Cumberland night, she could barely make out the white ribbon of sandy road through the forest. *If he catches me, I'm dead,* Carol thought. He was getting closer. She smelled his bourbon musk.

"Get back here, Carol!" he yelled.

The hairs on her neck bristled. *Be ready to fight,* Carol told herself. *Gouge his eyes. Kick him in the balls. Rip off his ears.*

She glanced sideways and caught a glimpse of his shadow closing in. Her heart leapt into her throat. Arms flailing, jaw clenched, she looked out through fogged slits at her slow-motion nightmare. She felt his hot breath on the back of her neck.

Then a pale sliver of moonlight pierced the clouds, and she glimpsed the house's silhouette through the trees. She bore down, wringing out the last sap from her legs.

Carol raced up the steps, swung open the door, dashed into the back room and locked it. She huddled in the corner. For a moment, everything was still. Then she heard footsteps clomp across the

porch. His bloodshot eyes appeared at the back window. Adrenaline knifed through her.

Louie rattled the door handle. Then a long silence followed. Carol shivered in the corner, wondering if she could make it till daylight. She counted the seconds, one by one. Finally, dawn drowned the stars in a pale azure. She steeled herself, crept to the window, and peered into the twilight. He was gone.

Slowly, she cracked open the door and snuck across the hall to Patti's bedroom.

"Oh my god, Carol! What happened?" Patti said.

Carol's right eye was black and ballooned. Dried blood stained her upper lip. Carol sat on Patti's bed shivering and tried to explain. A few minutes later, they heard Louie walk up the porch steps and creak open the front door.

"Everybody take it easy," he said.

"What the hell did you do to her?" Patti shrieked.

"I don't know what you're talking about," Louie replied, eyes to the ground. "She must have tripped on a tree root."

Patti packed her bags and walked with Carol back to her cabin, elbows linked. They barricaded the door behind them and didn't leave the cabin all day.

Louie returned the next morning. Carol was washing dishes when he tapped at her kitchen window. She jumped backward from the sink.

"Stay away from me, Louie!" she shouted through the glass.

"I'll do whatever it takes to make it right."

"I don't want anything from you."

He hovered on her porch, pacing. Carol hid in the windowless bathroom until she heard him leave.

Later that afternoon, Carol called her parents from the Park Service phone, and they promised to come down the next day. Then she and Patti took a stroll along the beach, walking barefoot in the surf, feeling the warm sun on their skin. They kept to the firm sand below the tide wrack, a tangle of shells, seaweed, and horseshoe crabs—their spiked maroon flanks and long, sharp tails still wet. Carol nudged a horseshoe crab's jagged, helmet-shaped shell with her foot.

"That looks mean," Patti said. "Does it bite?"

"Naw. Most folks use it for fish bait."

Carol explained how horseshoe crabs crawl ashore to nest under the full moon for only a few nights each spring, coating the island beach with pastel-green eggs that look like Tic-Tacs. At the same time, a small shorebird called a red knot synchronizes its eighteen-thousand-mile migration from South America to the Arctic with the horseshoe crab's egg laying orgy to fuel its journey. Today, both species are threatened.

Patti stayed behind to photograph horseshoe crabs and collect seashells while Carol headed home to feed her animals. On her hike back to the cabin, Carol rounded a bend in the road and suddenly felt chills ripple across her goose-bumped skin. The hairs on her forearm stood on end. Just then, Louie appeared from behind an oak.

"We must find a way to get along," he said.

Carol tried to act calm. "You gotta lay off the liquor, Louie. You don't have control of yourself anymore."

"I'll stop drinking if you'll come back to me."

"We can be friends. But my feelings go no further."

His face dropped. "It's all just fun and games to you, isn't it!" He yanked her braids and pulled her face against his. "I swear I'll kill you for doing this to me!"

Carol wrestled free of his grasp and ran for her cabin. When she got inside, the electricity had been cut. Through the window, she watched Louie disappear down the road.

"I'm sorry, Carol, but I need to go," Patti said when she returned from the beach. She was supposed to be writing a story about Carol's turtle research, not the violent stalkings of her ex-lover.

"Please stay one more night," Carol pleaded. "My parents will arrive tomorrow. Don't leave me here alone."

Patti agreed to stay. Carol lit candles and cooked a supper of stir-fried venison and greens on the woodstove. After a soothing glass of wine, their jumpy nerves began to calm.

Then they heard a scratch on the screen of the porch window that stopped the food in their throats.

"Open the door, Carol!" Louie shouted.

"You're scaring me, Louie!" Carol shouted, her voice trembling.

"Go away! Please go away!" Patti screamed.

There was a long silence. Through the porch window, his eyes roved from Carol to Patti in a cold, inscrutable stare. Finally he turned and walked out into the darkness.

Just before dawn, they heard another noise in the yard. It was Jesse, coming by for his morning drink. He sat on a pine stump smoking a cigarette. Relieved, Carol poured him an extra-tall glass of bourbon and told him what had happened.

"I sho don't wanna be here when yo daddy sees yo face."

Her parents drove through the night to catch the morning ferry at the St. Marys dock. Pelicans perched atop the barnacle-covered concrete pilings as they climbed aboard the *Cumberland Queen*, a paint-chipped, double-decker boat carrying 150 passengers—Boy Scout troops, backpackers, young couples, and day-tripping seniors.

On the one-hour ride over to the island, the ferry meandered through jade-green marshes lined with snowy egrets. The ferry crossed the sound and hugged the southern rim of Cumberland, where horses grazed in the marshes near the Dungeness ruins. Passengers jockeyed for position along the starboard deck to snap photos. At Sea Camp dock, two deckhands tied the boat to the piers. As Carol's parents disembarked, a manatee and her calf grazed in the grassy shallows beside the dock.

Carol felt like an eight-year-old running into her mother's arms.

"You're coming back to Atlanta for a while," her dad told her.

Patti left on the ferry, and Carol returned to her cabin with her parents to pack up her belongings. That afternoon, Carol and Earl tinkered with the jeep while Anne grilled pork tenderloin from a hog Carol had shot on the beach a few days earlier.

Around sunset, Louie knocked. To his surprise, Earl opened the door.

"I was hoping to talk privately with Carol," Louie stammered.

"You need to stay away from her," Earl said, pointing a finger at him.

"We've got to work it out."

"You've got to move on." Earl folded his arms across his chest. "This is between Carol and me."

"You knocked my daughter unconscious. What kind of a man suckerpunches a woman?"

Louie glared at Carol, standing in the doorway. "You know, there's some folks on this island who think she got what she deserved."

13

"My world is falling down around me," Carol wrote in her journal after four months away from Cumberland. "What a waste! So many good things I could be doing on the island instead of twiddling my thumbs here."

Carol was thirty-nine and living with her parents in Atlanta. Not much had changed since she last lived under their roof. They followed their same routines: drinks at five, dinner at six, the television blaring in the background to drown out the uncomfortable silence. Earl and Anne bickered constantly, but they teamed up to berate Carol for living alone on a wild island and not settling down with a suitable husband.

Carol didn't think she would ever return to Cumberland. She would never be safe there with Louie stalking her. So she started exploring the north Georgia mountains again. She went mushroom gathering and ginseng hunting with her old homesteader friend Mamie and started scouting for property in Appalachia. Grudgingly, she even made plans to rent out her Cumberland cabin.

But she deeply missed the island. The island was her center of gravity, her north star. It was where she found her bearings. Without it, she felt lost and unanchored.

She ached for the island every evening when the moon rose. As it shone through her open window, she listened to the song of the sea in a whelk shell that sat beside her bed. In those moments, she closed her eyes and could almost feel herself crouched in the dunes, listening to the purr of the ocean, whispering to a nesting sea turtle as she counted her eggs.

Then Louie's shadow stalked across the moon, and she awoke, sweating and shuddering. On the island, fear had followed her everywhere. She couldn't go back to that life. Slowly, gently, she let go of the island, like sand slipping through her fingers.

* * *

On a cloudy April morning in 1980, Carol was dissecting a D.O.R. possum in her parents' basement and listening to the news on the radio: Mount Saint Helens had begun to smolder, rookie Wayne Gretzky had scored his record-setting fiftieth goal, the United States had announced it would boycott the Olympics in Moscow, and President Carter had just broken off diplomatic relations with Iran.

The phone rang, and Carol picked up.

"Hey, Carol. It's Jesse."

"Jess! It's great to hear your voice. Have you been feeding my chickens?"

"Oh yea, every mornin. They sho miss you."

"I miss them too. More than you know."

"You can come back now, Carol. Louie's found hisself a new woman. You ain't got nuthin to worry about no mo."

Carol packed up immediately and headed for Cumberland the next morning. When she arrived back on the island, she dashed straight for the ocean, dunking herself in the wild waters. All of the anguish left her. Saltwater dripped down her cheeks, and she tasted the island again.

Her hair was still wet when she arrived back at her cabin. It hadn't been burned down like she expected—not even a broken window. Carol flung open the fence gate and stood in the yard, letting her senses soak it all in again: the scent of fresh cedar, a puff of wind tickling the pines, the olive braids of Spanish moss hanging from live oaks. Everything was silent and still.

Too still. Where were her chickens?

She walked over to the coop and found half-eaten carcasses and feathers strewn everywhere. Raccoon tracks surrounded the coop.

She stormed over to see Jesse, who was working on his boat at the Candler dock.

"What the hell, Jess? My chickens were eaten by coons. How'd you let that happen?"

"I'z sorry Carol."

"If you lied about feeding my chickens, did you lie about Louie, too?"

Jesse hung his head.

"Dang it, Bailey! How could you do this?"

"It was Louie's idea. He missed you."

"He's threatened to kill me, Jess!"

"Truth is, I missed you too."

Carol sighed. She couldn't stay mad at Jesse. She sat on the dock beside him and dipped her toes into the water. But a sinking dread had already begun to settle back in.

The next day, she went to the National Park Service headquarters to talk with the chief ranger. "I wish we could help," he said. "But park rangers can't get involved with domestic disputes." She visited the St. Mary's Police Station on the mainland, but they told her Cumberland Island was outside of its jurisdiction. She asked the Camden County Sheriff's Department to issue a restraining order against Louie, but they said it would be difficult to enforce. It seemed no one could protect Carol from a man threatening to kill her.

Sure enough, Louie showed up drunk at her door a few days after she had returned. Carol told him to leave.

"I've talked with the cops about taking out a peace warrant," she said.

"You sign a peace warrant, you sign your death warrant!" he snarled.

She was afraid to close her eyes that night. She finally got out of bed at 3 A.M. and went to work on her turtle research, hoping that a return to routine might calm her. The window above her desk faced Louie's road. With every leaf flutter or twig snap, she glanced wide-eyed out the glass into the darkness.

"There is no feeling like trying to work at your desk and waiting for a bullet to hit your brain," she wrote in her journal that morn-

ing. "I wonder what it will feel like. Will I hear the sound of the gun firing? How many fractions of a second will it take for the bullet to pass through my skull?"

Jesse didn't show up for his sunrise cocktail. So Carol hopped in her jeep and headed out to the beach early. The sun was blood red, casting liquid fire across the ocean. Dozens of dead sea turtles littered the beach from her four-month absence. Vultures had picked over most of them.

At the South Cut beach crossing, Carol noticed two figures atop the dunes. Hikers usually didn't venture this far up the island, so she walked closer. It was Ebby and Betty, watching the sunrise from the tallest dunes on Cumberland.

"I need your help," Carol said to Betty. "Please keep Louie away from me. I don't want trouble. I just want to be left alone."

"You think I can control what he does?"

"Can you at least help reel in his drinking?"

Betty looked vacantly out across the ocean. "You knew what you were getting yourself into," she said flatly.

Carol made plans to leave the island again. Returning to her parents' house in Atlanta was unthinkable, so she contacted her aunt in Rochester, New York. Her aunt's health was declining, and it seemed like an opportune time to reconnect and lend a hand. From Rochester, she could explore the wildlands of the Adirondacks, searching for quiet hollers and deep forest coves. She began packing for another extended absence.

She slept in the dunes that night, afraid to stay in her cabin alone with Louie skulking about. The next morning, just before heading back to the cabin to pack up, Carol spotted vultures congregating on the beach. A dead loggerhead had washed ashore, and Carol recognized it instantly by its massive, barnacled back. She checked the turtle's tag to confirm: it was the giant turtle that Carol had ridden bareback a few months earlier.

"I'm sorry, girl." Carol said. "We're a rotten bunch."

She glanced at her watch. The sun was already high in the sky, and if she stuck around to necropsy her, she would miss the boat off

the island. But she couldn't leave her bareback turtle to rot. So she decided to stay on the island one more day. She gripped her knife and plunged in.

"Shucks, girl. You're loaded with eggs." Carol scooped them out of the disemboweled turtle. She filled her hat with eggs and carried them deep into the dunes to bury them.

Carol returned to the carcass. As she was untangling the turtle's ropy intestines, a young, sandy-haired backpacker hiking up the beach approached.

"Can I have a look?" he said.

He squatted down for closer inspection. Carol was impressed. Most casual observers cringed at the stench and gore, but here was a kid genuinely interested in what the turtle could teach him. His name was Pete DiLorenzo, and he had been camping on Cumberland for a week.

"This island is paradise," he said. "I feel like I'm strolling through Eden."

All his life, Pete had been a devout Christian. Lately, though, his faith had been faltering. The twenty-two-year-old had fallen into drugs and alcohol and lost his way. His camping trip to Cumberland had cleansed his spirit, and he felt born again.

It turned out that Pete was also from Rochester. Short on cash, he planned to hitchhike back to Rochester after his camping adventures on Cumberland. He was a Jesus freak, but he seemed like a nice enough kid, Carol thought. And she didn't want to be alone with Louie stalking her. So Carol offered him a ride to Rochester, as long as he didn't mind waiting until tomorrow to leave. Pete eagerly agreed, and he hopped in the jeep with Carol. As they drove past the road to Half Moon Bluff, Louie, watching from the woods, saw a handsome young guy with wavy blond hair riding next to Carol.

That evening, Pete set up his tent in the yard beside the chicken coop while Carol cooked supper. She was relieved to have company with Louie still prowling around. When Pete came inside for dinner, Carol locked the door behind him from the inside, leaving the key in the knob. Ever since Louie had punched her, Carol had been locking herself in. She checked the window to see if Louie was lurking.

"Would you like a drink?" Carol asked.

"I'm trying to lay off the liquor," he said. "Been sober for five weeks."

"How about some water then? It's the sweetest water on the island, straight from a spring."

Pete sat at the kitchen table sipping his water while Carol marinated a mess of coon and collards.

"Do you belong to a church?" he asked.

"I worship in the cathedral of nature."

"I mean a real church."

"There's nothing more real than nature."

"What about a house of worship?"

"Well, I sweep and clean that abandoned church every month," Carol said, nodding to the First African Baptist Church across from her cabin. "Does that earn me some points?"

He smiled. "I guess what I'm asking is: what do you believe in?"

"Truth," she replied.

Suddenly, they heard footsteps on the porch. It was Louie, carrying a broken canoe paddle with a sharp, splintered end. He rattled the locked knob. Then there was a bang-bang-bang against the door.

"Open up!" Louie shouted.

Carol's heart exploded out of her chest. "Go away!"

"Open the goddamn door!"

Pete clenched his water glass tightly and looked wide-eyed at Carol.

The door shook in its frame. Louie kicked in the bottom door panel. Pete jumped out of his chair and crouched behind the table. Carol shrieked.

"Please, Louie! Leave me alone!"

"Who's in there with you, dammit?"

He broke through the rest of the door panel. Scraps of wood fell to the floor. Louie's full figure appeared behind the empty door frame.

"Are you already screwing someone else, you fucking whore?" he shouted.

Instinct took over. The sawed-off shotgun that Louie had given her was tucked behind the bathroom door, loaded. Carol was on autopilot. She ran to the bathroom and grabbed the gun.

Pete cowered in the corner, hands clenched in prayer. Louie was waving the canoe paddle and shouting.

"You just want to have fun? I'll show you fun!" He began to step through the empty door frame and into the cabin just as Carol returned to the kitchen.

"You fucked with the wrong guy!" he shouted, and busted through the door toward her.

Carol had only one shot. There would be no time to reload if she missed. She had to make it count. She raised the shotgun and steadied it, braced snugly against her hip, like her father had taught her.

She held her breath and squeezed the trigger. The gun fired, kicking hard against her hip. The report rattled the floorboards and shook Pete's water glass on the table.

Then the room went silent. A haze of smoke lifted from the barrel. She had shot Louie squarely in the chest. The impact knocked him back, and his body slumped to the porch.

Carol reloaded and prepared to shoot again, then stopped herself. No, no, no, don't act like a psycho, she told herself. But she kept the gun sighted on Louie.

"Is he dead?" she asked, frozen with fear. Pete peeked over the table at the motionless body in the doorway.

"I think so."

"Tell me he's dead, because I can't look. I can't look."

Pete walked over to the door. Louie lay lifeless, pooled in blood. His chest was still.

"Yeah, he's dead."

Carol lowered her gun and collapsed to the floor. The gunshot still echoed in her ears, and she couldn't stop shaking. For a few moments, she swirled in and out of consciousness. Everything felt uncoupled from its shoring. She could only hitch herself to one hard truth: She was alive, and Louie was dead. It was over. It was finally over.

Or so she thought.

14

Crumpled on her cabin floor, Carol buried her face in her arms, afraid of the feeling rising up inside her: relief. Months of mortal fear had already begun to lift. Now there was the world to face. She wiped her eyes with her sleeve and wobbled back to her feet.

"Are you okay?" Pete asked.

"I don't know," said Carol.

A sparrow trilled in the twilight. Carol staggered out to the porch and knelt beside Louie's body. His eyes were lifeless and blank, like the deer her father had shot in the meadow when she was four. She pressed her ear to his blood-soaked chest. It was silent.

A veil of cloud drifted across the setting sun as Carol and Pete walked to the Candler estate to call the police on the two-way radio.

"I need to report a homicide on Cumberland Island," Carol said.

"Where is the victim?" asked the dispatcher.

"On my porch."

"Who are you?"

The knot in her throat hardened. "Carol Ruckdeschel—the woman who shot him."

She and Pete returned to the cabin and waited for the police to arrive. The last pangs of dim-blue twilight clung to the sky. Carol sat beside Louie's body and held his cold hand in hers. Then she leaned over and whispered in Louie's ear: "I'm so sorry."

It was nearly dark when Sheriff Jimmy Middleton arrived, along with the coroner, two park rangers, and two deputy detectives, who photographed the body and investigated the crime scene: "Victim shot in chest," the police report read. "Wound directly in heart. Broken canoe paddle with long, sharp splinter. Porch door panels smashed out. Strong odor of alcohol about the victim's body. Ejected double-ought shotgun shell on kitchen floor."

The most important clue was discovered by the sheriff: two of the shotgun pellets had clipped the edge of the empty door frame,

showing that the panels had already been broken out when the gun was fired.

Jesse stumbled up, whiskey bottle in hand. His bloodshot eyes were wet. He hunkered down on the stoop beside Carol's porch, where the sheriff questioned him.

"We been drinkin all afternoon, Louie an me. Mostly whiskey."

"Did he talk about Carol at all?" the sheriff asked.

"Louie talk bout Carol all da time. He hit her afore. He socked her once an' gave her a black eye." Jesse shook his head. "I wuz posed to look after Carol. I promised her daddy I'd watch out fo her. I done let him down."

In the dark, Carol stood in stunned silence, staring down at her blood-soaked porch. She had killed another human being. Nothing could ever wash away that stain.

"All right, ma'am. You'll need to come with us," Sheriff Middleton said.

"I can't leave. I need to feed my animals. And what about the turtles?"

"Ma'am, you'll have to spend the night with us. There will be a hearing tomorrow at the courthouse."

Carol climbed into the truck, with Louie's corpse in a body bag behind her.

Before leaving, the sheriff and one of the park rangers drove down to Louie's house. A light was on inside, and the sheriff saw a shadow move across the room. They crept up to the porch. The deputy peered in through the porch window.

"Sir, the man inside has a gun," he whispered.

The sheriff scowled, then kicked open the door. The man inside jumped back.

"Give me that goddamn gun!" the sheriff shouted. The frightened young man handed over the pistol. The sheriff handcuffed him and shoved him onto the couch.

The young man said his name was Steven Waye. Eyes glued to the floor, he evasively answered the sheriff's questions with gruff, short responses. He was on leave from Jacksonville's Naval Air Station. He'd arrived on the island two days earlier.

Sheriff Middleton transported Steven Waye back to the mainland, where he was released to the custody of the U.S. Navy Patrol. He disappeared later that night.

Middleton called the Jacksonville Naval Air Station the next morning to inquire about the suspicious sailor.

"We have no record of a Steven Waye," they replied.

Some authorities suspect that Louie, already plotting his attack on Carol, brought the sailor to the island to be his alibi. But no one knows for sure. Steven Waye was never heard from again.

The deputy drove the makeshift hearse slowly through the dark forest. Louie's body bag was draped in a brown blanket in the back of the green Park Service pickup, while Carol sat with the deputy in the cab. They finally reached the Dungeness dock, where Louie's body was loaded onto a National Park Service boat. Carol arrived at the county courthouse in Woodbine, Georgia, around midnight.

She spent the night in an empty jail cell. Carol lay in the top bunk, adrenaline-flooded, body locked, eyes frozen open, staring at the graffiti on the ceiling above her. The seconds ticked slowly. She waited for dawn, passing the time by reading the prisoners' scrawl and wondering if soon she would be adding her own.

The guards cut off the lights for the evening. In the windowless jail cell, the raw darkness reminded her of the cave beside the Chattahoochee River where she and her dog had camped.

All night in the jail bunk, she lay rigid, like petrified wood, rewinding through the scenes of her life. Why did this happen? What had she done wrong? She understood in great detail the reproductive habits of turtles and the mating calls of frogs, but she couldn't figure out how to interact with her own species. Every relationship had ended in disaster. She had tried to shield her heart after relic hunter Jim toyed with it and Professor Charlie totaled it. She pushed John Pennington away. She kept Louie from getting too close. But distance only seemed to cut deeper.

The next day, she ate nothing and stared blankly at the walls. Then, in the early afternoon, she heard footsteps and a clatter of keys.

"Showtime, miss," said the jailer. He led her to the courthouse, a two-story brick building with palm trees flanking the flagpoles out front. Inside, the tap of the jailer's hard-soled shoes echoed through the tile foyer. Carol's muddy leather boots were quiet.

He swung open the wooden double doors to the courtroom. Heads swiveled, and silence fell across the windowless, fluorescent-lit room. She felt the eyes of the five jurors boring into her. Carol sat alone behind a wooden desk, folded her hands in her lap, and gazed down at her thumbs.

Her parents were in the gallery, solemn and stiff. Rebecca, her turtle-tagging friend from Little Cumberland, was also there. Pete sat dazed in the back of the courtroom. News reporters, park rangers, police officers, and curious onlookers filled the remaining seats.

At 2 P.M. on April 18, 1980, the day after the shooting, the inquest was gaveled to order by coroner Danny Saturday, a plumber by trade. The five-person jury—four middle-aged white males and an older African American man—sat behind a wooden table to his left. They had been summoned to determine the official cause of Louie McKee's death.

The five jurors first listened to Sheriff Middleton and his deputies recount the events and display the evidence, including the splintered paddle and the gray molding of the broken door frame.

"The molding had two shotgun holes," Deputy Harvey Amerson explained. "The panel itself did not—indicating that Ms. Ruckdeschel fired the weapon after McKee had busted out the panel."

The pellet holes also confirmed that Carol had pulled the trigger from the point where the gun was found—near the bathroom, about sixteen feet from the porch door.

"There was a strong odor of alcohol about the victim's body," the sheriff added. "McKee had been drinking with Jesse Bailey about an hour before the incident."

Carol kept her trembling hands folded beneath the wooden table. Her head throbbed. Her heart pounded. She could hear the swish of her own blood.

Next, Harold Wood, a law enforcement ranger on Cumberland Island, came forward to testify. He began by explaining that "McKee had a drinking problem." Then he said that "McKee and Ruckdeschel

had an affair going," and that "McKee had beaten her up some, the last time reported in December 1979, when he gave her a black eye and threatened to kill her."

Pete was too emotionally shaken to testify. He listened from the back of the courtroom as his statement was read to the jurors: "While I was sitting in the kitchen talking to Carol, I heard someone walk on the porch and try to open the door. I saw and heard this man breaking in the door angrily yelling something, and by the time he had broken the main panel in the door out, I heard a shot behind me, and he fell. Carol and I spoke for a moment. Somewhat shaken, I went and looked at the man on the porch and figured he was dead because he was not breathing. Then we went to the phone to contact the police."

The words all blurred together in the flat fog of Carol's brain. She felt the hardness of the wooden chair against her bones. Head down, she picked at the grit beneath her fingernails. Every now and then, she glanced up at the nervous young coroner and the expressionless, deadpan jurors.

Finally, District Attorney Glenn Thomas was called on to speak. The room was dead silent as he stood before the jury. Carol felt her stomach drop to the polished tile floor. The only man in the courtroom wearing a suit, he scanned the crowd and finally pivoted to the five stone-faced jurors.

"The statutes regarding justifiable homicide are numerous and complex," he began. His voice was like gravel in a blender. He launched into a long speech summarizing federal and state self-defense laws. At the end, he stood rigidly behind his desk and leaned forward on his fingertips. Carol's head pounded with her pulse. Sweat coated the palms of her clenched hands. After a long pause, he said: "It is our conclusion that Ms. Ruckdeschel reacted spontaneously and automatically to threats of serious bodily harm."

The jury agreed. They ruled unanimously that Carol's actions were in self-defense, and Louie's death was a justifiable homicide. No charges would be filed against her.

Upon hearing the verdict, Carol had hoped the cannonball in her chest would lift, her blurry vision would clear, and her cloudy-headedness would dissipate. But Carol felt nothing. Nothing at all.

Blank and benumbed, she walked out of the dark courtroom into the blindingly bright light of a spring afternoon. She thanked Rebecca for coming. She said goodbye to her parents. Then she went home and washed the blood off her porch.

Afterward, she sat on the porch steps, watching color drain from the darkening sky. From the direction of Louie's house, she could almost hear the sound of Ebby's fiddle: not the fast-paced, foot-stomping fury of a Saturday night shindig, but a slow, soft, mournful song that trickled through the moss-draped oaks.

That's when the tears finally came—tears of regret, tears of relief, tears of the deepest sadness she had ever known. She cradled her knees against her chest and rocked back and forth, sobbing. She wept for Louie. She wept for herself. She wept from the bottom of her being, until her heart was wrung dry.

Emptied of emotion, Carol curled up on the porch and listened to the night. Ebby's fiddle went silent. In its wake was the tenor of distant tides washing ashore, scouring the island, rinsing it clean.

Word of the shooting spread like wildfire. Island families vilified Carol, calling her "a vulture who preys on people for her own selfish goals." Park rangers kept their distance.

"She shotgunned her boyfriend when she got tired of him," said one islander who worked at the Greyfield Inn. "All of her lovers end up dead."

"She thinks she owns the island, and she'll kill anyone who gets in her way," said a Carnegie heir.

"She's like a black widow spider. After she breeds, she kills and eats her mate," said Douglas McKee, Louie's brother.

Betty McKee was outraged that her ex-husband's killer walked free less than twenty-four hours after shooting him. "It wasn't right," Betty said. "I don't know how she got away with it. She seemed to receive special treatment. If I'd done it, I woulda been locked up for life."

Betty had known Louie since he was three years old. He had always been a gentle, thoughtful person, she said. For twenty years,

Dungeness, the Carnegies' fifty-nine-room mansion, burned down in 1959.
WILL HARLAN

Steel magnate Thomas Carnegie (left, with his brother Andrew) bought most of Cumberland in 1881. WIKICOMMONS

John F. Kennedy Jr. married Carolyn Bessette in the one-room church across from Carol's cabin in 1996.
WILL HARLAN

Plum Orchard is the island's largest and most controversial Carnegie mansion.
WILL HARLAN

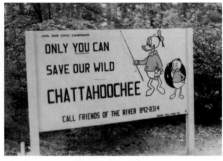

Jimmy Carter paddled the Chattooga River in 1970. He later protected it as a Wild and Scenic River. DOUG WOODWARD

In the early 1970s, Carol led Atlanta activists in safeguarding the Chattahoochee River corridor from development. ROGER BUERKI

Carol spearheaded efforts to protect half of the island as wilderness, but others have lobbied to remove the designation. WILL HARLAN

Cumberland's eighteen-mile seashore is one of the country's largest and most biologically diverse. SASHA GREENSPAN

The island's towering dunes are home to hundreds of endangered sea turtles' nests each summer. SASHA GREENSPAN

Lined by live oaks, the main road was recently removed from wilderness to accommodate vehicle tours. SASHA GREENSPAN

Thousands of feral hogs have overrun the island and destroyed endangered turtle nests. EMILY DIZNOFF

Feral horses attract tourists, but many horses are starving and suffering. WILL HARLAN

Carol often wades through swamps to investigate the habitat of alligators, Cumberland's largest predator. CAROL RUCKDESCHEL

Carol has studied and protected the island's imperiled wildlife for forty-two years.

A loggerhead sea turtle crawls ashore to nest. SASHA GREENSPAN

Hatchlings emerge from their eggs and scamper to the sea. SASHA GREENSPAN

Only one in 10,000 turtle hatchlings survives to maturity. SASHA GREENSPAN

A female loggerhead lumbers back to the ocean after nesting in Cumberland's dunes. SASHA GREENSPAN

Carol's field notes are accompanied by exquisitely detailed drawings, including this sketch of a loggerhead turtle hatchling curled in its egg. CAROL RUCKDESCHEL

Lucy Ferguson, founder of Greyfield Inn, was the matriarch of Cumberland for decades. CAROL RUCKDESCHEL

Lucy's granddaughter, Gogo Ferguson, was once Carol's close friend—and is now an adversary.

Carol rebuilt her cabin using driftwood. Leaders and lovers have squared off with Carol on her porch. WILL HARLAN

Greyfield Inn is operated by the Carnegie family on 200 privately owned acres. EMILY DIZNOFF

Carol, circa 2002, works
in her lab.
SASHA GREENSPAN

Carol handles a snake she caught in her
chicken coop.

Carol and her mother,
Anne (left), hike together
near Lake Whitney.
BOB SHOOP

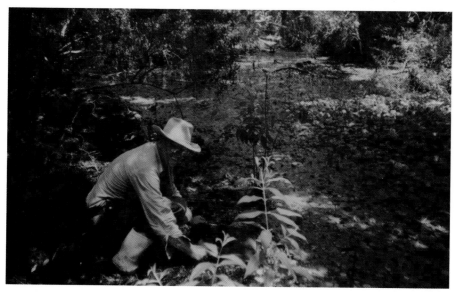

Bob Shoop collects specimens for the museum he helped build with Carol. WILL HARLAN

Bob and Carol were pioneers in sea turtle research. WILL HARLAN

Carol reaches inside a sea turtle carcass to examine its gut contents. SASHA GREENSPAN

Shrimp trawlers near Cumberland often capture sea turtles in their nets. SASHA GREENSPAN

Nuclear submarines prowl offshore and dock directly across from Cumberland at Kings Bay. WIKICOMMONS

Carol guards her wild island. SASHA GREENSPAN

Betty had been married to him, and never once had he been abusive toward her, she maintained. Even their divorce had been civil and gracious. Betty had spoken with Louie the day before the shooting, and he didn't seem ill-tempered or angry. Whatever he may have said or done on Carol's porch that evening, Betty said, it certainly didn't warrant being shot in the chest at close range.

"As a Christian woman, I must forgive her," Betty said. "But I won't forget."

Even Sam Candler was aloof and standoffish after the shooting. "I was a little bit afraid of her after that," he admitted. "I couldn't trust her. She was never part of the island families to begin with. She became the black sheep of the island."

Their words were like battery acid on Carol's heart. She became even more of a reclusive hermit.

"I am the bad guy. Everyone sees me as evil," she wrote in her journal. "I have to remind myself constantly that I know the truth. No one can understand it, because they've never been in a position like that, scared for their life."

Carol had read the statistics: every nine seconds in the United States, a woman is assaulted or beaten. Over eleven hundred women are murdered by their husbands or boyfriends annually—an average of three women each day. She was almost one of them.

But the numbers were cold comfort. She would have to bear away her sorrow with no one in her corner. Carol's few friends mostly abandoned her. Gogo was especially leery.

Island residents asked Carol if she really had to shoot him. *Couldn't she have shot him in the leg?*

He was breaking down her door and threatening to kill her, she would reply. If she had missed, she would be dead—and maybe Pete too.

For the next few months, Carol went subterranean. She buried herself in work. Holed up in island seclusion, she wandered alone through the marshes and slept in the dunes with the turtles. Once again, she had only animals as her companions. In her journal, she wrote: "Never get close to anyone. Ever."

* * *

Louie's estate only made things worse. Carol still had partial owner-
ship in Louie's property at Half Moon Bluff. She wanted nothing to
do with a haunted house.

But then Grover Henderson claimed Louie's house for himself.

Grover was the south Georgia lawyer who had already acquired
Beulah Alberty's house, across from Carol's cabin. He was one of the
legal representatives for the Carnegie and Rockefeller families on
Cumberland. He also served as the local Camden County attorney
until he was involved in a car accident while under the influence of
alcohol. Scrutiny following the accident revealed that he had been
using government funds for lavish travel and billing the county for
personal expenses.

According to Carol Grover drank heavily, talked loudly, shot out
the eyes of alligators at Lake Whitney, poached deer, and cut down
trees in the national park. Carol had spotted him trawling for fish
at night, out of season, using giant spotlights to lure fish to his nets.
He dumped his garbage—including three broken-down vehicles—on
park lands. When the National Park Service began trapping hogs on
the beach, Grover ran over the traps with his truck.

Grover had already tried to take Carol's property once before.
Soon after she had purchased her ramshackle cabin from the Trim-
mings family, Grover coerced Bobby Rischarde, a black man who
owned property adjacent to Carol's, to claim the cabin belonged to
him, because he had occasionally mowed the weeds around it. Grover
was behind the scheme. He hoped to chase Carol off the island and
have the Settlement to himself.

But his plans backfired when Carol showed up one morning
with Frances "Sister" Trimmings and a tape recorder in her pocket.
Sister strutted across the yard and stomped up to Bobby and Grover.

"What's this you claimin' this property?"

"Sister. Uh . . . good to see you again," Bobby stammered.

"Who dat house belong to?"

"Uh . . . I looked after it some. Kept the grass cut for you."

"You knowed this house was mine and I done sold it to this
woman," Sister said, poking Bobby in the chest.

"Oh yes ma'am."

"So why are you tellin' folks that it belong to you?"

Bobby looked sheepishly at Grover, whose sunburned cheeks flushed even redder.

"You got a lawyer?" Grover asked Sister.

"That's all right about the lawyer. I wanna know how you come by dat house," Sister said. She pursed her lips and leaned forward into Grover's face.

"I'd rather ask your lawyer that," Grover said, stepping between them. "I mean, that's what you pay him good money for."

"It's a real simple question," Carol interjected. "Bobby, did you ever own that house?"

"No, ma'am. It was Grover here that done all the complaining and kicking. He didn't want you there, you understand."

"Oh, I understand," said Carol.

"I'd be more than happy to talk to your lawyer about this," Grover said.

"As Grover's neighbor, I didn't say nothing and went along with it," Bobby explained, shuffling his feet in the sand. "But then this morning I had a different view about the place. Since you is here, it belongs to you. I want to live in a world with friends."

"Now wait a minute, wait a minute," Grover sputtered.

"You done wasted enough of my time already. I don't wanna hear no more from you," Sister said to Grover, and marched out of the yard.

Now Grover was back for round two. Just a few weeks after the shooting, Grover moved into Louie's vacant house at Half Moon Bluff.

"I swore never to step foot in that place again. But I couldn't just stand by and let Grover swipe it," Carol said.

She reluctantly decided to sue Grover. Carol couldn't afford a lawyer, so she represented herself. Even though Grover was the newly minted county attorney, he was already facing a grand jury

investigation for traveling on the taxpayers' dime. So Grover decided to hire the best attorney in south Georgia to represent him: Bobby Lee Cook, widely considered to have been the basis for the television show *Matlock*, though a bit more greasy than Andy Griffith. Cook had succeeded in getting dozens of felons acquitted with his courtroom theatrics and shrewd cross-examinations. By tearing into witnesses and breaking them down on the witness stand, he helped mobsters, Klansmen, and porn racketeers get off the hook. He was a bulldog trial lawyer who had a long-standing reputation as a winner, and he saw Grover's case as an easy slam dunk. He built his defense around a Georgia law that specifically prevents murderers from benefiting from the death of their victims.

But Carol had done her homework, too, and discovered that the law did not apply to acts of self-defense. In the end, Carol triumphed over Matlock. Louie's house belonged to Carol, and Grover was sent packing.

Carol didn't ever want the house to begin with. So she gave it to her parents, who had loaned her the money to build her cabin. But that didn't change the facts: she had acquired the house of the man she had killed. It sparked rumors that she had intentionally shot Louie to get his island property.

"She murdered her way onto the island," said Renee Noe, a National Park Service ranger. "She used men to get what she wanted."

Other park employees joined in. "Did she really need to blast a shotgun through her lover's heart at point-blank range?" said Zack Kirkland, a veteran park ranger on Cumberland. "He was holding a canoe paddle, not a gun or knife. Did that really warrant a death sentence?"

Even the media turned on her.

"She engineered the whole thing. Louie's death made her life very comfortable," said Robert Coram, a former Cumberland Island park ranger and reporter for the *Atlanta Constitution*. "I am convinced that she lured Louie onto the porch and killed him cold-blooded, without remorse. She is an amoral sociopath devoid of feeling who

wanted the island for herself. She killed Louie to protect her privacy. She literally got away with murder."

In a 1981 story in the *Atlanta Weekly*, Coram wrote: "Men seem to sense in her a primitive woodsy vitality of extraordinary appeal. She has been married twice and caused two other men to leave hearth and home to be with her. . . . Another man later left his wife to be with her. She shot and killed him with a gun he had given her. . . . It was Carol, the vigilant protector of Cumberland, who brought the worst of the world to the island."

Two books were written about Carol that further maligned her. One was a conspiratorial account written by Ard Eulenfeld, a friend of Louie McKee. In his book, Eulenfeld claimed that Carol masterminded Louie's murder, and then Jimmy Carter and the CIA provided the cover-up. He recounted a fiddle party where Carol once playfully slithered like a rattlesnake, stalking her prey. She supposedly flicked her tongue and writhed across the floor, then suddenly coiled and struck, biting Louie in the crotch.

"She latched onto Louie McKee, got all she could out of him, then shot and killed him at the back door of the cottage he had built for her," he wrote. "Every man she touches winds up dead. She must have some kind of hole on her."

Later, bestselling author and former Cumberland Island park ranger Nevada Barr published a novel about a bloodthirsty villainess with long braided pigtails who ate roadkill, slept her way onto a Georgia barrier island, and murdered her lover. In the novel, she also used money designated for sea turtle research to support her cocaine habit. Carol later sued Nevada Barr for libel and won, but the damage had been done.

Carol had come to Cumberland to find a deep connection to a place where she belonged. Now, she lived in torment and isolation. Instead of Louie stalking her, she was constantly shadowed by shame and sorrow. *I did nothing wrong*, she told herself, over and over. But everywhere she went, she felt the sting of venomous words and glares. Once again, Carol decided to pack up her belongings and leave the island. She had nowhere to go, but she couldn't bear to stay.

The night before she planned to leave, she wandered out to the beach to say goodbye. As she crested the dunes, she stopped suddenly, awestruck: the ocean had come alive with light. Bioluminescent plankton shimmered across the water. Not even the star-filled sky could compete with the ocean's neon glitter. Flecks of electric blue light washed onto the beach, breaking apart beneath her feet as she walked beside the water. Her footprints glowed in the summer sand.

Carol waded out into the shining sea. Amid the fiery foam of the curling breakers, she made up her mind once and for all: she wasn't ever going to be chased off the island. This was the only home she had ever known. This was her habitat, her feeding grounds, and the tangled web of life she studied was her family, who accepted her as she was, no matter what. This was where she belonged.

Carol still felt pangs of guilt for living in the middle of a protected national park. She was infringing upon its wildness by residing within it. But she was temporary, she reminded herself. As lifetime rights expired, including hers, the human thumbprint would fade, and the wild island would heal. She wouldn't live to see it, but at least she could help nudge it in the right direction. She would keep her ear to the sand, watch over the island, and guard it with her life.

For years, she had taken from the island: oysters from the marsh, driftwood from the beach, data from dead animals. The only way she could stay on Cumberland was to give something back. She could fight for the wild. She could speak for the turtles and gators. She could be a voice crying out for the wilderness.

She had sheltered beneath her shell for too long, cloistered in her cabin, hidden away from humanity. Now it was time to stick her neck out and fight for life beyond her own.

The underwater light show flashed around her. She vowed to carry the light inside her, like warm coals in her chest, to illuminate the dark days ahead.

Later that night, after unpacking her boxes, she wrote in her journal: "It is my fault that Louie is dead. I must face that guilt every day, for the rest of my life. I'll have to learn to live with that. But I'm sure as hell not gonna run away. With every fiber of my being, I'm gonna stay and fight."

* * *

Cumberland needed her more than ever. In the late 1970s, the National Park Service planned colossal developments on the island to accommodate one million tourists annually. A bridge from the mainland was proposed. Carol quickly learned that the National Park Service could develop the supposedly protected island almost as ruthlessly as Charles Fraser. Cumberland's status as a national seashore was not enough. Even well-intentioned agencies like the National Park Service had become more focused on visitation revenues than preserving wild places. Parks could be loved to death, especially a sandbar in south Georgia that was about to be inundated by a million people.

Once again, Cumberland Island needed to be saved—and once again, it needed a woman to save it. Carol realized that the only way to prevent overcrowded beaches, noisy vehicle tours, bulldozed dunes, cluttered concession stands, and garbage-strewn boardwalks was to designate the island a wilderness.

part four

last of the wild

15

Right now, trillions of critters are grazing on each of us. Microbes are feeding in our gut, swimming over the surface of our eyes, and drilling into the enamel of our teeth. There are more organisms on our tongue than all the stars in the galaxy. Without them, we'd be dead.

The human body is an untamed wilderness of undulating mountains, folded valleys, tangled hairy jungles, and cavernous maws brimming with microscopic life. We are vast. We contain multitudes. Each of us is an ecosystem, a walking biome. There are ten times more cells of other organisms in our body than our own. That makes us 90 percent nonhuman.

"We are wild country," Carol says. Our bodies are as lush and diverse as the world they inhabit.

Because wilderness is so deeply rooted in us, it's one of our most fiercely conflicted ideas. Like our own hearts, wilderness is dark and light, deadly and divine, sinister and sublime. Wilderness can be a place of sacred and inspired transformation: Moses went to the mountaintop; John the Baptist was a voice crying out from the wilderness; Jesus wandered the wilderness for forty days and transfigured himself there. In every major religion, wilderness is where the great spiritual pilgrims went to seek revelation: Muhammad met the angel Gabriel in the wilderness near Mecca, Buddha found the path to enlightenment beneath a tree, and Lao-tzu retreated to a remote mountain cave.

But wilderness can also be a dark and shadowed realm, home to witches and evildoers. Fear of nature lingers in our mythologies, from the serpent in the Garden of Eden to the Blair Witch and other woodsy horror-flick slashers. Even beloved fairy tales like Little Red Riding Hood and Hansel and Gretel perpetuate phobias of bogeymen lurking behind every tree. Today, the great outdoors is still haunted by the dueling banjos of *Deliverance*. The

moral of most of these stories is pretty consistent: if you go into the woods, bad stuff happens.

However, we're usually scared of the wrong things. We're hundreds of times more likely to die driving to the trailhead than actually hiking in the forest. Fear of snakes keeps millions away from the woods, but only fifteen people die of snake bites each year in the United States. Bears and sharks kill a combined eight Americans annually.

If we're looking for something to fear, we should take a glance in the mirror. There are over seventeen thousand murders annually in the United States, and less than .001 percent of them take place in the woods. Our neighbors are far more dangerous than any animals in the forest. Wilderness is far safer than our own backyards.

Some say wilderness is everywhere. Others argue it doesn't exist. Wilderness might describe an untouched forest or an unmowed field, a roadless area or a roadside rest stop.

Wilderness actually has a very specific definition, enshrined in what Carol calls "America's most astounding piece of legislation," the Wilderness Act of 1964—the first law ever to give nature priority over people. It defines wilderness as "an area where the earth and its community of life are untrammeled by man . . . an area of undeveloped land retaining its primeval character."

Wilderness areas are the last pristine pockets of nature. They sustain themselves, without human manipulation. People can visit but not live in wilderness. No roads, vehicles, or structures are allowed. Logging, mining, and development are also prohibited. It is machine free: not even bicycles or chainsaws are permitted. Simply put, wilderness is pure nature, where the human imprint is minimized.

Such a division between humans and nature is relatively new. For 99 percent of human history, we have seen ourselves as part of nature, not separated from it. Most indigenous cultures have no word for wilderness, because they never divided themselves from the natural world.

Our hunter-gatherer ancestors weren't noble savages, nor were they tree-hugging environmental saints. They cut down trees for firewood, and they routinely burned down forests to improve hunting and replenish the soil. They butchered sea turtles and ate their eggs. When they competed for limited resources, they slaughtered each other. For the most part, however, they lived within the resource limits of their environments.

Everything changed about ten thousand years ago, when we began domesticating animals and plants and concentrating into agricultural societies. Food was stockpiled and distributed in cities, and hierarchies developed around the surplus. The human population began to swell. Forests were cleared for farmland. Ordered rows of grain crops and settled societies replaced nomadic hunter-gatherer life in the wilderness. Fences were built. Animals were corralled. Boundaries were mapped. For the first time, we drew a line separating our controlled spaces from the wild beyond.

We benefited immensely from bringing nature under control. Food and shelter were more secure, life expectancy increased, and social organization enabled the arts and education to flourish. Everyday living became cleaner, safer, healthier, and more convenient.

But we also took a big risk: we bet our entire evolutionary future on controlling nature rather than living within it. We began distancing ourselves from the untamed wilderness and favoring the domesticated. Dogs replaced wolves. Cows replaced buffaloes. Wild grasses were plowed under to plant wheat.

We can't fault our ancestors for wanting a bit of security—a steady and predictable surplus, a corncrib to get them through the long winter, a hog to slaughter if food got tight. Both the wild and the tame have their place, even in the natural world. But things went wrong when we wanted to control not just a small garden patch but all of nature. Modern civilization severed the web of life and turned it into a chain, with humans at the top, the puppeteer pulling on nature's strings.

Conquering nature became a central tenet of human faith and philosophy. Control—for both religion and resources—even drove us to domesticate our fellow human beings.

We have so thoroughly conquered nature that most of its resources support not the diverse species of life but a monoculture of man, seven billion strong and doubling every half century. We're on our way to oceans without whales or sea turtles. Empty forests. A world without wild animals.

For two million years, we played by the same rules of nature as everyone else: Diversify. Adapt. Cooperate. Waste nothing. Stay within resource limits.

Then, fairly recently, we decided that the world belonged to humans and the rules of nature didn't apply to us any longer. We tamed the wilderness and controlled the earth. We tried to butcher the turtle on which Turtle Island rests.

But she didn't die.

In 1969, NASA scientist James Lovelock noticed something unusual happening in the earth's atmosphere: inexplicably, its balance of oxygen and other gases was regulating itself like a thermostat. But what was doing the regulating? He looked at other planetary processes—including the stable concentration of ocean salinity and the cycling of nutrients—and came to a startling conclusion: the earth is alive.

He proposed that the earth is a superorganism—one giant living system that includes not just animals and plants but rocks, gases, and soil—acting together as if the planet was a single living being. Its bodily systems, such as the water cycle and nitrogen cycle, are balanced to maintain life on earth. The throb of the tides was the systole and diastole of the earth, and water coursed like blood through its veins. We proud humans may simply be microbes on the surface of a superbeing whose entirety we cannot fully comprehend. Like the bacteria in our body, is it possible that we, too, are part of a larger living earth, a speck on the eyeball of the universe?

Tree roots break the sidewalk. Dandelions spring through the cracks. Insects grow resistant to pesticides. Rivers flood our tallest levees and break through our mightiest dams. Beaches keep moving, despite jetty walls and truckloads of imported sand. "Our domination of nature is a delusion," Carol says. "We cannot exempt ourselves from nature's ironclad laws. We cannot grow infinitely on a finite planet."

Mother Nature is a tough old broad. Like the humble tortoise lining up against the hotshot hare, she will outlast us. We can't sustain our blustery sprint to the front of the pack. Our current reign has lasted fewer than ten thousand years—barely a blip in the earth's four-billion-year history. Our supremacy is short-lived, and our species' future is uncertain. Only one thing is for sure: we need Mother Nature a lot more than she needs us.

Nowhere is the human relationship to nature more schizophrenic than in *Homo americanus*. The United States is home to the most technologically advanced civilization and the most raw, untamed wildness in the world. Over the past five hundred years, Americans hated and feared wilderness, then loved it, then nearly killed the thing they loved.

The Americas were already inhabited by at least ten million indigenous people when Columbus dropped anchor. But those folks didn't count to Europeans—except as slaves. They viewed the continent as a blank spot on the map, virgin terrain to be reaped for its abundant resources.

The first pilgrims aboard the *Mayflower* looked across the waters and gloomily beheld "a hideous and desolate wilderness full of wild beasts." Puritan colonists viewed themselves as Christian soldiers in a divinely ordained war against pagan wildness. A century later, American pioneers also believed it was their divinely ordained duty to tame the wilderness. They were spearheads of progress, fulfilling America's Manifest Destiny to expand westward across the continent. After the American Revolution, frontiersmen blazed paths across the Wild West. Indigenous people—and species like the buffalo and passenger pigeon—were corralled or killed to make way for America's transcontinental conquest. We carved our civilization out of the wild, endlessly expanding frontier.

Along the way, though, wilderness became deeply ingrained in American identity. The wilderness had forged rugged individuals and a pioneering spirit. The challenges of frontier travel ennobled our character and toughened our resolve. The vigor and vitality of

wilderness life distinguished us from our stodgy, effete European parents and tested the mettle of our young nation. America had succeeded in transforming the wilderness, but the wilderness had also transformed us.

Then, in the late nineteenth century, westward expansion ran out of room. Industrialized America had finally sprawled from sea to shining sea. The American frontier—the border between civilization and wilderness, order and chaos, the cultivated and wild—disappeared forever. The howling wolf and trumpeting elk went silent.

Sentiment toward wilderness began to shift. Without the frontier, Americans began to view wilderness as an asset rather than an adversary. Instead of being reviled, wilderness became revered. "We need the tonic of wildness," wrote Henry David Thoreau, the first prophet of the wilderness gospel, who built a one-room cabin and grew beans beside Walden Pond in 1845.

Carol built her cabin in the wilderness for many of the same reasons as Thoreau, who went to the woods "to live deliberately, to front only the essential facts of life, and see if I could learn what it had to teach, and not, when I come to die, discover that I had not lived." Like Thoreau, Carol was a student of nature and a geographical extension of the wilderness that surrounded her. Both explored a life stripped down to its essentials. They wanted "to live deep and suck out all the marrow of life."

Thoreau believed wilderness provided a necessary counterbalance to the materialism and urbanization of industrialized America. It was a place of self-renewal and contact with the raw material of life. "In wildness is the preservation of the world," he famously wrote.

Thoreau was among the first to advocate for protecting America's vanishing wildlands, proposing that the nation formally preserve "a certain sample of wild nature . . . a network of national preserves in which the bear and the panther may still exist and not be civilized off the face of the earth." Wilderness preserves could provide a perpetual frontier to keep overindustrialized Americans in contact with the primitive honesty of the woods.

In 1872—the same year that Tom and Andy founded Carnegie Steel—America designated its first national park: over two million

acres in northwest Wyoming were set aside as Yellowstone National Park.

A second national park soon followed, thanks to the inspiration of Sierra Club founder John Muir.

He so loved the Sierra that he proposed a fifteen-hundred-square-mile park around Yosemite Valley and spent decades fighting for it. When Yosemite National Park was finally signed into law in 1890, Muir wrote, "Thousands of tired, nerve-shaken, over-civilized people are beginning to find out that going to the mountains is going home, that wildness is a necessity, and that mountain parks and reservations are useful not only as fountains of timber and irrigating rivers, but as fountains of life."

But a few pristine parklands were not nearly enough. By the beginning of the twentieth century, nearly the entire continent had been clearcut, from the California redwoods to the eastern chestnut. The federal government bought the slashed stumplands left behind by timber companies and formed the U.S. Forest Service, which would eventually manage nearly two hundred million acres of forestland. However, the government continued to allow logging, dam building, cattle grazing, and mining in these forests.

"The earth and its resources belong to its people," proclaimed the U.S. Forest Service's first chief, Gifford Pinchot. He wanted to democratize the forest resources. Pinchot advocated the wise use of public lands to maximize benefits for all Americans. According to Pinchot, sustainably cutting timber from the forests made them even more healthy and productive than a hands-off approach.

Pinchot and Muir clashed in epic turf wars that still rage today. Is nature a resource to be used or a sanctuary to be protected? Pinchot bashed Muir for locking up natural resources: "The mere preservation of a romantic and picturesque spot should not take precedence over the urgent needs of great masses of human beings for the necessities of life." Muir decried Pinchot's economic motivation to turn every tree and waterfall into money: "These temple-destroyers, devotees of ravaging commercialism, seem to have a perfect contempt for Nature. Instead of lifting their eyes to the God of the mountains, they lift them to the Almighty Dollar."

By the middle of the twentieth century, national forests were used mainly for timber harvesting, and many national parks had become tourist attractions managed to maximize visitation. Neither jived with the pure wilderness protection ideals of Thoreau and Muir. Stronger measures for wilderness preservation were needed.

Along came Aldo Leopold. He was a U.S. Forest Service ranger who initially supported Pinchot's use-oriented management of forests. A seasoned hunter, he had long believed that good game management required killing predators that preyed on deer. Then one afternoon, hunting with a friend on a mountain in New Mexico, he spied a mother wolf and her cubs, took aim, and shot them. "We reached the old wolf in time to watch a fierce green fire dying in her eyes," Leopold wrote. "There was something new to me in those eyes—something known only to her and the mountain. I was young then, and full of trigger-itch. I thought that because fewer wolves meant more deer, no wolves would mean a hunter's paradise. But after seeing the fierce green fire die, I sensed that neither the wolf nor the mountain agreed with such a view."

The wolf's fierce green fire inspired Leopold to extend ethics beyond the boundaries of the human family to include the larger community of animals, plants, and even soil and water. He enshrined this natural code of conduct in his famous land ethic: "A thing is right when it tends to preserve the integrity, stability, and beauty of the biotic community. It is wrong when it tends otherwise." Carol inscribed Leopold's land ethic in her journal when she was a teenager and has steadfastly followed it throughout her life. She believes that it changes our role from conqueror of the earth to plain member and citizen of it.

Leopold led the effort to create the first federally protected wilderness area: a half million acres of the Gila National Forest in New Mexico was designated as wilderness in 1924. Leopold had laid the groundwork for a national wilderness system, interconnected oases of biodiversity permanently protected from human development.

Wilderness became the most fiercely contested idea in conservation history. It was vigorously opposed by the lumber, oil, cattle, and mining industries, which echoed Pinchot in criticizing the lockup of

natural resources. It revived religious arguments against the pagan wild. Timber baron William Hunt lashed out at the "woodsy witch doctors of a revived ancient nature cult," and Cumberland Island developer Charles Fraser later characterized wilderness advocates as "druids who worship trees and sacrifice human beings to those trees." Other wilderness opponents argued that the land belonged to man, not animals. Nature was not a divine cathedral but a mosquito-ridden hell. It needed the human hand to transform it into something useful and beneficial.

As the debate over wilderness raged, a reclusive female marine biologist helped launch the modern environmental movement. In 1962 Rachel Carson published *Silent Spring*, which showed that pesticides like DDT kill far more than the pests at which they are aimed. They nearly wiped out the bald eagle, symbol of American freedom and wildness. Carson became one of the most important scientists of the century who strikingly linked nature's health with our own. "Man is a part of nature," she wrote, "and his war against nature is inevitably a war against himself."

Carson was the first modern female voice of the wild—and an inspiration to young Carol Ruckdeschel. Rachel Carson was her favorite author and scientist. As a teenager, Carol read everything that Carson had written, including three books about islands, the sea, and biodiversity. Carson combined a romantic love of nature with the cool analytical mind of a trained scientist and the controlled passion of a political activist—a model that Carol would follow on Cumberland more than a decade later.

Carson was also one of the first to link science to wilderness. Wilderness offered an evolutionary baseline of how healthy ecosystems maintain themselves, she argued. Wilderness areas were places for pilgrimage into our species' past, where we could temporarily strip away the thin veneer of civilization to rediscover the deep evolutionary flow that shaped us.

Her research fueled the passage of the 1964 Wilderness Act, which would permanently protect the purest and most pristine pockets of nature in America's existing public lands as "an enduring reservoir of wilderness." The bill passed almost unanimously. Upon signing the Wilderness Act into law on September 3, 1964, President

Lyndon B. Johnson said, "If future generations are to remember us with gratitude rather than contempt, we must leave them more than the miracles of technology. We must leave them a glimpse of the world as it was in the beginning, not just after we got through with it."

It was the first piece of legislation to acknowledge an inherent value to nature and—even more radically—to give nature precedence over civilization on these last scraps of American wildlands. The United States was the first country ever to set aside lands for their intrinsic natural values. Today, America's wilderness is the largest and most biologically diverse system of protected lands in the world.

Wilderness has been called America's best idea yet. It's also one of our most controversial—and Cumberland Island is a magnifying lens for the wilderness wars. Over a century after Pinchot and Muir first clashed, their philosophies remain locked in battle over the future of America's wilderness: wise use versus wild sanctuaries. Wise use is prevailing, but the devoted cult of wilderness has succeeded in expanding the wilderness preservation system. Today there are 704 wilderness areas totaling 107 million acres.

That's still not much. Only 2 percent of the continental United States is protected as wilderness. The United States has more theme parks than wilderness areas. East of the Mississippi, there are more acres of pavement than wilderness. Now more than ever, wilderness is an endangered geographical species. And nowhere is it more imperiled than on Cumberland Island.

16

A heated wilderness debate in the early 1980s was already raging on Cumberland Island when, on a coal-black night, Carol saw flickering light through the trees—fire.

Lightning had ignited a pine near Lake Whitney, and soon the entire forest was ablaze. Park rangers were evacuating the island, and fire crews were clear-cutting giant swaths of forest as firebreaks. Island families frantically packed up belongings and loaded them onto boats.

Jesse Bailey, half-drunk and hungover, sprawled out in a stupor beside the road. Strong southerly winds were whipping the wildfire closer to the Candler property, and a park ranger came racing up the road to help them evacuate by boat.

"Dammit, Jesse, get out of the way!" he shouted.

The midnight horizon was eerily orange. The Candlers backed up trucks to their houses and loaded them with rugs and keepsakes. The fire swept closer. Jesse didn't move.

"You better get on that boat," the ranger warned Jesse. "The whole north end is going up in flames."

"The fire will stop when it hits them big oaks," Jesse said.

Sure enough, the fire arrived at the wall of live oak trees ringing the Candler compound and abruptly fizzled. A few flickers of flame flared in the duff, but the blaze had burned out before their eyes.

Living on barrier islands his entire life, Jesse knew that oaks were a natural firebreak. Long before fire hydrants and helicopter fire crews, Jesse and his kin had learned how forest fires moved. They welcomed wildfires, which were a regular and restorative part of island life—as natural and necessary as rain showers, as regular as the tides in replenishing life.

Smokey the Bear was wrong. Fire had been suppressed and extinguished on public lands since 1911, causing choked combustible understories of brush to accumulate. Wildfires are natural and healthy, but when smothered for a century they swell into raging infernos that are far more severe and catastrophic. Worst of all, fire suppression doesn't work. Under fire suppression policies, wildfires have grown larger, hotter, and more destructive. Acreage burned by wildfires has quadrupled since 1980.

Scientists and land managers are starting to realize the essential role of wildfire in maintaining healthy forests. After wildfires, the thick understory is cleared, allowing light to reach the forest floor and new growth to emerge. Tick and parasite populations are dramatically reduced. Soil fertility is enriched by the ash. Birds flourish, their nests protected from predators below by the burned-out understory. Some species of trees, like the pond pine, even require wildfire to regenerate. Its pine cones only shed seeds in the presence of searing heat.

Although the island wildfire had stopped before reaching the Candler compound, farther south it continued to blaze. Carol was staked out nearby, photographing the fire. Smoke burned her throat. She felt heat from the fire pulsing through the scorched pines. Fingers of orange and black seeped across the forest, cracking and popping in mossy wet logs.

Then she heard the helicopter overhead. It had scooped saltwater from the ocean into a one-thousand-gallon bucket that hung by a cable from its skids. The chopper was dumping saltwater onto the island's freshwater ponds, lakes, and forests and spraying the wilderness with poisonous fire retardants.

Carol was incensed. Smothering an entire freshwater-dependent forest with saltwater and retardants would devastate the wildlife there. She wanted photographs of the deadly rain of saltwater and toxins, so she crept closer to the heart of the fire.

She hid behind an oak as the chopper returned from the ocean with its full bucket and hovered directly overhead. Carol snapped her camera three times before a wall of water fell toward her. She scrambled out of the way and dove just a few feet from the thunder-

ing slam of half a ton of water. Trees snapped and crashed beneath the weight of the deluge.

A few days later, Carol stormed into the superintendent's office and slapped the photos on his desk. "You're supposed to be protecting the island, not poisoning it!" she said.

"I did what was necessary to ensure public safety," the superintendent replied.

"The island needs fire. Without it, you'll lose the endangered wood storks and a bunch of other wildlife. The longleaf pines will disappear."

The superintendent cleared his throat. "To be perfectly candid, Carol, as long as we don't lose any houses or human lives, it really doesn't matter."

Wildfire had fanned the flames of the wilderness wars on Cumberland in the 1970s and early 1980s. In the name of fire safety, the park could bulldoze ancient forests, cut new roads, and spray chemicals across the island. The National Park Service could be just as dangerous as developers, Carol believed. They weren't stewards of nature for the common good. They were deliverers of a nature experience to their customers.

The National Park Service had recently announced plans for developing Cumberland Island into a vast tourist resort for one million annual visitors. Plans included a conference center, hotels, and a network of paved roads and beachfront developments. A wastewater treatment plant would be built atop the island's most treasured archaeological site near Brickhill Bluff. A fleet of twelve ferries would run nonstop from the mainland. Tour buses would shuttle visitors all over the island and out to the beach, where they would congregate along boardwalks with concession stands and gift shops.

At first, Carol wanted to bury her head in the sand. But she had vowed to fight for Cumberland. She couldn't let one of the country's last wild islands become yet another road-filled resort. Cumberland sheltered over one thousand different kinds of plants and animal species, including a dozen endangered species. The island

was an integral hub along the Atlantic Flyway, an aerial highway for migrating birds. It was home to the most fecund saltwater marshes and largest old-growth live oak forest in the country.

She had made a promise and she intended to keep it: If she was going to stay on Cumberland, she was going to give nature a voice in the fight. She dove headfirst into the fray.

From the start, it was a gamble. She was a wild card, and the deck was stacked against her. The National Park Service, state and local leaders, the Carnegie families, and even several environmental groups already supported the tourist resort proposal.

Politically, Carol was clueless. She was a loner living in the wilderness. She had no people skills, she didn't understand the National Park Service bureaucracy, and she certainly wasn't familiar with federal agencies' revenue streams or cost-benefit analysis. She knew little about environmental law and even less about public policy. Most of her friends were four-legged and either furry or flippered.

Unlike the deep-pocketed Carnegies, she couldn't buy influence or political power. She couldn't call her congressmen—she didn't even have a phone. She had no constituency and spoke for no organization or voting block. She was a nobody, and she knew it.

Her only hope was to rally the American people. Ironically, the best chance for saving Cumberland was for the public to choose self-restraint over self-indulgence. Could they love an island enough to leave it alone? Would they be willing to voluntarily limit their visitation to keep Cumberland wild? It seemed unlikely, but it was her only play. She was betting everything on wilderness, and she anted up the next three years of her life.

Though she didn't have a rolodex of political heavyweights, she did have one friend in a very high place. Her old boss and fellow river rat Jimmy Carter was now president of the United States.

She had an ace up her sleeve, but she couldn't play that card until she had a seat at the table. She wrote letters to conservation leaders in Atlanta and quickly assembled a team of grassroots activists who could build a movement. She got the newspapers and national media interested in the island. Most importantly, she launched a grassroots letter-writing campaign aimed at not only stopping the

park's development plan, but also creating a federally designated wilderness on Cumberland.

"Environmentalists are always on the defensive," Carol observed. "Their only hope is to stop the next rotten deal or to block the next bad bill. They can never win with that strategy."

Carol believed the best defense was a good offense. The National Park Service had proposed a tourist playground. In response, Carol proposed designating the entire northern half of the island as wilderness.

"People are tired of fighting against things. They want something to fight *for*. An island wilderness is something that people can believe in," Carol told her core crew of conservationists in Atlanta.

Among them was a twenty-six-year-old creative writing major and Sierra Club volunteer named Bill Mankin. He had just recently joined the Sierra Club, barely scraping up $10 to cover his membership dues. At his first meeting, the Atlanta chapter nominated him to lead the Cumberland Island committee. It seemed like a safe, easy way to get his feet wet. The national seashore had just opened, and everyone was enchanted by it. Surely there was not much controversy yet surrounding the nation's newest national seashore. Then he met Carol.

"She instantly drew me in," Bill said. "Whenever she talked about the island, she glowed with fire, and everyone around her wanted to catch some of her warmth."

Bill became the lead coordinator for the Cumberland Island wilderness campaign in Congress. He traveled to D.C. on his own dime to meet with representatives and lobby for wilderness on Cumberland. But it was Carol who fueled the fight.

"The wilderness was Carol's idea," he explained. "She was the inspiration for our perspiration. She knew everything that was happening on Cumberland, even behind closed doors. She was the island's watchdog and bulldog."

Carol had literally drawn a line in the sand. Nearly all of the island's historic structures were on the southern half of the island, including the Dungeness ruins and the Stafford slave chimneys. The National Park Service and the Greyfield Inn could run vehicle tours on the southern half of Cumberland. But under Carol's plan, the

northern half would be forever preserved as federally designated wilderness.

"The park is gonna keep hatching plans to develop the island. We'll be fighting them constantly," Carol reasoned. "But if we can get the island designated as wilderness, then we've got it protected permanently. Instead of fighting endless battles, let's try to win the war."

Not everyone liked Carol's approach. Nearly all of the environmental groups initially supported the park's development plan. Many thought Carol's wilderness proposal was too radical and unrealistic. Only one environmental leader from Atlanta, Hans Neuhauser, liked Carol's game plan and eventually joined her team.

"Carol is extreme, but so are the problems we face," he said. "She puts herself way out there, where most people are afraid to go. She is uncompromising—sometimes frustratingly so. But we need people like Carol to hold the line."

Hans was a giant hulking German with a gentle voice. A pillar of the conservation community, Hans was well connected in the political arena and helped draft a Cumberland Island wilderness bill for Congress based on Carol's recommendations.

"She drew the wilderness map for the island," Hans explained. "She had the on-the-ground knowledge for the Cumberland campaign. She spearheaded the grassroots effort. I talked to lawyers and legislators, but it was Carol that inspired the movement."

Newspaper reporter Robert Coram also played a key role in Carol's wilderness campaign. Though he disliked Carol for breaking up with his friend John Pennington, Coram joined forces with her in criticizing the park's tourist resort plan. He wrote a series of scathing editorials in the *Atlanta Constitution*, which earned him a Pulitzer nomination. The National Park Service was soon flooded with thousands of letters and phone calls opposing its development plans and supporting a wilderness on Cumberland.

"Leave Cumberland Island alone. Georgia's crown jewel sparkles in its own light," wrote Sandy Colhard, a Marietta housewife. "Turning Cumberland into a tourist trap would be like painting a road sign over a Picasso," wrote Benjamin Murphy, an artist from Savannah. Most of the four thousand responses were summarized in

a single statement by Roger Buerki, a carpenter from Atlanta: "This is a plea from the heart: keep Cumberland wild."

The feds were stunned by the flood of public response. They received more letters about Cumberland than even the big heart-throb parks out West like Yosemite and Yellowstone. "We didn't expect this," said National Park Service spokesman Paul Winegar. "I know of no national park anywhere in the country that arouses the feeling Cumberland does."

Already the National Park Service had spent millions buying the national seashore, and the service had hoped to recoup its investment through visitation revenues. Cumberland Island superintendent Paul McCrary had spent years drafting the tourism and development proposal for the national seashore. He sure as hell wasn't about to let Carol's ragtag band of wilderness warriors wreck his plans.

McCrary envisioned the country's newest national park becoming its most visited. Fortunately for McCrary, most of the higher-ups in the National Park Service still supported his development proposal, despite the rising tide of public opposition to his plan.

McCrary was short and stout, with tightly cropped hair and an angular face. He despised Carol and the whole idea of wilderness. Carol didn't think much of him, either. "He's a mouth breather. If his IQ were any lower, he'd have to be watered twice a day," she said.

Ultimately, the director of the National Park Service, William Whalen, was dispatched to Cumberland to determine the park's final plan: a vehicle-accessible island enjoyed by the masses or a protected wilderness off-limits to development.

A soft-spoken, curly-headed thirty-six-year-old, Whalen was the youngest director in National Park Service history. Too much emphasis had been placed on iconic parks like the Grand Canyon and Glacier, he believed. In his first two years, he had successfully refocused the agency toward developing more accessible national parks such as the Golden Gate National Recreation Area outside of San Francisco and the Martin Luther King National Historic Site in Atlanta. Whalen created more than thirty new national parks closer to urban centers, and he even coined the agency's new motto: parks for people.

Cumberland Island was expected to attract throngs of visitors from Atlanta and Jacksonville until Carol's grassroots gang started throwing around the *W*-word. Wilderness had not been part of the original plan for Cumberland. Whalen braced himself for a bitter feud. He stepped off the ferry onto Cumberland wearing his crisp, ash-gray National Park Service uniform shirt with the trademark arrowhead patch on its sleeve, tight-fitting olive slacks, and a wide-brimmed straw hat.

McCrary drove Whalen all over the island, mapping out plans for tour routes and visitor centers. They discussed budgets and time-lines. Then, near the end of his visit, Whalen met with Carol alone. This hike was Carol's last chance and only hope of saving her wild island.

The forest was alive with chickadees trilling and woodpeckers drilling. They walked a twisting filament of trail beneath mossy oaks out to the beach. Atop the dunes, Carol launched into her laundry list of reasons for protecting wilderness: pharmacy, cathedral, art gallery, life support system. Whalen interrupted her in mid-sentence.

"I've heard all this before, Carol," he said, waving her off. "Here's what I really want to know: Why bother with protecting all of this just for the animals to enjoy?"

"Animals love life just as much as we do. They deserve some of the last crumbs of wildness we have left."

"But animals don't pay taxes to support this park. Don't get me wrong. I love nature. I've devoted my life to it. But there are practical, real-world considerations. Wilderness is pretty and peaceful, but it's a relic that's mostly irrelevant to modern life."

"Then we're headed for forests without animals and a completely tamed planet of people and their pets. Instead of 'lions and tigers and bears, oh my!' we're reducing our world to poodles and gerbils and goldfish, oh well."

Whalen gazed out across the glassy ocean, a mirror of the peach skies above. Pink tufts of cloud hugged the horizon.

"The National Park Service is not a charity organization," he said. "We have to balance our budget. Visitation supports our work. Most Americans will probably never visit a wilderness area. They

want something easier and more accessible. Don't hard-working Americans deserve a scenic drive on the beach? A comfortable place to rest and relax on their few days of vacation from grinding city life? After all, they're the ones footing the bill for this place."

Carol felt words crowding at the exit to her brain, all fighting at once to fit through the door. Which ones should she let through the gate? She took a deep breath.

"At our core, we hunger for something deeper. We long for contact with raw wildness, where we can see our connection to the bigger picture. In wilderness, we find something far greater than ourselves. That can't happen in a tourist playpen."

"I get that. But my job is to get people into parks, not exclude them from pristine wilderness areas."

"Wilderness doesn't exclude people. It just requires that we change our behavior when we're in it. It's like going to church. People don't live there. They just visit once a week. As soon as they enter, they're more mindful, more respectful. Even if they don't listen to the preacher's words, they get the feeling behind them, the feeling of being a part of something larger. Communion. A feeling of belonging."

"We can get that feeling just as easily from a paved nature trail in a city park. Why do we have to set aside giant swaths of wilderness?"

"We need the whole web, not just a few strands."

For several minutes, they stood silently, listening to the lilt of the tides, the setting sun throwing sparks across the waves. Then they heard the grumble of a distant motor. McCrary drove up the beach, scattering flocks of shorebirds, and swerved to a stop beside them.

"We better get you back to the dock," McCrary said. Whalen climbed in the air-conditioned truck and held the door open for Carol.

"I think I'll walk," she said.

She trudged back to the dock, flat as a deflated beach ball. Her words had not been convincing. Her wilderness campaign had fallen short. Whalen seemed set on a people-centered park instead of a nature-centered one.

Carol arrived back at the dock just as Whalen was boarding the ferry to leave. She walked to the end of the creaking wooden pier to

say goodbye. The ferry captain blasted his horn, and his deckhands untied the boat from the dock.

"Wait—" Carol said to Whalen. "I think you're making a big mistake. You already have dozens of populated parks and not a single island wilderness—"

"I've already made my decision," Whalen said, cutting her off again. The boat began to pull away from the dock. "I made it this afternoon, when you finally stopped talking, and we stood silently on the dunes, hearing only the wind and the waves."

The following week, newspaper headlines announced: "Park nixes development plans for Cumberland." Instead of one million annual visitors, the park would maintain a limit of three hundred visitors per day. Instead of nonstop, round-the-clock ferry service to the island, the park would offer only two trips a day. No new buildings or accommodations would be constructed on the island. No vehicle tours would be offered. Most importantly, the National Park Service would support wilderness for the northern half of the island.

According to one editorial, "Carol Ruckdeschel almost single-handedly stopped the development and vehicle shuttle plans for Cumberland Island. . . . Superintendent McCrary must have an extreme case of chapped rear." He was transferred to another park soon after.

The public had rallied, and the leaders had listened. For once, the system had worked. They had defeated the park's development plan.

But the wilderness war had yet to be won. The Cumberland Island Wilderness bill still remained hopelessly stalled in Congress, mainly due to pushback from locals. So the wilderness purists rolled up their sleeves and got muddy rolling around in down-and-dirty south Georgia politics.

Bill Mankin met with legislators to push forward the wilderness bill, sleeping in his car and brushing his teeth in McDonald's bathrooms. Hans Neuhauser garnered key political support from Georgia representatives and spoke before congressional committees

about the wilderness bill that he and Carol had basically written. Carol continued rallying grassroots support for wilderness.

The Carnegies initially went along with the wilderness proposal. Only later, after skirmishes over Plum Orchard's restoration and Greyfield's vehicle tours, did they object to the wilderness designation.

Other wilderness opponents—mainly from Camden County—argued that wilderness was elitist and anti-American. It outlawed motorized access, including ATVs and motorboats, two favorite toys of Camden County hunters and anglers. Fit, healthy hikers vacationing from the city could enjoy the wilderness while locals could not even land their boats on the beach to fish. Camden County commissioner Jack Sutton called the National Park Service "a private-property-consuming monster" and led a boat-in protest against the wilderness.

He and other commissioners also decried the loss of revenue from wilderness designation and claimed that wilderness discriminated against the elderly and disabled. How were people in wheelchairs supposed to reach the island's remote north end?

Without local support, it seemed the wilderness bill was dead. Cumberland Island needed the help of yet another strong woman: Lady Luck.

Carol's calls and letters to President Carter had not been returned. It seemed that the Oval Office was a lot harder to reach than Governor Jimmy's office down the hall. The president already had a full plate of problems. He was busy dealing with a national oil shortage, a nuclear meltdown at Three Mile Island, and a hostage crisis in Iran. But if the Cumberland Island wilderness bill languished much longer, it would be dropped by Congress.

So Carol penned a heartfelt letter to the *Washington Post*: "Wilderness is more than tents, backpacks, gorp, rattlesnakes, mosquitoes, and ticks. It is also darkness, silence, and simplicity in a natural setting. It is a chance to shed daily responsibilities and expose our bodies and minds to natural stress, to assume a new role with quite different values, to re-create ourselves. Wilderness is a touchstone of reality."

Remarkably, the *Post* published her op-ed, and President Carter read the editorial. He placed a handwritten note on his press secre-

tary's desk that read: "I agree with Carol, and I would like to see the north end of Cumberland Island preserved as wilderness."

Carter's support for wilderness on Cumberland Island provided the political muscle to move the bill forward. However, it was Carter's successor Ronald Reagan who grudgingly signed it into law in 1982.

Carol and her crew had permanently protected the entire northern half of Cumberland Island as wilderness. Soon after, the United Nations designated the island a Global Biosphere Reserve, one of only 384 in the world—joining the ranks of Yellowstone, Patagonia, Denali, and the Serengeti.

Carol had wagered on wilderness—and won. But by holding her ground she would lose a friend in Gogo.

17

Carol soon lost another friend, too.

In 1982, island families had big parties planned for the Fourth of July weekend, and they asked Jesse to fetch oysters for their guests. Jesse headed out into the marshes, steering his johnboat through the twisting tidal creeks. His dog, Jessico, sat in the bow, jowls flapping, ears blown back by the wind. Jesse harvested a boatload of oysters, then motored back to Half Moon Bluff. But the outgoing tide was too low to reach the dock, so he tied his boat to a tree about a hundred yards below it. He sloshed through knee-deep water and hauled his catch up the bluff, Jessico trotting beside him.

One of the big bashes was at the home of Laurence "Laurie" Miller, who lived along Half Moon Bluff, not far from Louie's old house. Jesse delivered a heaping sack of oysters to Laurie, who invited him to stay until high tide. Jesse couldn't get his boat home anyway with the water so low. At the party, the liquor flowed freely.

Jesse also brought oysters to a gathering hosted by Grover Henderson, who was already deep into his drinks. Grover handed Jesse a tumbler of scotch and began ribbing him.

"So let me get this straight—that dirty dog of yours dines on pork chops and spare ribs, while you eat mullet and whatever else you can drag out of the water."

"Dats right," Jesse said. "Carol gives me pork from da hogs she shoots."

"Why the hell do you feed your dog pork chops?"

"My dog likes pork chops."

"Your mangy mutt eats better than you, Bailey."

"I eat all right."

The tide had risen high enough for Jesse to get back home. Loaded to the gills, Jesse wobbled back down the bluff with Jessico.

The next morning, Jesse didn't show up at Carol's for his morn-
ing drink. She assumed he was still hungover. Then a few hours later,
Jessico came charging onto Carol's porch, barking frantically.

"Where's Jess?" she asked. She looked into the dog's panicked
eyes and knew the answer.

Carol dashed down to the bluff, Jessico nipping at her heels.
Jesse's boat was still tied to the tree. Jessico barked at the edge of the
deep high-tide pool where the boat floated. Carol threw a handful
of sand in the pool, and Jessico jumped out after it. She knew right
then: Jesse was out there.

Carol walked the entire creek, feeling for Jesse's body with her
bare feet. Meanwhile, Laurie Miller trawled the braided tidal tributar-
ies with his boat. Carol searched for hours, swarmed by bugs, caked
in mud, cooked by the hot summer sun. Crabs pinched her toes as
she scoured the soft, squishy bottom.

By midday, the tide began to ebb. Carol was wading chest-deep
in the creek when she came around a sharp bend. Suddenly, there was
Jesse's body, beached on an oyster bed, left behind by the receding
tide. He was lying facedown, his arms shredded by the sharp oysters.
The blood was red and fresh.

Waves of emotion swept over Carol. Laurie soon arrived in his
skiff beside the oyster bed.

"We should probably leave the body for the authorities," Laurie
said.

"I'm not leaving Jesse out here," Carol replied.

She lifted his waterlogged body from the oyster bar and into
Laurie's skiff.

The sheriff and coroner arrived, and they pieced together what
had happened. It was low tide when Jesse had tied up his oyster-filled
boat. Jesse drank too much and stayed too long at the parties. By the
time he stumbled back down the bluff, the high tide had lifted his boat
almost seven feet. Jesse tried to wade out to his boat, but he didn't
know how to swim. He drowned in the deep hole beside his boat.

Nearly everyone on the island showed up for his funeral. Hun-
dreds crammed the clapboard church on Sapelo Island to remember
the humble sixty-four-year-old Gullah fisherman. Jimmy Carter,

whom Jesse had taken fishing in Cumberland's creeks, sent his deepest sympathies in a handwritten card, along with a photo of the two of them tossing a cast net off the Candler dock. The letter and photo rested proudly atop his pine box casket.

Conspicuously missing from the funeral service was Carol. She didn't want to grieve amid the public parade of islanders, and her sorrow was still too raw. But her absence fueled rumors that Carol had killed Jesse, too.

She waited until after the ceremony to visit Jesse's grave alone. Sapelo Island's Gullah community had mostly been replaced by high-end vacation estates, but the cemetery was still there. All of the deceased, including Jesse, faced east toward Africa.

Carol brushed away a gnat and knelt beside his freshly dug grave, the sound of the sea trickling through the trees. Jesse had taught her more than anyone in her life—not just how to fish or find oysters, but how to observe, how to listen, how to be present.

"You knew so much, without even knowing that you knew so much," she whispered. "I could sit with you on the dock, watch the water, and not say a word, and that was good enough."

Beside his grave she placed a sprig of pennywort, his favorite garnish. "You died in the creek. That was where you always wanted to be."

Back home the next morning, Carol stood on the dock at Half Moon Bluff and threw Jesse's old cast net out in the creek. The net came alive on her first toss. She could barely lift it out of the water. It was filled with flopping mullet, more than she had ever caught.

Jesse's empty glass still sits on the pine stoop near her porch.

Before long, Carol had another friend waiting on her porch steps. She returned from a turtle necropsy one morning to find Bob Shoop, the ocean-eyed biologist from the turtle conference, leaning against her gate.

"I'm working on a study of frogs," he said. "I was hoping you could help me find a few island specimens."

Carol walked over to the chicken coop and scattered scratch for her hens.

"You're looking for more than frogs."

Bob flashed his wide, floppy-lipped grin. "I brought my tent— although I think last time we met, we ended up sharing a room."

"You can sleep in the lab," she said, throwing him a blanket. "It's behind the chicken coop. The roosters wake up at 3 A.M. with me."

Early the next morning, Carol and a bleary-eyed Bob bush-whacked across the island searching for frogs and other critters. They spotted an endangered diamondback terrapin foraging in the marsh. They grabbed the elephant-like legs of a giant gopher tortoise just before it scrambled into its burrow, a long underground tunnel nearly ten feet deep. Near Lake Whitney, Bob caught a corn snake slithering across the trail, pinning its head with a stick. He held it behind its jaws and examined its stout, coiled body. "This fella just gorged himself," he said, pointing to the bulge in his belly.

Carol was impressed—but not to be outdone. Later that morning, she spotted turkeys strutting across the forest. She crawled out toward them, clucking like a female turkey. It got the attention of the males, whose heads turn blue when sexually aroused. One blue-headed tom pounced on Carol's back, his velociraptor claws kneading her shirt. Carol quickly reached up and grabbed him by the legs.

"Men are so predictable," she said.

Together they caught leopard frogs beside Lake Retta. Carol had a live frog in each hand when she saw another one hopping nearby. So she held one frog in her mouth while she grabbed the third.

Around noon, they came upon two small, steep-sided ponds, which looked more like puddles at first glance. Carol thought she might find mud turtles burrowed on the bottom. She removed her boots and waded out into the waist-deep water, searching the bottom with her bare feet, until she kicked something hard hunkered down in the muck.

"Here's one!" she said. Bob waited at the pond's edge while Carol grunted in the mud.

"Golly, it's heavy. I can't pry it up. Can I use your stick?"

She wedged the stick down into the mire.

"There," she said, handing the stick back to Bob. "It feels bigger than a mud turtle." She lifted it to the surface.

It wasn't a turtle—it was the back leg of a giant alligator.

Carol froze. Bob ran. He didn't even realize he was running until he found himself fifty feet away, hiding behind an oak.

Carol wanted to run, too. But she was waist-deep in murky water, holding the gigantic foot of a primordial beast. On the other side of the pond, the alligator lifted its head above the water and locked eyes with Carol. She slowly, slowly eased the leg back under water. She took a full minute to move a millimeter. Sweat dripped down her forehead, off her chin, and into the water, rippling the surface tension of the still, coffee-brown pond. She gently lowered the clawed toes, the webbed feet, the scaled leg. After ten minutes, she had finally dropped the leg all the way down in the mud. Then she began her painstakingly gradual crawl out of the pond, not even fluttering the water with her imperceptibly slow motion. Bob watched through the trees as Carol ponderously pulled herself up the steep bank, her eyes fixed on the gator. Its yellow, unblinking eyes hovered just above the surface. Finally, after a half hour, she was completely out of the water.

As she backed away, the twelve-foot gator suddenly leaped into the larger pond beside it, revealing its enormous size and explosive speed in less than a second.

Carol leaned back on her elbows and breathed for the first time. How did a twelve-foot alligator curl into that mud puddle, she wondered. How did she hold hands with it and not get chomped? And where the hell was Bob?

That night, they replayed the day's adventures over popcorn and margaritas on Carol's porch. Between their rocking chairs, an orb weaver spider had stretched an enormous silk web, an architectural work that rivaled a Carnegie mansion in its intricacy and Carnegie steel in strength. Carol wedged shims beneath the rockers to prevent them from disturbing the web. She and Bob sat in the unmoving rocking chairs and watched a straw-yellow moon rise over the trees.

She learned that Bob was recently divorced, flew airplanes, rode horses, and loved snakes and turtles as much as she did. He recounted near-death adventures catching venomous cotton-mouths and rattlesnakes in Louisiana swamps. He once tracked endangered diamondback terrapins through marshes so thick with mud that one grad student sank up to his hips. Bob had to pull him out by his arms, yanking him out of his boots and jeans. The student hiked back in his underwear. Another time, Bob discovered a rare salamander on private property, and when he went to photograph it, his camera flash gave him away. The shotgun-wielding landowner chased him through the forest. Bob climbed a tree and waited him out.

"Clearly you're good at hiding," Carol said.

"And waiting."

"How long do you plan on staying anyway?"

"Somewhere between a week and a lifetime."

They listened to the footfall of the deer in the forest and watched bats flicker across the dusky sky. As night swallowed the island, they sat side by side, soundless and still, the silk threads of the spiderweb stretched between them.

Bob may have run from the alligator, but he stuck by Carol. He didn't leave the next day, or the next.

He was still feeling the previous night's drinks when Carol's roosters roused him at 3 A.M. Carol was already at her microscope.

"Goddamn roosters," Bob mumbled.

"One of them—Willy—is impotent. Not many folks have an impotent rooster, but I can't bring myself to kill him."

"I can help you with that."

"How about you help me catch the chicken snake instead?"

A six-foot snake had coiled in the rafters of Carol's coop. Bob held open a cloth sack while Carol coaxed it down, talking softly and reassuringly to the snake: "Easy now, big guy. This dingy coop is no place for such a handsome fella. There you go. Good boy."

"That's real sweet," Bob said. "Too bad snakes are deaf."

She eased the snake into the sack. They released it at Lake Whitney on their way out to the beach.

Bob was stunned by the number of dead turtles littering the seashore. They necropsied five loggerheads together that morning. Carol was thrilled to have help from someone who didn't mind getting his hands dirty. While heaving the turtle carcasses into the dunes for the vultures to clean, they spotted a sixth stranded animal just down the beach.

"Another one?" Bob asked. They walked closer.

"That's not a turtle," Carol said. A ten-foot alligator was stumbling through the surf.

"What's he doing out here? Gators can't tolerate saltwater for very long."

Then Carol noticed: his eyes had been shot out. Some islanders' favorite evening activity was shining spotlights across Lake Whitney and shooting at the glowing red eyes that surfaced.

"Look how emaciated he is. He probably hasn't eaten in a few months," Bob said.

"We've gotta catch him," Carol said, grabbing a coil of rope from her jeep.

"Are you serious?"

"We can't leave him out here to die."

The alligator couldn't see, but he sensed their approach and snapped his jaws at them.

"If you straddle his body to prevent him from rolling, I'll rope his mouth shut," Carol said.

"Okay," Bob replied.

For the next five minutes, Bob stood behind the alligator, summoning the courage to mount it. Carol stood in front, waiting.

"Go ahead," Carol said.

"Okay." Bob was paralyzed. The gator dug his claws deeper into the sand and lifted his snout toward them.

"I am utterly unable to bring myself to do this," Bob said finally.

"What happened to all that bar talk about big powerful males?" Carol said, shaking her head. "You're sperm donors and nothing more."

She walked behind the gator and pinned his mouth shut with a stick. Then she straddled the gator and, in one quick motion, sat squarely on his scaled back and began wrapping rope around his jaws. The gator tried to roll her, but Carol held him in place, squeezing him between her knees. She cinched the rope around his jaws until he was muzzled.

They loaded the gator onto a trailer behind the jeep and drove him to a small freshwater pond deep in the wilderness. Once they set him beside the pond, Carol straddled the gator again and unfastened all but the final loop of rope around his jaws.

"Here's the hard part," she said.

She was crouched, spring-loaded, on the balls of her feet. She yanked off the rope and jumped away in the same motion. The gator lunged blindly and snapped his jaws in the air. His teeth nearly nipped the back of her jeans.

"Whoa! He almost took a bite out of your ass!" Bob shouted.

"Good thing I ate a light breakfast."

That evening, they sat beside the pond on the hood of Carol's jeep and drank White Peggies—a special drink Bob concocted from moonshine, triple sec, grapefruit, and lime. The alligator hovered on the pond's surface. They listened to the gator's deep, guttural bellows, rolling like rumbles of thunder across the water.

"He's got a good voice," Bob said.

"And he's blind, too," said Carol. "Let's name him Ray."

As dusk settled over the forest, a patch of stars glittered through the canopy. Bob sipped his Peggy and then said, "I heard about the shooting."

"I don't want to talk about it," Carol said, slurping the last stringy pulp from her glass.

"If you hadn't shot him, you'd be dead yourself," he said.

"That's true. But it doesn't make it any easier."

"Think of all the women who didn't do what you did and got killed instead. You chose not to be one of them. You fought back against a dangerous drunk. You've got some big ovaries."

"That's not how most folks see it."

"You're not the villain. To millions of women getting banged up and battered, you're a goddamn hero."

After another day of observing frogs with Bob, Carol served up an armadillo quiche on the half shell topped with figs, ginger, and pecans. They stayed up late swigging bourbon and swapping stories on her porch.

Bob told her about a recent prank he had pulled at the University of Rhode Island, where he was a tenured professor. He had enrolled a fictitious student named Steven Koranda in a fellow professor's class. Bob swiped copies of the professor's tests, completed them himself, and then snuck them back onto the professor's desk. Koranda aced every exam despite never attending a lecture, and his essay responses cited obscure studies that not even the professor had read. The bewildered professor expressed his exasperation at Friday faculty meetings: "Who the hell is this Koranda kid? He's either a cheat or a fucking genius." The other professors shrugged their shoulders and choked back laughter. Bob was poker faced.

Bob also inaugurated a long-standing tradition at Friday seminars: mystery meat. Each week, he brought a different specimen from the field. Every grad student and professor tasted the meat and guessed its origin. Wagers were placed, potlucks ensued, and seminar attendance soared.

Often the meat came from turtles or snakes he was studying, but Bob also had a fondness for roadkill: sautéed otter, roasted mink, fried porcupine. Carol had never before met another roadkill connoisseur.

She couldn't make sense of it all. In her darkest, loneliest hour, a handsome turtle biologist who ate roadkill had shown up on her porch. Carol didn't want to admit it, but she liked having him around. She didn't need him—or anyone, she kept reminding herself. But it sure was nice to have someone to talk to.

Bob stayed for a full week. Carol lived like a hermit, but she didn't act like one, he quickly realized. She was gregarious, animated —hell, she was downright chatty—and she laughed often, especially

at herself. She was playfully prankish, too: she hid a garter snake beneath his pillow and swiped his clothes and towel while he was in the outdoor bathtub.

On Bob's last day, they rode horses bareback on the beach. The horses brayed and whinnied, tossing their heads as they galloped through the surf, hooves splashing, nostrils flaring. Finally, Bob's horse threw him into the soft sand. Carol was barely holding on to her horse by its mane. She dropped into the sand near Bob.

"Marry me," Bob said.

"Maybe next week."

Bob returned to Rhode Island for the semester, but he visited Carol every other weekend, flying his single-engine plane down to the island. He helped her publish scientific papers, necropsy turtles, and track gators. More importantly, he helped her heal.

"Whenever I slipped into a funk, Bob pulled me out of the ditch," Carol wrote in her journal. "He brought me back to life."

In between visits, she started to miss Bob. He had untied the knot that was her body. But her feelings scared the hell out of her. She was forty-one years old and comfortable in her solitude. She enjoyed the ease of her everyday routines. Life was safe and steady in her island seclusion.

In 1983, Bob finished his spring semester of teaching and planned to stay the summer doing research with Carol. Carol met him at the island's grassy runway. As soon as he swung open the plane door, she held up her hand to stop him.

"Before you step foot on this island again, let's get a few things straight: I can go it alone. I don't need anyone."

"Okay."

"So you gotta play by my rules when you're here, or you can fly right back home."

"And what are your rules?"

"Give me space. Expect nothing from me. No more than two drinks a day—I can't deal with another raging drunk. Get along with my animals. And no jazz music when I'm around. I know

you're from New Orleans, but damn, it's just acoustic masturbation to me."

Bob smiled, hopped down from the plane, and kissed her. "Agreed."

After years of being feral, it was hard for Carol to take the bit again. She wasn't used to sharing her space. She had to cook twice as much food and wash twice as many dishes. Bob's dirty laundry festered on the floor for weeks. He farted and belched and read scientific journals in his underwear.

But Bob and Carol soon became two of the world's most renowned sea turtle biologists. For the next twenty years, they lived and worked together, publishing dozens of sea turtle studies in leading scientific journals. Carol and Bob also wrote two widely celebrated sea turtle books. They spoke at symposiums and presented papers to policy makers. And they were the only turtle biologists in the country to openly criticize the National Marine Fisheries Service, which was responsible for protecting sea turtles. Carol believed the agency cared more about protecting shrimpers' profits than endangered species.

Carol's favorite sea turtle research came in the summer of 1984, when she and Bob flew the entire Southern coast from North Carolina's Outer Banks to the Texas border conducting aerial surveys of nesting sea turtles. Bob flew his plane low over the beaches while Carol counted crawls and turtles out the window. It was the largest turtle survey ever conducted, and it confirmed that the Southeast was critically important and imperiled turtle habitat. The largest nesting site in the world for loggerhead turtles was also swarming with commercial shrimp boats. Dead sea turtles were washing ashore in record numbers.

Near the end of the aerial survey, they stopped in New Orleans. Bob was bubbling with excitement to show off his old stomping grounds. At the airport, Bob bragged about the city's public transportation system. "You don't need taxis in New Orleans," he assured her. "A bus runs every five minutes."

An hour later, the bus finally arrived. It was dark by the time they stepped off at their stop. Bob had reserved a room at a nearby motel, but it was nowhere in sight. After calling for directions, they circled through parking lots and walked across a six-lane interstate to get to the motel, which was nestled beneath criss-crossing highway ramps and bridges.

"It might be a bit noisy trying to sleep," Carol pointed out.

"Sound rises, so we should be okay," Bob replied.

The motel was small, two-storied, and clean. It was on no obvious street. The only vehicle access was from a potholed road between the interstate bridge pillars. Carol waited outside while Bob went in to register. Faces peered at her from behind the curtains of dark rooms. A large black man, bedecked in gold chains, emerged from one room, folded his arms across his chest, and stared at Carol.

Just then, Bob came out to explain the situation.

"It turns out that it's an all-black motel. But that's okay. We can still stay here."

"There's something else not right. I'm getting the jitters."

"You haven't been in the big city for a while. You'll get over it."

Carol waited outside again while Bob went in to pay. Shadowed figures appeared behind the gold-chained man staring at her. Then she noticed that each room had a blue light on the door. Carol stepped inside and whispered in Bob's ear: "This is a brothel."

His cheeks flushed. He smiled sheepishly. "Oops," he said.

Bob called a taxi, which showed up an hour later. The driver was a young college kid who laughed when he arrived: "How drunk were you guys when you showed up at a whorehouse?"

"We haven't been drinking actually," Bob said. "Though we would like to be."

On the interstate, Carol shouted suddenly, "Stop the cab— D.O.R. possum!" Carol shouted. "Let's grab it for breakfast tomorrow."

"I've already got coon packed in the cooler," Bob said.

The driver noted Carol's braided pigtails, men's button-down shirt, deerskin pullover vest, and giant knife sheathed to her horse-leather belt.

"Are you guys some kind of act?" he asked.

They flew back to Cumberland the next day in Bob's plane. As soon as they landed, Carol dashed out to the beach and splashed saltwater on the back of her neck. Then she stood in the surf, soaking in the island with her senses wide open, until the rise and fall of her breath synchronized with the tides. After flying the entire Southern coast, there still was no place like home.

But home was about to have a new neighbor.

In the Cold War 1980s, a new naval base was built on the mainland directly across from Cumberland Island for submarines armed with nuclear missiles. Kings Bay was the largest peacetime construction project ever undertaken by the U.S. Navy. Sea turtles would be dodging nuclear submarines on their way to nest on Cumberland. Carol would soon have another fight on her hands—this time, with the world's mightiest military.

18

Lucy stepped to the microphone, and the crowd fell silent. In the summer of 1987, hundreds of people from across Georgia had gathered in St. Marys for Lucy Ferguson Day, honoring the eccentric millionaire who had fought for years to protect her island, especially from the National Park Service. "It's hard having a name like Carnegie," she said. "They always want to take everything away from you. But I guess even Cumberland can't be one person's private garden forever." Lucy reminisced about her days riding horses on the beach and exploring the pathless woods with her children. Near the end of her speech, she said, "There are too many people on Cumberland, too many cars going up and down the road."

A few months later, Lucy fell and broke her shoulder. She became a shadow of her former self. Her sight faded. She lost weight and the will to fight. She sat quietly and placidly for hours, gazing across the fields of her island estate.

"Even though we clashed," Gogo said in *Cumberland: Island in Time*, a 2000 documentary, "as we grew older, I certainly understand now. She was just a feisty woman right to the end." Carol, meanwhile, continued to visit Lucy regularly, collecting scraps of island lore.

Near the end of her life, Lucy was interviewed by the *Atlanta Journal-Constitution*. Sitting on the veranda of Plum Orchard, she reflected, "I sometimes think about life on Cumberland, when everything was high and handsome, and wonder if we were snobs. I remember thinking the lowest thing in life was to be a servant. I thought the rich played together. The lines were very strict. Now there are no lines."

On a rainy September evening in 1989, Lucy ate a bowl of ice cream, then closed her eyes. Just three days shy of her ninetieth birthday, she died in her sleep. Her ashes were interred in the Carnegie family cemetery near Dungeness.

* * *

With Lucy gone, Gogo became a more important voice for the Carnegie family. Though not as rugged as her grandmother, she was every bit as gritty when it came to defending her family's heritage. "Cumberland has been our home for seven generations. We feel a strong sense of responsibility for its future," Gogo said. "There are too few places like Cumberland, with all of its diverse assets, left in the world." But she never anticipated that a former custodian who dissected dead turtles might have such an influential voice in shaping the island's future.

It was unclear who would become the next matriarch of Cumberland, the bejeweled Carnegie heiress or the renegade turtle biologist. Both women loved and drew upon the wild creatures of Cumberland, one for her art, the other for her science. But they disagreed sharply on how best to protect the island.

Carol envisioned an evolving island wilderness whose human impact would gradually diminish as lifetime rights expired. Gogo worried that the Carnegies' legacy would be lost beneath an overgrown forest, that an expansive wilderness would interfere with preservation of the island's historic buildings, including Plum Orchard mansion.

Gogo argued that Cumberland didn't even qualify as wilderness, under a strict definition of the term: it had already had a network of roads and people living in it. Twenty-one families still lived on the island—eight of them in the wilderness, including Carol. How could she advocate for an uninhabited wilderness that she herself violated.

At a series of island meetings in the mid-1990s, Gogo and Carol's conflicting views came to a head. At one island showdown with the park superintendent, Gogo was dressed in a black blouse and slacks, with silver-plated coral cuffs and scallop shell earrings cast in fourteen-karat gold. Carol wore loose-fitting jeans and a khaki button-down with the sleeves rolled. The air-conditioning had broken in the meeting room. Tensions rose and tempers flared in the stifling midsummer heat.

All Americans deserve access to the island—not just rugged backpackers, Gogo argued, with a nasal, northern intonation. Not everyone can hike long distances, she pointed out. It was unfair to lock up wilderness for an elite few.

"Should we run vans down to the Grand Canyon, or jeeps to the top of Denali?" Carol replied in her spry Southern cadence.

Cumberland Island is more than a nature preserve, Gogo replied. More people tour the island's historic structures than hiked in the wilderness.

"There's plenty of room on the island for both wilderness and history," Carol said. "Run all the vehicle tours you want on the south end, but keep the northern half wild."

What about Plum Orchard? asked Gogo. She didn't want her family's heritage to rot into the ground just because it was north of an arbitrary wilderness boundary.

"Which is more valuable: a mansion built for Andrew Carnegie's brother's fifth son, or the largest barrier island wilderness in the country? Wilderness is the ultimate historic resource. It's far more precious than another big wooden house."

That big wooden house is where my family grew up, Gogo bristled. She accused Carol of trampling her family's heritage to preserve a wilderness that didn't even exist. Wilderness wasn't supposed to have roads or residents, but Cumberland had both.

"Both will gradually fade away as lifetime rights expire. It's an evolving wilderness, sure, but those wounds will heal with time."

The exchange grew more heated. Gogo contended that Carol just wanted to protect her privacy and keep people away from her cabin in the woods.

"This is not Carnegie National Monument. It's the Cumberland Island Wilderness," Carol fired back.

Gogo pointed her finger at Carol. The Carnegie family had lived on Cumberland for five generations, Gogo reminded her. Carol showed up in her muddy boots just a few years ago. Who was she to tell her family how the island should be managed?

The clash on Cumberland between Carol and Gogo soon escalated into all-out turf war, pitting nature against history, with the National Park Service caught in the middle.

The island boasted a world-class wilderness and global bio-sphere reserve that protected eighteen miles of pristine seashore, wild dunes where endangered sea turtles nested, and the largest old-growth maritime forest in the country. Cumberland Island also had mansions, archaeological sites, cemeteries, slave chimneys, and Indian burial grounds. Which should the National Park Service prioritize?

Wilderness meant allowing nature to rule, which cost essentially nothing. Nature did all the work for free. Historic development was the exact opposite: it was fundamentally about combating the forces of nature. The only way to preserve historic structures was to prevent nature from destroying them. And that cost money—a lot of it.

The public had spoken years earlier: people wanted wilderness on Cumberland Island. But the Carnegies wanted to preserve their family's historic legacy—along with their commercial uses of the island. Carol still believed that a world-class wilderness and historic structures could coexist on Cumberland. Nearly all of the island's historic sites and structures were located south of the wilderness boundary, but a few historic hot spots—like Plum Orchard mansion —were farther north, surrounded by wilderness.

Plum Orchard became the battleground for Carol and Gogo's epic tug-of-war between wilderness protection and historic preserva-tion. The forty-two-room mansion was adorned with marble-faced fireplaces, grand pianos, mahogany tables, and parquet floors. Call buttons in each room once summoned maids and butlers. An eleva-tor in the west wing, just past the library and gun room, led upstairs to bedrooms with handpainted wallpaper, walk-in closets lined with walnut cabinets, and steam-heated racks to warm bath towels. In the east wing, leading off the piazza, was a white-tiled, twelve-foot-deep indoor swimming pool flanked by indoor squash courts.

Plum was one of over one hundred structures on Cumberland Island listed on the National Register of Historic Places. Since the National Park Service could never afford to preserve all of them, it evaluated the historical significance of each: the Stafford Chimneys were rated "one of the most important black history sites in the

country," while the Plum Orchard mansion was deemed "of limited local significance."

Despite the National Register's assessment, Gogo believed that Plum Orchard should be fully renovated. She felt that the National Park Service was shirking its responsibility to preserve the historic structures that had been entrusted to them.

Carol thought the mansion should be minimally preserved as a museum, but that the National Park Service should not waste millions trying to restore it. "People can go lots of other places to see old mansions," Carol said. Jekyll Island, immediately north of Cumberland, boasts a dozen millionaire manors from the robbor-baron era. But there was no other place in America as spectacularly wild and biologically diverse as Cumberland. Retta Richards, daughter of the Carnegie heir who donated Plum Orchard to the National Park Service, agreed with Carol. Retta's recommendation went even further: Let it rot. "Plum Orchard should die a natural death," she said of the aging mansion.

By the mid-1990s, Plum Orchard mansion was starting to deteriorate. Its porch eaves sagged, the paint was peeling, and the roof leaked. Carnegie history was crumbling into the sand. That didn't sit well with Gogo. She couldn't bear to watch her family's heritage fall apart. So she hatched a plan to restore the mansion by establishing a private artist retreat at Plum. "I watched Plum Orchard . . . deteriorate as a result of park underfunding and neglect," Gogo explained. "My vision was to . . . put it to an appropriate and worthwhile use. We sought the advice of many artist retreats, such as the McDowell Colony, to create a retreat where . . . artists could work on projects within the solitude and beauty Cumberland provides." It would be an ideal way to wed her love for the arts and the island. She hoped the arts center would help preserve the fading mansion by bringing artists and patrons to Cumberland. The plans originally included a performance center, galleries, and artists' workshops adjacent to the mansion. Gogo assembled a board of influential friends to support her artists' retreat. There was discussion of how to accommodate visitors to the artists' retreat given the three-hundred-visitor limit Cumberland Island.

However, Plum Orchard was surrounded by federally designated wilderness, which prohibited vehicle traffic and placed stringent protections on activities surrounding the mansion. In 1995, the Plum Orchard Center for the Arts, of which Gogo was the president met with park superintendent Rolland Swain to negotiate a deal. The park agreed to lease Plum Orchard mansion for an artist resort.

The ink had barely dried on an undisclosed memorandum of understanding, a tentative deal, when Carol stumbled upon it.

Once a week, Carol waited until the maintenance crew had left before rummaging through the island garbage, her unofficial shopping mall. Over the years, she had scored some great finds in the trash. She had rebuilt her chicken coop with scrapped wood and collected an entire castoff wardrobe. On this day, however, Carol unearthed her most valuable find: several boxes of discarded correspondence including a memo between Superintendent Rolland Swain and the organizers of the planned artists' retreat.

Carol was torn. Gogo was once a close friend, but this deal was even more rotten than the moldy food scraps festering beneath her. Millions of dollars, both private and public money, would be spent renovating the mansion for an artists' colony, whose visitors would have to be driven through the island wilderness. The last thing Cumberland Island needed was more vehicles and development.

So Carol alerted the press. Newspaper editors, public interest watchdogs, and conservation organizations immediately expressed concerns about development in the middle of the island, surrounded by wilderness.

The suggestion that the Carnegie heirs could favor anything inappropriate to the island clearly annoyed Gogo. "Some people think this is some kind of grandiose plan for the rich," Gogo told *Preservation* magazine, "but Plum represents five generations of my family. The critics should be glad they're not looking at another Hilton Head."

Environmental groups filed a lawsuit over the Plum Orchard Center for the Arts proposal on April 17, 1996, and two months later the National Park Service quashed the tentative agreement. Rolland Swain left his post as superintendent soon after.

Gogo was devastated. She had a lifelong love of the arts, and the island had been the inspiration and source of her jewelry business. There was no better place for artists than the solitude, scenery, and serenity of Cumberland.

Carol wrote to Gogo, "It saddens me to lose your friendship over what amounts to a political issue, but I respect your ideals and goals and your right to fight for them, as I hope you respect mine. . . . You and I share a deep love for Cumberland Island, if it is expressed in different ways, and I hope that our differences of opinion will melt into the past and we can again be friends."

Carol never received a response.

"Carol was . . . part of the community at the time," explains Gogo, but then "all the families of private land closed their gates to her."

So she drove down to Gogo's house one evening to apologize. Though she denies it, according to Carol, Gogo swung open the door and called her a backstabbing bitch.

"I'm sorry, Gogo. I love you like a sister, but you know how deeply I feel about wilderness. It's not personal. We disagree politically, but I still consider you a friend."

Gogo replied that friends don't put politics ahead of feelings, and they don't put their personal agenda ahead of their friends' passions. The slammed door rattled the frame.

To replace the outgoing superintendent, the National Park Service brought in a rookie, Denis Davis, to manage the country's most contentious and complicated national park. On his first day as park superintendent, he met with Gogo at Greyfield, and then later with Carol on the beach.

"They were two of the most strong-willed women I had ever met," Davis recalled. "I knew right then that I was in trouble."

He was impressed by Gogo's unwavering commitment to her family's heritage, and he admired Carol's encyclopedic knowledge of the island. "Carol loved the ecology of the island and knew more about it than anyone in the park," Davis said. "I wish there were more Carols on Cumberland who loved the island for the reasons that she loved it."

But it was a struggle to work with her, Davis said. She was obstinate in her defense of wilderness, rigid in her interpretations of policy, and brutally candid in her criticism of park management.

"She would approach me directly and say, 'This is wrong.' I often found myself saying, 'Oh come on, Carol, be a little more flexible.' But for her, wilderness had already been compromised on Cumberland, and she wasn't willing to give another inch."

She was a thorn in the side of the National Park Service, Davis admitted, and every other previous superintendent expressed a distasteful opinion of Carol. But Gogo, he said, could be even worse.

Davis organized a series of meetings aimed at bringing together island families and conservation advocates. He believed both the natural and cultural resources of the island were important and could be preserved. In the first ten minutes of the first meeting, the park service mediator was removed as mediator and replaced by an island resident married to a Carnegie heir, who set the agenda. A compromise agreement that grew out of these meetings only resulted in more lawsuits.

Undaunted, Davis spent three years drafting a compromise management plan for preserving historic structures and protecting the wilderness. Thousands of letters supporting the plan poured in from the public. He received an award from the National Parks and Conservation Association for his efforts. Then, weeks before the plan was finalized, Davis was transferred.

"I was forced out," Davis said, which his superiors later told him was due to political pressure from Gogo's family and Congressman Jack Kingston, who represented the coastal Georgia district.

Kingston claimed that Davis was not concerned enough with historic preservation. As proof, Kingston said that the superintendent had demonstrated his contempt for historic resources by putting vinyl siding on his mainland home in the St. Marys Historic District. In fact, it was a man named Dennis Davis, not the park superintendent Denis Davis, who had altered the historic home.

"The real reason I was transferred was because the Carnegies felt I was too sympathetic to conservation," said Davis.

* * *

After her rift with Gogo, Carol was blackballed by the Carnegies and Candlers. Most of the island families had already snubbed Carol after she shot Louie McKee, but her role in establishing wilderness and torpedoing the Plum Orchard artist retreat permanently ostracized her. "Carol is an eccentric whack job who turned on us," said Molly Prochazka, Gogo's cousin. "She's a radical one-sided wilderness hermit who weaseled her way onto the island. She's not one of us. It makes me nervous to have residents on this island who don't have our history."

Carol was an outsider who snuck in the door at the last minute, a penniless loner living in an old black shantytown. Even her longtime friend Sam Candler abandoned her, calling her "an isolated environmental extremist who has cut herself off with her militant, radical stance on wilderness."

Carol was hurt, especially by Sam, but tried not to show it.

"Trying to save the last one percent of wild places is not radical," she said. "Radical is wiping out half of the world's species in less than a century."

She still had plenty of animals to keep her company, including a family of vultures that congregated on her roof. And instead of feuding with the Carnegies, she brawled with Bob.

Carol and Bob loved to butt heads. Every evening on the porch, while sipping White Peggies, they fiercely argued ideas and disputed each other's research. Their porch debates became legendary. Scientists from across the country traveled to the north end of Cumberland to sit ringside on rickety wooden porch chairs, grab a handful of popcorn, and listen to the heated exchanges between the PhD biologist and the gutsy turtle girl with a high school diploma. Carol and Bob wrangled over controversial ideas such as animal altruism, overpopulation, and their favorite topic, human nature.

Carol believed that humans were fundamentally greedy and selfish. Like all animals, we competed for limited resources, and the fittest survived to pass on their genes.

Bob argued that humans were far more cooperative and empathetic. Across cultures, we had demonstrated a universal hunger for fairness and equality that sprang from our long nomadic history

as tightly-knit tribal bands. For at least half a million years, we hunted and gathered food communally, shared resources around a campfire, and jointly nurtured the young and the elderly. People weren't purely selfish, Bob maintained. We were hardwired to work together and help each other.

Carol and Bob were mixing drinks on the porch one evening when a jeep loaded with Greyfield tourists rumbled past. Carol smiled and waved. Bob shook his head and grumbled about rich snobs.

"The Carnegies are the top predators on the food chain," Carol said. "You can fault them for a lot of things, but not for being wealthy."

"They exploited hardworking Americans to make their millions," Bob replied.

"Looking out for number one—that's how nature built us to survive," Carol said.

"That's a lopsided view of nature," Bob said. "Nature has been wrongly portrayed as only viciously cutthroat and merciless. Yet even Darwin believed that cooperation was just as fundamental as competition."

Bob rattled off a list of examples: bees fly millions of miles to feed their colony and die in defense of their queen. Ants similarly work together like a single superorganism to find food and shelter. Vampire bats disgorge blood meals to share with the sick or hungry. Dolphins swim beneath injured animals—including humans—and carry them to safety. And bacteria—the oldest and most numerous organisms on the planet—cooperatively share survival information with each other. Perhaps most amazing of all are the humble slime molds. They live as individual amoeba scattered widely across the forest floor until they are starving. Then hundreds of them simultaneously crawl together and merge to form a slug, so they can seek out food as a collective organism.

Humans, too, are a kind of superorganism, Bob contended. *Homo sapiens* have thrived primarily because we cooperate better than other species. Even primitive humans took care of the elderly, weak, and disabled, as evidenced by eighty-thousand-year-old skeletons of handicapped Neanderthals found in Iraq's Shanidar Cave. But it was care for our young that especially distinguished us as a cooperative

species. When our ancestors climbed down from the trees and started walking upright, it meant giving birth to babies that were small and six months premature. Human infants were—and still are—the most vulnerable beings on the planet, with the longest developmental period in the animal kingdom. Years of around-the-clock care required strong partner bonding and the help of a clan. It took a village—or at least a pair of parents working together—to raise a child.

"Ultimately the secret to our success was cooperation—and perhaps even the first primitive flickers of love."

Carol rolled her eyes. "Love isn't stopping us from raping Mother Nature," she said. "Any other animal with our forebrain would overpopulate and overconsume just like us. It's a dog-eat-dog world."

They continued the debate early the next morning. Carol was working in her lab picking worms from coyote scat. On the wall above her microscope was a bulletin board of her favorite quotes.

Jane Goodall: "The least I can do is speak out for those who can't speak for themselves."

Rachel Carson: "Those who contemplate the beauty and mystery of the earth find reserves of strength that will endure as long as life lasts."

Mary Oliver: "What is it you plan to do with your one wild and precious life?"

Around dawn, Bob swung open the screen door to the lab.

"Smells good in here," he said. Then he asked her to join him on his morning five-mile run. "Come on—it'll be a lot more fun than playing with poop."

Carol was naturally fit. When she wasn't tromping to gator holes or hiking to turtle nests, there was always wood to cut or traps to check. But she had not run in years. Reluctantly, she set down her tweezers and agreed to run the first mile with him.

As they trotted along, a veil of fog cloaked the island in gray. After about a mile, Carol asked, "When are we gonna actually start running?"

"What do you mean?"

"This isn't running. This is shuffling our feet."

"You thought I ran a five-mile sprint every morning?"

"The only kind of running I know is for my life. I'm either chasing something or being chased."

They jogged beneath hoary, hefty oaks as the sun burned off the morning mist. A soft breeze stirred the ribbons of Spanish moss.

Then, halfway through the run, Carol noticed tracks in the sand and tore off like a bloodhound, disappearing into a tunnel of palmetto. Bob followed her boot prints and eventually came upon Carol sniffing around the remains of a deer. The kill was written in the sand. Carol pointed out two pairs of coyote tracks leading up to the lunge, then traced their paths as they dragged the carcass beneath a tree to eat it.

"See? All of your warm, fuzzy, lovey-dovey, holding-hands hogwash doesn't stop hungry coyotes from killing Bambi," Carol said.

"Predator eats prey. There's no denying that," Bob replied. "But these coyotes hunted together to take down this deer. It's also a dog-help-dog world."

He recounted the saga of the Donner Party, a wagon train caravan of eighty-seven frontier pioneers who were stranded in the Sierra Nevada for an entire winter. Their numbers dwindled as survivors resorted to cannibalism to avoid starvation. Only forty-six came down from Donner Pass alive the following spring, and it wasn't the virile young males. The survivors were mostly those who were embedded in families. The same was true of the *Mayflower* colonists who first set foot on American soil: death was disproportionately higher among the unattached. Families fared better than even the healthiest, fittest individuals.

"Groups nourish us and give us something to live for," he said. "In the long run, it's survival of the friendliest."

"What about cheaters?" Carol asked. "There will always be selfish individuals stealing from the altruistic suckers. Nice guys finish dead last—or just dead."

"But nice groups win every time," Bob replied. A tribe of cooperating members will always triumph over a tribe of selfishly motivated ones, he pointed out. "We are a social species more naturally inclined to work together than rip each other's hearts out."

"I don't know about that," Carol said, and began sprinting back toward the cabin. Bob strained to keep up, while Carol barely broke a sweat. Even in her heavy boots, she outkicked Bob.

"I win," she said.

After the run, they gulped freshly squeezed grapefruit juice on the porch and watched a family of vultures perched atop the museum's tin roof. Dad regurgitated food into the mouth of his tottering fledgling, a runt with a broken leg. The runt repeatedly lost his balance and slid down the tin roof, its long claws scrabbling at the metal. Mom snatched him by his nape each time just before he plunged off.

Below the vultures, hordes of horny toads stirred in the shaggy stubble surrounding Carol's small pond. Hundreds of spadefoot toads had waited for the previous night's rain to begin breeding explosively in Carol's waterlogged yard. They mated once a year, crawling out of underground burrows to copulate in shallow rain puddles. The frogs frantically mounted each other and smeared fertilized eggs across the soggy yard, their breeding calls roaring to a deafening pitch. It was a cacophony of spadefoot screams and vulture claws screeching against tin.

"Ain't life the greatest," Bob said.

That evening, before Bob left for Rhode Island for the semester, he proposed to Carol again.

"I'm damaged goods," she said. "In case you're keeping score, I'm 0 for 2 in the marriage game."

"We can do it quietly. No one else needs to know."

"We already live like a married couple," Carol said. "Your dirty laundry is everywhere. The spot where you pee off the porch is stained with piss dribbles. I don't think you've ever washed the dishes or cooked dinner. You've got everything a husband could want. What do you need a piece of paper for?"

* * *

Curled in Carol's lap on a drizzly spring evening was her cat Pal, named after Stuart Woods' bestselling thriller *Palindrome*, which takes place on Cumberland Island. The novel's female heroine is Liz Barwick, a bold, brave loner living on Cumberland who is beaten up by her lover. Liz soon befriends the carefree, promiscuous granddaughter of a wealthy family who runs the Greyfield Inn. Liz's lover stalks her on the island, and eventually, he is killed. Carol found the novel entertaining, even though it hit uncomfortably close to home.

Carol was drinking a tumbler of scotch and listening to the drip-ping forest—when Pal's ears perked up. A low-flying plane buzzed just over the cabin. Carol leaped up to look: a pilot was scud running below a tattered veil of clouds when suddenly he clipped the trees and crashed. She saw an orange flash on the horizon.

The plane had skidded across the island and burst into flames, leaving a smoldering trail of shrapnel. Carol dashed across the marsh and was the first one on the scene. She climbed into the blazing wreckage to search for the pilot. Smoke burned her throat as she crawled through the twisted tube of melting metal, the plane pop-ping and groaning. Finally, she found the pilot, dead in the blood-splattered cockpit. Carol tried to remove his charred body, but his intestines spilled out onto the seat.

For weeks afterward, the grim images replayed in her mind. What astonished her most, she realized, was not the gore or blood-shed. It was that human guts looked shockingly like a turtle's. Inside, we were made of exactly the same stuff.

Carol witnessed more carnage later that summer. One sweltering afternoon, Carnegie handyman Roger Daniels went skinny-dipping in Lake Whitney overflow creek, a deep channel that emptied into the ocean. Though the creek was only a few feet deep, an alligator had holed up at the bottom of it. Roger was sitting in the water when the gator swam up from beneath him. His bare white butt looked like a floating carcass from below, and the gator hit it. The alligator bit hard, ripping open Roger's left testicle and a chunk of ass cheek. Then it let go and swam away. Roger dragged himself out of the water, and blood dripped into the sand. A little while later, Carol arrived.

"Are you okay, Roger?"

His face was pale. He covered himself with his jeans and mopped up blood with his T-shirt.

"I'm all right," he said.

"What happened?"

"I just got gator bit."

Roger tried to stand. Blood leaked down his leg. His left testicle was hanging out of his scrotum.

Remarkably, Roger never went to the hospital. He was too embarrassed even to get stitches. More remarkably, he fully recovered and eventually fathered a child. He is the only person on Cumberland in recorded history ever to be attacked by an alligator.

The National Park Service wanted to keep it that way. Two rangers were sent to kill the gator that had bitten Roger. When Carol heard about it, she raced down to the Whitney overflow and arrived just as the rangers were loading their rifles.

"Howdy, fellas. What's going on?" Carol said.

"We gotta put down this alligator," said the chief ranger. "It's endangering public safety."

"All alligators endanger public safety. This alligator is just being an alligator."

"Carol, this is park business. You need to leave." The men raised their rifles to their shoulders.

"No, fellas. You need to leave." Carol stepped out into the knee-deep blackwater and stood between the rifles and the gator. She felt the water stirring beneath her.

"Come on, Carol. Don't pick a fight with us."

"You're in a wilderness. You can't shoot the animals that live here."

The men looked to the chief ranger. They lowered their rifles and returned to their trucks.

The next day, an island resident shot the gator instead.

A few months later, the park took aim at another alligator: a ten-foot male living in the swamps near Willow Pond. On her Park Service walkie-talkie, Carol heard the chief ranger dispatch a crew to kill it.

Carol knew the Willow Pond gator well. She had been studying him for years. Once she had accidentally stuck her head down into his burrow and found herself face-to-face with him. Instead of attacking her, the alligator backed deeper into his hole.

Carol hustled down to Willow Pond and once again put herself between the guns and the gator.

"Dammit, Carol. I'm getting tired of this. Get the hell out of the way," said the chief ranger.

"This alligator is a protected species in a wilderness area. You boys oughta know the law by now."

"This alligator is a nuisance to the public."

"How is it a nuisance?"

The rangers glanced sideways at the chief ranger.

"We're building a boardwalk to the beach through here. We can't have hikers strolling past a gator den."

"Then move your boardwalk. You're in a wilderness. You can't kill animals just because they're in your way."

"We'll just come back later and shoot it," the chief ranger grumbled, lowering his gun.

"When you do, make sure to bring a waiver from the Endangered Species Act that allows you to kill this alligator, along with a permit from U.S. Fish and Wildlife Service and a NEPA study that authorizes building a boardwalk through endangered species habitat."

This time, Carol prevailed. The boardwalk was rerouted, and the Willow Pond gator still lives today.

Alligators are the largest land reptiles in North America. Hunted for their hides, alligators were nearly wiped out in the twentieth century. They've made a comeback in recent decades, but they remain a threatened species. On Cumberland, gator populations continued to crash.

With more dead gators and turtle carcasses each year, Carol was running out of storage space. So she decided to turn her garage into a museum to house all of her specimen collections. Bob helped her construct it using driftwood that Carol dragged in from the beach. It

was a research facility, not an *ooh-aah* display museum. But scientists from around the world began hiking up the island to explore Carol's collections, which included everything from skinks and salamanders to spinner dolphins and sperm whales.

Visitors to the museum were often shocked by the surroundings. At first glance, Carol's quarter-acre compound resembled a shoddy Southern farm: a cluster of weathered buildings and a yard full of washtubs, rusty tools, dilapidated wheelbarrows, and piles of waterbuckled boards. Then there was the smell: the stench of rotting flesh wafted from dozens of water-filled plastic buckets scattered about the yard.

"Macerating is the best way to skeletonize marine animals," Carol explained to visitors. "You just put them in water and forget them. The flesh dissolves away, and a week later, even the biggest turtle skull is shiny clean. I bleach it in the sun for another day or two, and it's ready to go."

For some carcasses, she employed an army of carnivorous beetles to break down rotted flesh. Her flesh-devouring beetles and maggots were so valued that Carol scooped them into jars and brought them indoors on cold nights. Black vultures lining her cabin roof also assisted her in working the carcasses and picking the bones clean.

Carol's yard was a jumble, but her inner organization was meticulous. Thousands of museum specimens were neatly arranged, labeled, and cross-indexed. Also lining the shelves were decades of painstakingly precise field notes, with drawings of plants and animals that were detailed and almost photographic in their technical perfection. The windowless museum was lined floor to ceiling with handmade wooden shelves carefully arranged with skulls and specimens of nearly every critter on Cumberland Island, each with a handwritten label of its common and scientific names. In the back of the museum, dozens of heart-shaped loggerhead shells were stacked neatly like Russian dolls.

It was one of the world's largest sea turtle and marine mammal collections. In 1990, curators at the Smithsonian National Museum in Washington, D.C., heard about Carol's collections and asked Carol if she would share her specimens so they could be studied by the

world's top scientists. Carol was thrilled. She began providing them with specimens from the creatures that washed up on her eighteen-mile Atlantic doorstep.

"The whole point of my work is to make their deaths useful," Carol said. "Preserving and studying the carcasses at least provides some purpose to the carnage."

Helping Carol with the museum was a twenty-nine-year-old biology grad student named Creighton Cutts. He had been waiting his whole life to meet Carol. As a nine-year-old boy living in Atlanta, he had read about her in magazines: a wild woman fighting to protect a wild island. He visited Cumberland Island every year with his family, but he never met the reclusive wilderness woman. On a summer camping trip to Cumberland with his middle school buddies, he bravely waded out into a tidal creek to swim with a pod of dolphins. Afterward, he ran back to camp tell his friends, but he had already been trumped: a few minutes earlier, Carol Ruckdeschel had stopped by their camp with a rescued sea turtle hatchling.

Years later, Creighton returned to Cumberland to track bobcats for a University of Georgia research project. Bushwhacking through the forest late at night, he finally crossed paths with his lifelong hero beside Lake Whitney.

"Howdy, Creighton," Carol said nonchalantly as they passed each other on an alligator trail in the midnight darkness. He stood slackjawed: she already knew his name!

After the bobcat project ended, Creighton asked Carol if he could stick around to help her with research. Bob was leery of the handsome young apprentice at first, but he liked Creighton's wild and mischievous instincts. Once, when he overheard the chief ranger threatening to revoke Carol's collection permits, Creighton stealthily unhooked the fuel line from the ranger's four-wheeler. Another time, he caught a juvenile alligator near Lake Whitney and wrapped its jaws closed with shoestring from his boots.

When Bob returned to Rhode Island for the semester, Creighton worked elbow-to-elbow with Carol in the museum. With Bob

gone, he also began accompanying Carol on turtle necropsies and all-day gator tromps. At night, he drank cocktails with her on the porch.

"Are you and Bob married?" he asked one night, doe-eyed and drunk.

"No—although he proposes to me every week," Carol said. "It doesn't matter. I'm a serial monogamist."

"I didn't think you were into monogamy."

"Monogamy is certainly fragile. But maybe that's why there's love: to override our instincts and hold us together."

One afternoon, Carol brought in a dead alligator she had found near Table Point. Creighton helped her necropsy it. When they opened up his stomach, they found that a plastic balloon had clogged its stomach. In the gator's gut they also found a spark plug, rusty fish hooks, and the collar of a dog. The leather collar had mostly disintegrated, but the metal tag still had the dog owner's phone number on it. Creighton called the owner from the mainland the next day. "I've got good news, and I've got bad news," he said. It turned out that the dog had gone missing years earlier on a hunting trip near Dover Bluff, ten miles away on the mainland.

Creighton was a fun-loving, adventurous entertainer who hit it off with everyone he met. At an island party, he quickly became chummy with Gogo's third husband, David Sayre. Creighton helped him build a house for Gogo on her Greyfield property. They constructed an airy, light-filled cottage with open rafters and turquoise floors. According to Creighton, Gogo wanted to use the crown molding from the Plum Orchard carriage house in her new home, so David and Creighton went to swipe it. First, they went in with a crowbar and loosened the nails so they could take it out more quickly at night.

A few nights later under a full moon, Creighton and David motored up to Plum Orchard, pulled out the molding, and loaded it onto their truck. Suddenly, a bright spotlight shone in their faces.

"Hold it right there, guys!" shouted a deputy park ranger, stepping out from the shadows. He handcuffed David and Creighton facedown against the warm hood of the truck.

"You know, fellas, it's a felony with a $5,000 fine and jail time for stealing historic materials on federal lands," he said.

Creighton was sweating blood. The deputy called in the incident to the chief ranger, and Creighton heard the chief ranger's garbled response.

"You gotta let them go," he said.

"I caught them red-handed swiping a truckload of federal property."

"That's Gogo's husband."

David smirked. The ranger bit his lip while his deputy unlocked their handcuffs.

According to David, he and Creighton had parked next to the dilapidated Plum Orchard carriage house and were simply noting the high quality of the lumber when a ranger pulled up and accused them of desecrating a historic monument. According to David, there were no handcuffs.

David and Creighton walked free that night. But the next day, the chief ranger drove up with a deputy to arrest Creighton separately.

"Sorry, Creighton," he said. "No free pass for you." The deputy ranger reached for his cuffs again.

Creighton cleared his throat. "Exposed nails. Rotted wood. Plum Orchard's carriage house could fall any day. It's a danger to the public. And you're allowing visitors in there? Without any warning signs? That's something the media oughta know about."

The chief ranger glared at Creighton, then walked back to his truck. Once more, the deputy clipped his cuffs back onto his belt.

Later, the National Park Service tried to seize Carol's museum specimens, claiming that they belonged to the park. "The Park Service didn't really want the collections—they were just pushing thumbtacks into Carol," Creighton said.

But before Park Service rangers could get their hands on them, Creighton was able to sneak Carol's collections to the Smithsonian. Had he been caught, he could have faced jail time and $25,000 in fines for transporting the bones of endangered species across state lines. For Creighton, it was a risk worth taking.

"Decades of Carol's fieldwork are now available to the public and to science instead of rotting in a Park Service closet," he said.

When Bob returned for the summer in 1992, he and Carol sat beside Lake Whitney, backs pressed against each other, listening to the evening symphony. Bats flitted and clicked overhead. The high ringing of cicadas and crickets was rounded by the steady soprano of tree frogs and the bullfrog's tenor. The alligators' bass bellows boomed across the water.

"Yes," Carol said.

"Yes," she said again, turning to Bob. "Yes, I'll marry you."

He tackled her in the sand and kissed her.

They quietly exchanged vows in the shadows of the First African Baptist Church. Carol and Bob lit a candle and promised to love each other for the rest of their lives. Moonlight shone through the whitewashed windows. The faint roar of the surf seeped through the cracks in the clapboard.

"You know what this means, don't you?" Bob whispered. "You realize you're stuck with me for good?"

"I do."

19

More dead sea turtles were washing ashore than ever before. Carol woke before dawn and spent the entire day cutting open their smelly carcasses, as she had done for decades, even though no one paid her to do so, even though few people knew about her research and even fewer actually cared.

"Do you ever lose hope?" Bob asked her that night on the porch, sipping his grapefruit moonshine.

"We're not saving anything here," Carol said. "We're just slowing down the rate in which things get worse. We live on a sinking ship. Get used to it."

"There's still a chance to patch the holes," Bob said.

"Not likely," replied Carol. "We're breeding faster than feral hogs and consuming more than the richest monarchs of the past, she pointed out. "We've occasionally been able to rally together during war or natural disaster. "So far, though, we haven't looked beyond our own lifetimes—or even the next election cycle—to squarely face the worst extinction catastrophe our planet has ever faced."

"The Permian extinction was worse," Bob said.

"This one is worse because it could have been avoided," Carol replied. "We could have saved the earth—and ourselves—but we were too damn lazy and cheap."

"If it's pointless, then why bother to keep at it?" Bob asked.

Carol rubbed her finger around the rim of her empty glass.

"At least I'll go down fighting for what counts," she said. "Someone has to carry the fire. Someone has to hold the light that has gone out of the world. Someone has to fight for life as if it mattered." She looked out at a smudge of stars glowing through the clouds. "The world is larger than us. We weren't always here, and we won't always be. Ma Nature always bats last."

* * *

Carol wasn't the only woman to wander into the wild and defend it against seemingly impossible odds. She was part of a tribe of legendary female misfits who fiercely guarded the creatures of their wilderness nests, often blurring the boundaries between animals and humans.

The leader of the clan is Jane Goodall, the primatologist who showed the world that a female scientist could work alone in the wilderness. Though she had no scientific training or even a college degree, she convinced legendary anthropologist Louis Leakey to hire her as an assistant at Tanzania's Gombe Chimpanzee Reserve in 1960.

She eventually won the trust of a single male chimp whom she named David Graybeard. Naming chimps was frowned upon by the other scientists, who warned her not to allow emotions to interfere with scientific study. However, Goodall believed that understanding animal behavior required the observer to see the animals as individuals, not interchangeable specimens. "It was not permissible to talk about an animal's mind. Only humans had minds," Goodall recalled in her autobiography. "Nor was it quite proper to talk about animal personality. Of course, everyone knew that animals did have their own unique characters—anyone who had ever owned a dog or other pet was aware of that."

She soon discovered that chimps hugged, kissed, and tickled each other. She even observed an adolescent chimpanzee adopt a three-year-old orphan who was not a close relative, a demonstration of altruism that was long thought to be beyond the capacity of animals.

"It isn't only human beings who are capable of rational thought and emotions like joy and sorrow," Goodall wrote. Chimps developed long-term affectionate bonds, used symbols to communicate, and even had a concept of self. She also watched David Graybeard use sticks to dig for termites—the first time another animal had been observed using tools.

Also working in Africa to protect wild primates was Dian Fossey, a zoologist who studied and lived with wild mountain gorillas for

eighteen years. She bucked the established scientific tradition of observing from a distance. Instead, she gained the gorillas' confidence and curiosity by acting like one of them. She thumped her chest, munched on stalks of wild celery, and mimicked their deep belches.

Fossey became the world's leading authority on gorillas and dispelled King Kong stereotypes by photographing them snuggling with each other, playing tag, and sliding down muddy mountain slopes. Her most famous photograph shows a gorilla she named Peanuts touching Fossey's hand, the first recorded peaceful contact between a human being and a wild gorilla.

She fought hard to safeguard the gentle giants from poachers. Government officials and local tribes wanted to convert gorilla habitat to farmland. In 1977, Fossey's favorite gorilla, Digit, was attacked by poachers. Digit took five spear wounds and fended off their dogs in ferocious self-defense, enabling the other thirteen members of his family to escape. Digit, however, was decapitated and mutilated. His hands were cut off and sold as ashtrays.

After Digit's death, Fossey became even more aggressively outspoken in protecting wild gorillas. Her 1983 bestselling book *Gorillas in the Mist* brought international attention to the poaching of mountain gorillas. She also became increasingly militant in her defense of gorilla habitat. She captured and humiliated poachers, destroyed their traps, held their cattle for ransom, and even burned their hunting camps.

Then, on the day after Christmas in 1985, Fossey was found hacked to death on the misty slopes of her Rwandan forest camp. No one has ever been prosecuted for her murder.

Protecting wildlife is dangerous work. Daphne Sheldrick, who has spent most of her life safeguarding wild elephants, has always understood that. Once, a startled four-ton elephant tossed her in the air and hurled her against a boulder with the swish of its trunk. Her shattered body lay in the dust, her legs broken and bleeding, as the elephant lumbered toward her. Its shadow loomed over her, and she braced herself for its final bone-crushing blow. The elephant lifted its giant foot, but instead of trampling her, it "began to feel me all over, barely touching me," Sheldrick wrote in her memoir. The elephant

"contemplated me lying helpless, merely inches from the tip of two long, sharp tusks. I knew then that [it] did not intend to kill me. It was at this moment I realized that if I were to live, I needed to fulfill the debt I owed to nature." For thirty years, she dedicated her life to rescuing orphaned elephants and other wild animals in Kenya's national parks.

Each of these pioneering women struck out into the wild to deepen her understanding of nature and find her place in it. They have inspired a new generation of wilderness women, among them Biruté Galdikas, who established Borneo's first national park to protect endangered orangutans; Eugenie Clark, who has studied and swum with sharks in Florida; P. Dee Boersma, who has devoted her life to defending penguins in Argentina; Eriqueta Velarde, who has spent thirty years on an island in the Gulf of California studying and saving rare terns; and Nobel laureate Wangari Matthai, who helped plant forty-seven million trees in rural Kenya despite death threats and torture. Another recent incarnation of the wilderness woman is Julia Butterfly Hill, who lived alone on a teetering, wind-blown platform in a 180-foot redwood tree for over two years to prevent an old-growth forest from being cut down by loggers.

But none of these wild women—not even Jane Goodall—has lived with the subjects they study as long as Carol Ruckdeschel, who has spent forty-one years immersed in sea turtle research on her wild island. She has necropsied over four thousand turtles on Cumberland. Through hurricanes and hundred-degree heat, Carol has been gutting sea turtle carcasses, studying death to better understand life.

Decades of her detailed data pointed to one obvious conclusion: turtles were in trouble. In the water, turtles dodged boats and nets. And on land, beachfront development was razing turtle nesting sites. Even on wild, undeveloped Cumberland Island, turtle nests were being destroyed—mainly by feral animals.

Ferals are once-domesticated livestock that have reverted to a semi-wild state. Island families had brought horses and hogs over to the island and then abandoned them. Now, over 250 horses and at least two thousand feral hogs were roaming Cumberland Island:

feral hogs routinely dug up and devoured sea turtle nests, and horses ate the dunes' fragile sea oats, whose roots held the island together.

Carol loved the horses. She rode them bareback on the beach and tracked the herds grazing in the forest behind her cabin. She filled a rusted bathtub with water for them during dry spells.

But she knew they were starving, diseased, and worm-ridden. Because they weren't native to the island, they weren't adapted to its harsh environment. Though galloping wild horses seemed romantic from a distance, up close they were malnourished and miserable.

Often, stallions fought each other over limited freshwater and food. One battle broke out behind her cabin. It was like a beer commercial: two stallions on their hind legs, biting and kicking.

One of the feuding horses was a strawberry roan that had gone a few rounds before with other stallions, and he had a slash across his snout and other battle scars to prove it. The other was a brown-speckled juvenile Appaloosa.

Carol watched the horse fight from her porch. The two rivals sniffed each other's muzzles and testicles, braying loudly to intimidate the other. Then the roan reared back and lunged with his forelegs, knocking the spotted Appaloosa off balance. The roan ripped a gash in the Appaloosa's neck and kicked him until he collapsed to the forest floor. The wounded Appaloosa whinnied to his mother and sisters, who were part of the onlooking harem. But they turned and followed the victorious stallion into the woods, leaving him behind, broken and bleeding. Carol nursed the Appaloosa back to health, but he never was able to rejoin his herd.

Carol began tracking the herds to learn their leaders, trails, and territories, and she observed their breeding and feeding habits. Foals are usually born between March and June on Cumberland. Each band of horses claims a home range of roughly one thousand acres, and their diet consists mainly of sea oats and saltmarsh grasses.

Carol even named a few of the horses. Her favorite was Pretty Butt, named for the white markings on his chestnut rump. After his mom died of encephalitis, Carol noticed Pretty Butt wandering the woods alone. He was gaunt, and ribs showed through his ragged coat.

Finally, one afternoon, she herded Pretty Butt into her fenced pasture, where she had built a small stable. He nibbled at stubbly patches of timothy, and gradually, he put on weight and gained strength. Carol broke him and rode him bareback around the pasture, then took him out to the shore at sunrise one morning.

"We galloped across a glowing, molten beach," Carol wrote in her journal. "Then Pretty Butt started to canter, and I knew I was in for it. He was tearing down the beach with me hanging off his side, but I wasn't gonna let him throw me. When he finally stopped, I was holding on with only one leg and a fistful of mane."

Another time, she and Bob were riding Pretty Butt through the woods when Pretty Butt froze suddenly in his tracks. Ahead of him was the fresh carcass of a palomino mare. The horse had become tangled in barbed wire and starved to death. Carol cut the horse loose and circled the carcass, deciding how to perform the postmortem. Intestinal fermentation had already set in, inflating the horse's belly into a giant balloon.

"The thing to do is to shoot her belly with a gun and let it blow," Carol said, but she had left her pistol at home. She'd have to do this by hand.

She crouched behind the horse's back and reached one arm over the belly. If the knife went in at this angle, she thought, maybe the stomach contents would blow the other way. Instead, they exploded in her face. A splattering gush of putrefying liquid and gas erupted from the horse's swollen belly and knocked her backward.

"Ugh," she muttered, wiping fusty sludge from her eyes. She mopped her face with her sleeve.

"What are horses doing on a muggy, buggy barrier island with very little freshwater?" Bob said. "It's unthinkably cruel."

Bob knew horses. He had grown up in Amish country and worked in a stable as a teenager saddling and shoeing horses. As both an equestrian and a scientist, he was outraged that stray, starving horses were roaming the island.

"Yep," Carol replied, "but the tourists want to see them."

* * *

Horses and humans have a long history together. Tens of millions of prehistoric horses once roamed North America, but they were likely hunted to near extinction and disappeared from the continent ten thousand years ago.

Surviving herds migrated across the Bering land bridge into central Asia, where they were first domesticated around 6,000 B.C.E. Initially used for food and even milk, horses were eventually employed in agriculture, transportation, and warfare. Horses played a pivotal role in the ability of Alexander the Great to conquer the Middle East and create the ancient world's largest empire in 330 B.C.E.

Spanish conquistadors reintroduced horses to the Americas in the sixteenth century. Most of the horses shipped across the Atlantic didn't survive the voyage. Their carcasses were thrown overboard in a becalmed stretch of sargassum-covered ocean that became known as the Horse Latitudes. To lighten their loads in the maddeningly still doldrums, beleaguered ships often threw live horses overboard, too.

Hernando Cortés used horses to vanquish the Aztecs in 1521. The Aztecs were awestruck when Cortés's soldiers arrived on horses, which they perceived as supernatural beasts. Cortés exploited their wonder to loot their gold and wipe out their civilization.

By the seventeenth century, Comanche and Apache tribes in present-day Texas and New Mexico began to acquire horses through trades with Spanish explorers. Eventually, horses escaped from their loosely tended, unfenced herds and spread across the Wild West.

In the United States, horses became emblems of unfettered freedom. Americans romanticized the horses' thundering stampedes, coats glistening and twitching, as they galloped free across sagebrush wilderness. Cowboys—from Buffalo Bill to the Lone Ranger—became quintessential American icons, mounting their horses and trampling underfoot the untamed wilderness. Like the horses they saddled, cowboys represented American ideals of ruggedness and vigor. Horse and human have become so entwined in American mythology that they have fused: perhaps no words better capture the unbridled American spirit than *mustang* and *maverick*.

When the frontier closed in the twentieth century and the Wild West was cross-fenced by cattle farmers, free-roaming horses no longer had endless wildlands to graze. Ranchers considered horses a nuisance. Some horses were rounded up by breeders in the East, who selected horses for racing and showing. The Carnegies brought trailer loads of polo horses and retired circus ponies to Cumberland Island to breed with a remnant herd of horses left behind by Oglethorpe and the British. One islander thought spotted horses would be pretty, so Appaloosa horses were introduced to Cumberland. Lucy brought over Arabian horses and her racing stallions to bolster the island herd.

All free-roaming horses in the United States today—including the 250 now on Cumberland Island—are feral. The government spends $75 million each year rounding up and corralling feral horses. In the West, over forty-two thousand stray horses are packed into crowded feedlots for slaughter annually. To deliver them to slaughterhouses alive, wranglers handicap them by sewing their noses partially shut with thongs of rawhide, cutting ligaments in their knees, and gut-shooting them. Most are then crammed into railcars and shipped to dog-food plants. The iconic American mustangs are being butchered to feed Fido.

Few other options remain for the once-wild horses. Their lands have been leased to cattle ranchers. Horse adoptions have steadily declined. Sterilization and castration programs have not been widely successful so far.

The feral horses on Cumberland Island face different but equally dismal fates. Most of the island horses are shabby, sickly, and emaciated. Three out of ten foals born on the island die in their first year. Most have worms and parasitic diseases. Their stomachs are eaten up with botflies. Some die of anemia and encephalitis; outbreaks are common on Cumberland. Carol has found dead horses tangled in vines and wedged between trees. Many more get trapped in the marsh mud and starve to death or drown. The horses breed beyond the carrying capacity of the island, and many suffer and die. The park stealthily stacks horse carcasses behind the Dungeness dunes, out of view of tourists.

The horses also devastate the island. Feral horses have so over-grazed the sea oats and vegetation near Lake Whitney that the denuded dunes are collapsing into the lake and filling in the island's largest source of freshwater. They also trample the nests of endangered least terns and other shorebirds, who bury their camouflaged, cream-colored eggs in scoops of sand along the dunes. In the forest, horses browse on Spanish moss, shearing it beyond the reach of native deer. In the marshes, feral horses shave the anchoring grasses that are essential for shrimp and shellfish nurseries. In short, they are an ecological nightmare.

But they are a tourist's dream. Nearly every camera-toting tourist who boards the island ferry hopes to catch a glimpse of a horse, partially because the National Park Service has promoted the island as a wild horse sanctuary. The horses are also a popular draw for Greyfield Inn's guests. Like Lucy before her, Gogo claims the horses' ecological impacts have been exaggerated.

Fearing public outcry and island family backlash, the National Park Service has been reluctant to remove the feral horses, even though they are mandated to do so. All feral animals in national parks—especially ones that threaten endangered species—are required by law to be removed. But tourism has trumped turtle habitat. The only steadfast voice for ending the suffering of the horses and the island has been Carol's.

"It's time for the feral horses of Cumberland to ride off into the sunset, for their own health and the island's," she said at a park meeting, despite the boos and catcalls of island families.

Not surprisingly, Carol's outspoken opposition to the feral horses has prompted a few dustups. One afternoon, Grover Henderson was fishing at the jetty when Carol passed by on her way to investigate a dead sea turtle.

"Why do you hate horses so much?" Grover asked her.

"They're suffering and starving. How can we wish that kind of anguish upon a creature just to fulfill our own misguided romantic notions?"

"That's a load of horseshit. Look at those horses grazing on the dunes. Do they look miserable? They got food in their bellies, a view of the ocean, a nice breeze to keep the flies down."

"Those horses are grazing sea oats, which hold the dunes in place. If people pull up sea oats, they can be arrested."

Grover staked his fishing pole in the sand and got up from his lawn chair. "Let me get this straight. You want to get rid of the horses to protect the grass? This is the biggest damn island in the South. The sea oats will grow back."

"Horses are also smashing the nests of shorebirds, starving out the deer, and mowing down the marshes."

"Cut the crap, Carol. We got thousands of acres of marsh surrounding the island. You don't have to be a PhD in flora n' whatever to see that. Where else can wild horses run free on an undeveloped island? This is as good as it gets."

"Not for the sickly, scraggly horses. Not for the dead stallions stuck in the marsh mud. The horses are not native to the island. They belong here about as much as they belong in downtown Atlanta."

"The horses will control their own population," Grover argued. "They'll die off. They'll get diseases. Let God handle the horses—not the government. I don't want the government doing anything except guarding the coast and carrying the mail."

One possible compromise solution to the horses is removing all but a small remnant herd on the south end of the island, where most of the tourists flock. The visitors get their horses. The horses' health dramatically improves. The island takes much less of a beating. Nests of endangered terns and turtles get a fighting chance.

It's worked on another barrier island. On Virginia's Assateague Island, a local fire department removes feral horses each year and sells them at a public auction. Assateague Island also uses contraception to control horse reproduction. Their smaller horse population is much healthier. Foals live longer, horses suffer fewer diseases, and their impact on the island is greatly diminished.

In the spring of 1996, the National Park Service began to consider plans to reduce the herds on Cumberland Island. "We are being selfish in wanting to maintain a large number of unhealthy horses

simply because we like to see them and feel that they are free," concluded the National Park Service's natural resource manager Jenny Bjork.

The park hoped that the south end herd solution would solve more than the feral horse headache. It would also help resolve the standoff between historic preservation and wilderness. Vehicle tours could circle the southern half of the island, so that everyone could see both the horses and the historic structures. They would stay out of the northern half of the island, which was already federally designated wilderness.

Most island residents supported a north-south compromise for the horses and the island. So did hikers and environmental groups. The park drafted a new management plans that limited the number of horses and confined them to the south end.

But then, in September of 1996, U.S. Representative Jack Kingston a friend of the Carnegie families on Cumberland intervened. Kingston added a one-paragraph rider to the federal budget bill banning all horse management at Cumberland Island National Seashore. The Park Service's south end horse plan was nixed.

And just a few weeks later, a humble structure on the north end would become a tourist attraction even more popular than the horses.

John F. Kennedy Jr. began visiting Cumberland Island in 1986. It was a quiet retreat for the handsome, adventurous son of the thirty-fifth president. For twelve years, he swam in the ocean, ran the island trails, paddled the marshes, and hiked deep into the forests.

John had met Carolyn Bessette in 1992, and she soon began joining him on Cumberland getaways. Together they dug for clams in the marshes, trekked beneath the moss-festooned live oaks, and strolled along the seashore hand in hand. They stayed at Greyfield and became good friends with Gogo.

John proposed to Carolyn in the spring of 1995, and they decided to marry the following summer on Cumberland Island, where they had spent some of their most cherished and romantic moments

together. John and Carolyn asked Gogo if she would help coordinate the wedding for them at the abandoned First African Baptist Church on the island's north end.

"I knew that it was going to be logistically very hard to do that," Gogo said, "but I also knew that it was the one gift that I could give: privacy."

Gogo kept the wedding plans a secret from the National Park Service, Greyfield Inn employees, and even most of her family. She even stealthily arranged the marriage certificate and bloodwork required by the state. Two days before the wedding, the county clerk was sent to the tiny airport in St. Marys, where she was to help a young couple complete pre-wedding paperwork.

When she arrived at the airport, the clerk met a young woman who was, according to the clerk, "the picture of an excited, anxious bride." As she filled out the marriage license, the clerk asked what her married name would be.

"Carolyn Bessette Kennedy," she replied. Suddenly, the county clerk understood the significance and the secrecy surrounding this license. Soon, another plane touched down, and out stepped John F. Kennedy Jr., who took his turn doing paperwork and giving blood.

It was one of many attentive details handled by Gogo, who pulled off one of the most successful covert celebrity weddings ever. Her secrecy and subterfuge kept gossipers perplexed and most of the media in the dark. Only one photographer from the French paparazzi managed to sneak onto Cumberland beforehand, and he was escorted off the island the morning before the wedding.

Gogo paid a friend to wash out the cobwebs and oil the floors and benches of the First African Baptist Church, which had not been used since 1963, when Beulah Alberty gathered all of the Settlement residents together to hold a memorial service for President Kennedy after he was assassinated. The National Park Service had recently applied a fresh coat of white paint to the clapboard church, along with a new red tin roof. Carolyn drove up to see the church beforehand. She hid on the floor of the car to avoid being recognized.

For the wedding weekend, Gogo hired former FBI agents to provide security for the couple and their guests at the Greyfield Inn. They installed a laser beam around the compound, which ended up being triggered by every horse that wandered through it.

On the afternoon of September 21, 1996, Gogo drove Carolyn from the Greyfield Inn to the wedding. Because of high tide, they could not drive up the beach, so they bounced up the washboard-rutted main road to the church. To avoid wrinkling her dress, Carolyn stood in the backseat and leaned into the front for fourteen jarring miles. As soon as she stepped out, she sunk down into the mud in her beaded satin sandals.

John delayed the wedding by several hours. He had misplaced his father's shirt and cuff links, which he had hoped to wear. Gogo's husband, David, scoured the Greyfield Inn and finally found them. It was nearly dark by the time John arrived at the church.

While the guests waited at the church, several of them—including Robert Kennedy Jr.—meandered over to meet Carol. She gave tours of her museum and introduced guests to Pretty Butt. A few guests wandered into the woods and were covered in ticks for days afterward. At dusk, Carol loaned the guests kerosene lamps and flashlights, which were used to illuminate the church.

Crowding into the chapel's eight wooden pews were forty guests, including John's longtime friend and CNN correspondent Christiane Amanpour, who had flown in from the Middle East. Caroline Kennedy's three-year-old son, Jack, was the ring bearer. When the bride appeared at the chapel entrance, Jack said loudly, "Why is Carolyn all dressed up?"

Carolyn wore a $40,000 pearl-colored silk crepe floor-length gown, a handrolled silk veil, and long silk gloves. A bun at the nape of her neck was pinned with a clip belonging to Jackie Kennedy. A gospel soloist sang "Amazing Grace" a cappella as she walked down an aisle carpeted with rose petals.

John, wearing a single-breasted, midnight blue wool suit, a white waffled vest, and his father's shirt, cuff links, and wristwatch, smiled as Carolyn arrived beside him. She handed her lily bouquet to her

matron of honor, Caroline Kennedy, wearing a high-waisted, navy blue silk gown.

Carol watched from the church steps with the Greyfield staff. During the long Catholic service, she walked over to her horse pasture, adjacent to the church. Pretty Butt nuzzled in beside Carol and dropped a pile of manure at her feet. A hulking, muscle-bound African American security guard chatted with Carol about her rugged life in the woods.

"Don't you get scared living out here?" he asked her.

Carol laughed. "You're ready to take a bullet for these folks, and you think my life is scary?"

During the ceremony, the priest read from the good book using Carol's flashlight. The couple exchanged gold wedding bands designed by Gogo. They kissed in the dimly lit chapel, then walked hand-in-hand down the aisle to an a cappella rendering of "Will the Circle Be Unbroken."

Outside the church, the couple smiled for photos while standing beside Carol's fenced pasture. As flashbulbs popped, Pretty Butt craned his neck over the fence and nibbled on Carolyn's bouquet.

Then the guests piled into vehicles and returned to Greyfield for the reception, while John and Carolyn lingered in the church alone for a few minutes. When they emerged, all the cars had left. Only a single park ranger's truck remained, which had been used earlier that day for a beach cleanup. The backseat was stuffed with trash bags full of beer bottles, moldy socks, and cigarette butts. The ranger quickly tossed out thqe trash and wiped the seats with a towel.

John and Carolyn arrived back at Greyfield after dark and stepped onto the floor for the first dance—to Prince's "Forever in My Life." Afterward, Ted Kennedy's teary-eyed toast was a powerful, poignant celebration of his family's storied legacy.

News of the wedding began to leak Saturday afternoon. By Sunday morning, the press was descending on Cumberland in chartered boats and helicopters, but the newlyweds had already left the island, ferried off in a plane flown by Gogo's cousin.

"I didn't realize until afterwards how wise we were in not telling anyone about the wedding. Just watching the flotillas of media trying to get onto the island was horrifying," Gogo recalled. "It just made me even happier to have done that for them. I think that I will always go down as someone who honors people's privacy."

Suddenly, the quiet north end of Cumberland Island became a bustling tourist attraction. The Greyfield Inn offered exclusive vehicle tours to the church for their guests, who paid up to $750 per night. They drove their guests through the wilderness and along the beach. Backpackers and beachcombers had to keep an eye out for truckloads of tourists guzzling past.

Greyfield benefitted from the wedding and the park. And unlike the twenty-one other island families who sold their land to the National Park Service when the park was established, Gogo Ferguson's family at Greyfield did not receive the lifetime rights to drive on parklands or in the wilderness that were part of those agreements.

Gogo defended the tours by arguing that her family had been exceptional guardians of Cumberland for generations and had earned the right to drive the entire island, including roads through the wilderness and on the beaches.

"The minimal use of vehicles has been a traditional use enjoyed by us for almost a hundred years, a small price to pay for the good stewardship we have provided," Gogo wrote in a letter to Congressman Jack Kingston. Kingston soon became an outspoken supporter of Greyfield's tours on Cumberland. "We are some of Jack Kingston's top clients," acknowledged one Carnegie heir. "We asked him to get involved on our behalf."

The National Park Service wasn't going to stop Greyfield. For years, Lucy had intimidated the park, and now Gogo was calling the shots, Carol believed. Numerous National Park Service superintendents felt the significant influence of the Carnegies, and the park wasp not about to tell them they couldn't drive through a wilderness that they once owned, especially now that the family had Congressman Kingston in their corner.

So Carol did. She spearheaded legal action to stop the tours.
A trio of conservation groups filed a lawsuit against the National
Park Service for allowing motorized commercial tours through the
wilderness. They won. In 2004, the Eleventh Circuit U.S. Court of
Appeals' unanimous ruling halted Greyfield's tours through the wil-
derness. Carol's small band of dedicated grassroots conservationists
had triumphed over a very powerful family.

But the victory was short-lived. Later that year, Gogo once
again asked Congressman Kingston to rewrite the law—this time
to strip wilderness status from the Greyfield tour route. She and her
family had contributed to Kingston's campaign Gogo wrote to him:
"Our hope is for you to sponsor legislation which would delay the
implementation of the wilderness."

A few months later, Kingston tacked a couple of paragraphs
onto a two-thousand-page omnibus spending bill. His legislation
removed the Greyfield tour route—including the entire beach and
the main road—from wilderness. The change went largely unnoticed
by Congress. Kingston's legislation was never voted on or discussed
in any committee. In the wee hours before the 2004 winter recess,
the spending bill passed, with the Cumberland wilderness removal
rider dangling from its coattails. Never before had wilderness been
removed from the federal system without any public input.

"People come before nature," Kingston said. "Access to the
island shouldn't be limited by a wilderness that never should have
been designated in the first place."

Cumberland's wilderness was fragmented by Kingston's leg-
islation, and vehicle tours increased dramatically, including a turtle
nesting habitat. The bill also called for eight busloads of tourists to
be shuttled to the north end daily, and Kingston earmarked millions
for the renovation of Plum Orchard mansion.

The Carnegie family had prevailed.

Kingston's legislation made it a lot easier for the Park Service
to manage the island and for residents to enjoy it. Both could drive
freely on the island without worrying about wilderness restrictions.
It also simplified and solved many logistical problems. Plum Orchard
and the First African Baptist Church could be reached by vehicle,

and the beach was no longer wilderness, which helped untangle the laws governing its use.

But the wilderness was critically wounded. So was Carol.

"This park is run by the rich," Carol fumed afterward. "They ignore the law. And when they don't like the law, they buy a congressman who changes it for them."

"You used the influence of Jimmy Carter to create the wilderness," Bob pointed out. "Now they're using Jack Kingston to dismantle it."

Some island families weren't satisfied with removing just the beach and main road from wilderness. "I'd like to repeal the wilderness entirely," Grover said. "I think it's a stupid idea, and I intend to fight it. It'll give me something to do in my retirement."

To demonstrate his opposition, Grover began riding his ATV on hiking trails in the wilderness. "The park tells me I can't ride my four-wheeler on certain trails. I ride whatever trails I want," he boasted. "Somebody asked me why I collect machine guns. I said, 'Cause I can.' I need no better reason than that."

Other island families have gone even further. Even though they were already paid millions for their land, the Carnegies have lobbied to extend their lifetime rights on the island forever. For the past decade, the Carnegies have been lobbying the White House and Congress to allow them to live on their taxpayer-owned estates permanently. The Carnegies claim they are seeking to lease back their historic houses because the park does not have the budget to preserve them. "It is certainly one very good option regarding important structures which require significant maintenance," said Gogo. So far, the National Park Service has stood its ground and refused. But Carnegies continue to urge influential leaders and legislators to grant them rights and residences without end.

"If lifetime rights are extended, the park is doomed," Carol said. "Extending rights—including my own—would be selling out a publicly owned national park to a privileged few."

Meanwhile, island families convinced the state of Georgia—which has jurisdiction over the beach—to issue them nearly four hundred beach driving permits on Cumberland Island. These permits

are special exemptions that allow them to drive along the seashore, which—even without wilderness protection—is supposed to be free of vehicles. More people drive on Cumberland Island National Seashore than any other island in Georgia. The most important beach for sea turtles and shorebirds in the state also has the most traffic.

Carol saw more tire tracks than ever on her island surveys. She learned to recognize the grooved tread of the Greyfield jeeps and the knobby tread of National Park Service trucks and vans.

In the early spring of 2007, Carol noticed the sandy tire tracks of park vehicles headed to the house of Ben "Doc" Jenkins, an island resident who lived between Greyfield and Stafford. Jenkins had just turned eighty-five, and his rights to live on the island were set to expire in two years. Unlike most other islanders, Jenkins had negotiated for a forty-year contract instead of lifetime rights. Now he was regretting that decision.

"I'm not leaving without a fight," Doc said. "They'll probably have to bring in the army to get me off the island."

Squat, squinty-eyed, and gray-bearded, Doc always had a cigar in his mouth, and his discarded stumps littered the main road. It wasn't clear if Doc was really a doctor. He had been accused of forging documents to get his medical degree. He practiced for decades as an ear, nose, and throat doctor near Atlanta until an investigation by the *Atlanta Constitution* revealed his alleged fraud. He fled to Cumberland Island in 1970, where he bought a house on the south end, paying in cash, just before the national seashore was created.

Then, in 2007, with his island living and driving privileges set to expire soon, Doc Jenkins hatched a plan to extend his stay. The tire tracks clued Carol in to the collusion. Just before dawn one evening, she crept up to Doc's house through the woods, slinking through the clattering palmetto along the spongy forest floor. She couldn't believe her eyes: through the Spanish moss, she spied a glimpse of an immense construction project next to Doc's house.

Carol contacted a couple of journalists, who staked out the construction site one evening and watched a National Park Service truck

pull up to the house. The new park superintendent, Jerre Brumbelow, stepped out of the truck, along with the longtime county sheriff Bill Smith. Doc Jenkins, with a cigar stub wedged in the corner of his mouth, waddled out to meet them. The superintendent and sheriff drank beers with Doc on the porch until nightfall. The journalists heard their guffaws and smelled Doc's cigar smoke from their spot in the forest fifty yards away.

Just after dusk, lights appeared on the water. Under the cloak of darkness, a barge approached the dock near Doc's house. Local inmates unloaded stacks of framing wood, concrete block, and other construction materials.

Carol and the journalists did some more digging and uncovered the subterfuge: Doc had teamed up with the sheriff and superintendent to secretly build a private vacation retreat on publicly owned parklands. As part of the deal, Doc would get his rights to live on the island extended indefinitely, and the superintendent would get his own private residence on the island. The sheriff covertly provided inmate labor from the county jail to build the facility. In return, the sheriff would get to use it as a fishing spot and island getaway for his family. They planned to disguise the facility as a center for disabled children. Sheriff Smith's son was a paraplegic. Superintendent Brumbelow and Sheriff Smith hoped to play on public sympathies so they could have a place of their own on Cumberland.

Carol's sleuthing helped stop the secret construction project. In 2008, a U.S. district court judge halted all construction until a federal probe could investigate. Doc continued construction in defiance of the judge's ruling and was held in criminal contempt. Eventually, a federal court permanently ended the illegal construction. Sheriff Smith was voted out of office and Superintendent Brumbelow was fired. It was the third island superintendent that Carol had ousted.

Afterward, animosity toward Carol intensified. She received hate mail and anonymous violent threats. Park employees and island families loyal to Brumbelow unleashed vicious tirades.

"You're a dirty dumpster diver with death breath," said one Brumbelow backer. "How the hell did you get away with murder anyway?"

"You can go fuck yourself and the fucking sea turtle you rode in on," said another.

She caught park employees snooping around her property. Law enforcement rangers began shadowing Carol on her island surveys, waiting for the slightest slip-up. One afternoon, Carol was inspecting a gator hole near South Cut Trail when a gun-toting ranger arrived suddenly. He barreled up in his big truck and slammed on his brakes, then jumped out of the cab with one hand on his holster, ready to arrest her. Carol was on all fours in the muddy slough inspecting deposits at the gator den's entrance.

"Whatcha got there, Carol?" he shouted.

"I don't know," she said. She lifted it up and handed it to the ranger. "Is it salty or sweet?"

The ranger held a log of gator shit in his hands. He stood silently for a full minute, trying to figure out if he could write her a ticket. Finally, he threw the dung down in the ditch and drove off.

20

Early one morning, Carol got a call on her walkie-talkie: "Dead turtle near Duck House Beach."

She raced out to the beach at dawn. A wafer of sun crested the horizon, and by the time she arrived at the Duck House dune crossing it had filled the purple sky dome with fiery orange breaths of light. The wind whipped streamers of sand across the shore. Then she saw the stranded carcass ahead. She squinted through the blowing sand at the dead turtle with the missing left flipper—and stopped in her tracks. It was Stumpy, the turtle whose nests she had helped dig and whose hatchling she had rescued years ago.

"I'm sorry, girl," Carol said. "I let you down."

The turtle's gut was loaded with shrimp. Her lungs were filled with blood. Lactic acid levels in her bones confirmed it: she had died in a trawl net. Dozens of shrimp boats lined the horizon.

Carol glared out across the water. "I swear to you, Stump. The slaughter stops here."

Over four thousand miles away, Stumpy's daughter had hitched a ride to Africa in the gyrating Gulf Stream to bask in turquoise lagoons and feed on crunchy crabs and juicy jellies.

The turtle had grown large, and her size attracted the males. They circled her and sniffed her cloaca. They tried to mount her, clawing at her carapace. But she was saving herself for the boys on the other side of the pond. The nesting beaches of Cumberland Island were calling her home. An ancient instinct had awakened. She set out to trace an ancestral memory across an invisible, indelible route.

Slow and steady, she flapped through the water toward home. It would take nearly a year for her to complete her voyage back across the ocean.

A lot had changed since her transatlantic crossing thirty years earlier. Much of the floating seaweed that had sheltered her in the Sargasso Sea had been harvested. Instead of a seaweed sanctuary, the still eye of the Atlantic gyre had become a trash dump. The Texas-sized Atlantic Garbage Patch was a swirl of confetti-like debris—mainly from cigarette butts, soda cans, beer bottles, and plastics. Worldwide, over one hundred thousand turtles, dolphins, and whales die each year from ingesting plastic. She chomped into a floating plastic bag, which resembled a jelly but didn't taste like one. She shook it loose from her jaws before it clogged her throat.

There were far fewer fish in the sea—and a lot more nets and hooks. Trawls had flattened the ocean's ancient forests of coral, sponges, and seaweed, leaving behind barren plains. The ocean was a lot more empty—and lonely.

There were fewer turtles, too. Many were sluggish and diseased, covered in warts and parasites. Others hung dead from longlines—burly fishing lines with baited hooks extending for miles across the open ocean.

There was one upshot: more jellyfish. The turtle gorged on swarms of moon jellies, purple-tentacled Portuguese man-of-wars, and lacy lion's manes.

At night, she swam for the shelter of one of the few remaining coral reefs, which were the mortar for massive metropolises of marine creatures. The reef was an underwater rain forest crowded with life. Sharp-toothed morays slithered across the stony polyps, scraping parasites from their skin. Reef sharks stopped by to brush their teeth: picking the flesh from their open jaws were zebra-striped angelfish living amid the corals.

The turtle let her head and flippers hang down loosely, a special posture to welcome cleaning barberfish. Their jaws tickled her skin as they removed barnacles—crustaceans that glue their shells to docks, boats, and the backs of turtles. Barnacles created drag and weighed down her streamlined shell.

The reef's night life was the marine equivalent of a hot tub orgy. All around her, coral colonies released sperm and eggs in a briny

bacchanal. Corals discharged their eggs and sperm in a synchronous mass spawning that occurred for only a few minutes, one night a year. Triggered by the moon and the tides, female polyps squeezed pink bundles of eggs from their translucent mouths, while male corals simultaneously released dense golden clouds of sperm. In a matter of minutes, millions of corals spawned, coating the sea in a soupy slick of pink goop.

Corals weren't the only critters spewing sex. Fish, jellies, sponges, and anemones bred in milky mobs of sperm and eggs floating in the ocean. Male sea horses gave birth, squirting out hatched babies from their brood pouches. And on the turtle's back, hermaphroditic barnacles still attached to her shell used their penises—the longest in the animal kingdom relative to their body size—to reach out and touch someone.

The turtle swam through a sea of love on her long journey home, where mating males eagerly awaited her arrival. She used the magnetite crystals in her brain, electrified by impulses from her optic nerve, like a compass to orient her home and to magnetically map the seafloor below her. She followed mountain chains and recognized deep abysses illuminated by bioluminescent fish, electric eels, and glowing squid. The sun and stars were also guideposts, which she checked every five minutes when she surfaced for air.

Not on her magnetic radar were oil barges, rigs, and platforms, some taller than the Eiffel Tower. Oil slicks stained the sea for miles. Also not expected were sprawling 6,000 mile dead zones where polluted river runoff had starved the ocean water of oxygen and killed off all life. Former turtle foraging grounds were barren water wastelands.

There was less life in the ocean but a lot more noise. Missile-carrying submarines plied the waters, emitting deafening sonar pulses. Air guns on oil ships fired round-the-clock fusillades loud enough to locate oil buried under the seafloor. Barges filled busy shipping lanes, pleasure boats crowded the coast, and colossal fleets of commercial shrimp boats trawled the open waters. The underwater ocean had become one hundred times louder in her lifetime.

On a late spring evening, the turtle lifted her head out of the water and spied the soaring dunes and emerald forest of her home island. She had swum nine thousand miles around the Atlantic to arrive back where she started: Cumberland Island. Just offshore, she burrowed into the soft sandy seafloor, folded her flippers across her back, and slept. She awoke to a massive shadow passing overhead. Above her drifted a pod of right whales and their nursing calves. Right whales sang to each other in shrill, fluted melodies that they mysteriously changed each year. They ate the caloric equivalent of five thousand Big Macs a day, and their heartbeats could be heard a half mile away. Right whales were the most endangered whales in the world, and their only known birthing grounds were just a few miles offshore of Cumberland.

After her transatlantic swim, the turtle had worked up an appetite, too. She had looked forward to a Southern shrimp feast, but there were few to be found. So she settled for a spread of jellies and crab. She also satisfied another craving: for the next few weeks, she rolled in the surf with dozens of male loggerheads in frenzied lovemaking. Before mating, the boys nuzzled and nibbled her. They stroked their flippers along her shell. They fought for her, thrashing and biting each other to claim the prize of the giant, brown-eyed, thirty-year-old virgin.

Once a victorious male emerged from the scuffle, he then began circling her. They spiraled for several minutes, eyes locked, sizing each other up. Finally, he made the move. He mounted her, his belly to her back. He clasped her shell with the curved claws of his front flippers. Then he twisted his longer tail down and around hers so that their rear vents met. His penis extended out and into her cloaca. She stored his sperm with the semen of a dozen other males in her month-long orgy, and she could store it up to four years after mating. But she didn't wait around. By summer, over one hundred eggs filled her oviduct. She was ready to nest.

Just before heading to shore, she was foraging near Cumberland Island along a seam of shrimp, when she suddenly noticed a wall of netted rope headed for her. She swam sideways but couldn't escape

it. The trawl engulfed her. The turtle thrashed against the net, flapping and snapping. She nipped at the ropes with her hooked beak, but the net was too thick and moving too fast. She was tangled in a panicked swarm of shrimp, crabs, and fish as the trawl dragged through the water.

Stuck in the trawl for nearly two hours, she couldn't surface for air. Blood filled her lungs. Her muscles swelled with lactic acid. The escape hatch in the back of the net was slowly moving toward her, but she was slipping into an anoxic coma.

The turtle was heavy with one hundred embryos that had taken her thirty years and thousands of miles to produce. She had dodged tiger sharks and toothed eels, sargassum barges and submarines, only to be swept up in a shrimp net a half mile from her home beach.

Out of oxygen, out of time, she shut down and floated limply in the water.

Shrouded in 4 A.M. darkness, Calvin Lang guided his seventy-five-foot trawler slowly down the black, ebbing water of the St. Marys River and out to the Atlantic. Hands on the pegs of the wooden wheel at ten and two, he knew by heart every coil and curve of the river and every rock along the ocean shelf. He could navigate these waters with his eyes closed. Calvin had been at the helm of a shrimp boat since he was ten years old, when his father bolted a milk crate to the floor so he could see over the wheel. Now he was wrinkled and leathered from six decades of piloting trawlers, but the sound of the sea still buoyed him.

Calvin lived by the changing tides, working to harvest nature's prize: wild-caught shrimp from coastal Georgia waters. With a seven-boat fleet and help from his wife and sons, Calvin Lang carried on the family shrimping business through good times and bad, working long, hard hours to net the tender, tasty shrimp.

Choppy water slapped against the hull of *Lang's Pride*. With masts extending at odd angles, like jointed appendages carefully

probing the sky, the shrimp boat bore an eerie resemblance to its prey. Out on the ocean, dozens of star-like specks were scattered across the water—lights from the decks of other shrimp boats. The first tint of twilight painted the clouds.

Calvin scoured map and memory to predict where shrimp might be waiting. It was low tide, so shrimp tended to cluster. And it was early in the season, so they were more likely to be close to shore. Beyond that, the hunt was pure intuition. Calvin could pick any patch of blue on the topo. There was no such thing as territory among shrimpers. And because shrimp gathered unevenly across the ocean floor, rippled with trenches and holes where the bottom dwellers could hide, one trawler could drag right beside another and catch three times as many shrimp.

Calvin throttled his engines to a hum just a half mile offshore of Cumberland Island, where the soft muddy shelf reliably sheltered seams of shrimp that had migrated out from the marshes. The rising sun traced the horizon with a thin white line. He lowered two nets into the water and began a steady two-mile-per-hour prowl. At the bottom of the trawl nets were quarter-ton steel plates chained together to form a plow. They dragged along the bottom of the ocean, dredging shrimp and other sea life into the nets.

On board with Calvin was a crew of two strikers, who helped work the nets. After lowering the nets into the water, they rested in the air-conditioned cabin for a few hours, snacking on Doritos and watching game shows on a portable television. Up in the pilothouse, Calvin scribbled notes as the sun climbed out of the ocean, glossing the sea in amber.

After two hours of trawling, Calvin and the strikers reeled in the squealing steel cables of the trawler's tow arms, hoisting the nets out of the water. Calvin tugged the nets' drawstrings and a shimmering cascade of creatures tumbled onto the deck. Amid a writhing two-foot mountain of fish were eels, crabs, jellies, rays, anemones, urchins, sponges, sand dollars, sea stars, squid, sea cucumbers, horseshoe crabs, a juvenile bonnethead shark, and a languishing loggerhead sea turtle, which they heaved overboard. From

the thrashing mound of marine life, strikers picked out two bushels of translucent, eight-inch white shrimp. They worked quickly, pinching off the heads of shrimp and throwing the meaty torsos and tails in a basket. Dozens of gulls and pelicans hovered overhead, picking off flopping fish from the pile.

Once their shrimp baskets were filled, the strikers swept the bycatch—most of it already dead—back into the sea. Alongside the trawler, porpoises splashed and thrashed amid the feast. Then Calvin dropped the nets back in the water, cranked the engines, and continued raking shrimp from the ocean floor.

Shrimp is the most popular seafood in the United States. Over forty million pounds are consumed annually in America—more than tuna, crab, cod, and clams combined. *Forrest Gump* got it right: there are a lot of ways to eat shrimp, from boils and barbecues to creoles and cocktails. That's why the average American eats four pounds of it each year, and it has been a staple of coastal diets for centuries.

Until recently, most of the country's shrimp was caught along the Southern coast. In the waters offshore of Cumberland, female shrimp release millions of eggs. Males release even more sperm in thick, creamy clouds. When they drift together and meet, eggs are fertilized and hatch twenty-four hours later. The mite-sized shrimp larvae then migrate to the marshes along Cumberland Island and Georgia's Golden Isles. These nutrient-rich nurseries allow the shrimp to grow quickly. Whenever Carol waded into the marshes' tidal creeks, she felt the spawning swarms of juvenile shrimp pricking her skin. At night, she saw their tiny red eyes darting all around her in the water.

By summer, the shrimp—now several inches long—swim back out to the ocean, where fleets of trawlers waited for them. Shrimpers drag their enormous nets only a few hundred yards from the beaches where sea turtles nest.

Fleets of commercial shrimp boats—some the size of small cruise ships—trawl the south Georgia coast. They tow their huge weighted nets across the seabed, pulverizing the ocean

floor. Miles of corals, sponges, and kelp forests that have taken centuries to grow are mowed down in a few hours, leaving behind vast ocean deserts. It's the most destructive activity in the ocean, outstripping even oil drilling in its impacts. An area twice the size of the contiguous United States is razed and denuded each year by trawling.

The trawlers' nets catch shrimp—as well as every other living sea creature in their path. For every pound of shrimp harvested in a trawl net, over ten pounds of bycatch is caught. Air-breathing animals such as dolphins and sea turtles drown in the nets.

Shrimping wasn't always so supersized. Up until the early twentieth century, most shrimp were caught with cast nets, like the one Jesse used to throw from the Candler dock. Shrimp boats were small, and their catch was targeted. Eventually, fishermen began utilizing rowboats and even real horse power to drag nets along the beach. Global fisheries did not reach ten million total pounds until 1900. Then, with the rise of fossil-fueled fleets, commercial fisheries doubled their catch by 1950. They began doubling their catch every decade, and by 1980, they raked in eighty million pounds of shrimp each year.

Carol found shrimp in the stomach of the first dead turtle she necropsied on Cumberland Island in 1973. She also noted the turtle's dented skull and broken pectoral girdle, a horseshoe-shaped neck bone. How could a turtle break its neck in the ocean? The only possibility was from falling out of a net onto a boat deck. Bloody lungs and lactate-filled muscles were other clues that pointed toward one obvious suspect: trawlers.

But shrimping was a $200 million industry in south Georgia. She needed more than one dead turtle to make her case. So she set about necropsying every single turtle carcass that washed onto Cumberland Island. Hundreds had been washing ashore every summer for years, but nobody had ever bothered to find out why. It was smutty, smelly work on animals with little commercial value. She studied their spilled guts to find out why they were dying.

Sea turtles were protected under the Endangered Species Act—a rudimentary bill of rights for nature. But in south Georgia, where

the shrimping industry—the world's largest commercial fishery—dominated the coastal economy, rules were rarely enforced, and shrimpers had routinely flouted the law to maximize their catch. Turtles were often killed so they would not repeatedly end up feasting on the shrimp in trawlers' nets.

As soon as the state opened its waters to shrimp boats in early spring, sea turtle strandings spiked. Carol could barely keep up with the work. Each turtle necropsy required two hours of rancid, sweat-drenched work on the beach and hours more back in her lab.

Carol's data from Cumberland was convincing: the number of dead turtles was steadily increasing each year, and all of the post-mortem evidence pointed to trawls. But Bob pointed out a hole in her data: all of her necropsies were from a single island. So in the early 1980s, Carol created the Sea Turtle Stranding Network. She contacted other biologists and volunteers on every island from the Carolinas to Florida to collect data on dead turtles washing ashore. She trained some of them to conduct basic necropsies. Others simply counted the number of turtle carcasses on the beach. After a few years, the volunteer network had amassed the world's largest stranded sea turtles databank. The patterns Carol had recorded on Cumberland played out on every other Southern shore. Trawls were killing endangered turtles.

Like other scientists, Carol was a data-driven, detail-oriented biologist who insisted on absolute accuracy and meticulous research. But unlike her colleagues, she combined her research with activism. Most of the scientists she met at turtle conferences tended to write technical papers for obscure academic publications. They were trained to divorce feelings from facts. They shied away from advocacy and rarely shared their research with the general public.

Carol was different. She didn't dress the part. She had no job or ego at stake. She just wanted to save the damn sea turtles. Even though everyone in the scientific community agreed that turtles were in trouble, few did anything about it.

"Scientists never scream," she said, nudging Bob.

So Carol decided to make some noise.

* * *

In the mid-1980s, Carol's Sea Turtle Stranding Network made national headlines, and Carol made new enemies. Shrimpers didn't like a female biologist poking her beak where it didn't belong. Shrimping fed families. Turtles got in the way of their trawls and ate the shrimp out of their nets. "The fewer turtles, the better," a south Georgia shrimper once told her.

Carol presented her data to the National Marine Fisheries Service, which was responsible for both promoting the shrimp industry and protecting endangered sea turtles. Managed by the Department of Commerce, the Fisheries Service usually followed the money instead of the Endangered Species Act.

Carol met with the fisheries administrator at the regional headquarters in Florida. "Loggerhead strandings increase dramatically as soon as waters are opened to shrimp boats each season," she told them. "Trawlers are the leading cause of death for sea turtles."

The fisheries administrator cast a sideways glance at the other officials in the room. "Miss, uh . . . Miss Turtleshell," he said, a mispronunciation of her last name, Ruckdeschel. (Turtleshell became a nickname that has stuck with her for life.) "Your data is persuasive. But our agency is also charged with managing the country's shrimping industry, which provides thousands of jobs and feeds the nation. We can't just close the coast to trawls."

"Why not? At the very least, create a trawl-free reserve along a portion of the coast," she said. A reserve would provide a baseline control to assess how sea turtles fared without trawls in the water, she argued. It would also allow shrimp and fish populations to recover and the seafloor to regrow. "It could provide a powerful point of comparison."

"Closures of any kind are not economically feasible," the administrator replied. "But we'll work with you to come up with other solutions."

Instead of creating a reserve, the National Marine Fisheries Service agreed to expand Carol's Sea Turtle Stranding Network. It

soon became a nationwide program with a full-time staff collecting dead turtle data from Maine to Texas. More dead turtles than ever were washing ashore. Even the National Academy of Sciences bolstered Carol's research, concluding that shrimp trawlers killed over fifty thousand sea turtles each year.

The feds couldn't deny the problem. But they couldn't solve it either. Trawlers had far more clout than turtles. They needed a middle-ground solution that slowed sea turtle deaths but still kept shrimpers happy.

They found it just a few miles north of Cumberland in the coastal town of Darien, the shrimp capital of the South. Its fleet of 250 trawlers was the largest in Georgia. At the beginning of shrimping season in Darien, hundreds of shrimp boats paraded through town, adorned with wreaths and lights. Clergymen blessed the fleet, sprinkling holy water across their decks as they passed beneath a bridge.

Several of those blessed boats belonged to Sinkey Boone, a legendary local captain whose family was synonymous with south Georgia shrimping. But Sinkey was more than a shrimper. He was a welder, net maker, purveyor of folk wisdom, and eccentric inventor. One afternoon, Sinkey Boone sat on the wet warehouse docks of Darien sewing a barbecue grill into his shrimp trawl. Fellow shrimpers puzzled at the fifth-generation shrimp boat captain intentionally cutting a hole in his net.

"Sinkey, I know you've been shrimping for a long time," said a fellow Darien shrimper. "But why in hellfire are you adding holes to your net? It's hard enough just to keep 'em patched!"

Frustrated by the amount of jellyfish clogging his trawl nets, Sinkey had recently developed a net with an oval-shaped metal grate sewn into it. Shrimp could pass between the grills, but jellyfish were stopped by the grate and diverted out an escape hatch. As an added bonus, the modified net shunted pesky sea turtles out of the nets, too. They were blocked by the barbecue grill and directed out the exit flap.

The feds visited Sinkey Boone's net-making shop on the Darien docks and liked what they saw. His new trawl net—which they called

a turtle excluder device, or TED—was the perfect solution to their turtle troubles. Shrimpers could continue trawling, but turtles would not drown in the nets. Fewer turtles would wash up on beaches, keeping Carol off their backs. And because the turtle excluder device was designed by one of their own, shrimpers would be more likely to use it.

In 1987, the National Marine Fisheries Service required a turtle excluder device in all commercial trawls nationwide. Sinkey began mass producing TEDs in his Darien shop, but shrimpers didn't take to them as well as he and the feds had hoped.

Shrimpers fought vigorously against feds and the TEDs, fearful that TEDs would cause them to lose shrimp and profits. Government studies had shown that TEDs cause less than a 4 percent reduction in catch, but shrimpers claimed the number was closer to 25 percent.

The shrimpers felt caught in the net of government regulation. They didn't take kindly to federal officials boarding their boats to ensure the TEDs were installed properly. And they didn't like turtle-hugging hippies like Carol telling them how to do their job. One shrimper described her as "a bleedin'-heart hippie woman runnin' around half-nekkid who'd rather put hard-workin' fishermen outta business than hurt any animals."

Shrimpers pointed out that trawls weren't the only turtle-killing nets. Thousands of turtles were killed each year by tuna fishermen using mile-long drift nets floating freely in the ocean. Even more were killed by longlines. But shrimpers' biggest beef was with the Endangered Species Act itself, which they believed prioritized turtles over people. Shrimpers argued that turtles weren't truly threatened. They claimed that their populations had rebounded, which is why more turtles were being caught in trawls.

"It's the shrimper who is endangered," said Clint Guidry, a third-generation shrimper. "Our way of life is under attack by people who don't know what the hell they're talking about."

In the summer of 1989, Southern shrimpers banded together to launch the TED Wars. An armada of shrimp boats, some flying skull-and-crossbones flags, formed blockades into Southern ports to protest TED rules. Gunshots were fired, windows were broken, and Coast Guard boats were rammed by shrimpers. Later, thousands of angry shrimpers mobbed a TED hearing in Louisiana, and the state police had to be deployed to maintain order. Some shrimpers took their frustrations out on the turtles, which began washing ashore with mutilated bodies.

After the violent summer of '89, the U.S. Department of Commerce caved in and suspended the TED rules. Environmental groups sued in court to reinstate them and won, but the judge left a gaping loophole: shrimpers did not have to use TEDs if they checked their nets every hour for turtles.

Even with the loophole, many shrimpers ignored the law and continued to drag nets without TEDs. They evaded enforcement by alerting each other via radio when feds were boarding nearby boats.

Meanwhile, environmentalists rallied behind TEDs and began pushing for their use worldwide. In 1998, Seattle protesters took to the streets in turtle costumes demanding that the World Trade Organization require turtle excluder devices in trawlers worldwide. That effort failed, but TEDs are still mandatory in all American waters.

With TEDs in place, Carol looked forward to studying living turtles instead of dead ones. She hoped her sixteen-hour days on the beach wallowing in mashed, maggot-ridden turtle carcasses were over. But deep down, she suspected that TEDs would not stop the slaughter.

Still, she made plans to study her other favorite reptile, the alligator, whose numbers were also crashing across the South. The island offered an ideal natural laboratory for studying them. And her blind buddy Ray enabled her to observe gator behavior up close. She was especially interested in how gators bromated, which involved burrowing in the mud and lowering their body temperatures. In this

torpid, slumberous state gators could go for months—even years—without eating.

But the dead turtles kept coming, even after TEDs were first required in 1989. Turtle stranding rates steadily increased over the next fifteen years. Thousands of sea turtle carcasses continued to litter the coast, and those represented just a fraction of the fatalities. Fewer than 5 percent of dead turtles actually washed ashore. Most carcasses sank or were eaten by sharks.

Despite mandatory TEDs, Carol necropsied more dead turtles than ever before. There was only one obvious conclusion: TEDs were not protecting turtles.

Carol was the first to publicly recognize the problem. Many shrimpers were still dodging the law and not installing TEDs properly—or at all. But the bigger failure was the TEDs themselves. Turtles caught in trawls often spent over an hour trapped in the nets before they were shunted out by TEDs. The panicked turtles, unable to surface for air, used up their oxygen thrashing, flailing, and trying to escape. They went into irreversible shock and either drowned or floated comatose until they eventually collided with the TED. The half-dead turtles were diverted out of the net, but by then it was usually too late.

TEDs were not saving sea turtles. The only solution, Carol realized, was an end to trawling. Trawlers were bulldozing the ocean and decimating marine life. Carol wrote letters, published papers, and gave anti-TED talks everywhere.

"Pirates like Blackbeard once sailed our coast. Today's pirates use massive trawls to plunder the ocean," she told audiences.

No one was all that interested. Even turtle-loving environmentalists preferred the happy, fairy-tale ending that they thought TEDs provided. They could have their turtles and their seafood, too. They stopped inviting Carol to their meetings and largely ignored her findings.

Eventually, though, government scientists begrudgingly acknowledged Carol's data.

"TEDs have not proven successful at reducing turtle mortality on Georgia beaches," admitted Brad Winn, head of the non-game division for Georgia's Department of Natural Resources.

"TEDs have not been as effective as we had hoped," conceded David Bernhart, a leading biologist at the National Marine Fisheries Service. They even recognized Carol's work in a landmark report on turtle mortality, which concluded: "We are compelled to singularly acknowledge the valuable contributions of Carol Ruckdeschel. Sea turtles have no greater ambassador."

In 2001, Carol invited one of the National Marine Fisheries Service's top officials to Cumberland. After examining the turtle collections in Carol's museum, they sat on the porch eating popcorn and drinking highballs.

"I was hoping TEDs would put me out of work," Carol said. "I'm busier than ever carving up carcasses."

"I can't argue with your data," said the official.

"Then close the waters to trawling."

"We can't rule out other causes for turtle mortality. Maybe shrimpers are cheating and not using TEDs properly. Maybe other fisheries are responsible, or collisions with boats, or disease."

"A marine reserve could answer all of those questions. Close a section of the coast to commercial fishing and see how it affects the number of dead turtles washing ashore."

"That's not an option."

"That's the only option," Carol said.

The official shifted uncomfortably in the hard wooden chair. "We haven't given TEDs enough time to work. It may take several generations before we see results."

"For over a decade, TEDs have proven to be a colossal failure," Carol bristled. "That's indisputable."

"They're keeping turtles out of the nets and off the decks. They're helping."

Carol's cheeks flushed with fury. "Can you point to a single example where TEDs have reduced turtle deaths? Name one place— just one—where TEDs have been effective."

There was a long silence. "We might be seeing some promising results from a test project in Costa Rica." The official tossed back his whiskey and looked out across Carol's yard, where dozens of turtle skulls macerated in five-gallon buckets.

"All right, Carol, I'll level with you," he said. "We don't have any evidence that TEDs have reduced turtle strandings."

"None?"

"None." The official leaned forward and whispered. "But turtles don't pay taxes or provide jobs. We gotta put the welfare of people ahead of turtles."

21

Sea turtles are the most endangered reptile in the world, and it's not just shrimpers to blame. Along the Southeastern coast, the largest loggerhead nesting site in the world, beaches were built up and brightly lit, and dunes were leveled for development. On Cumberland, feral hogs were almost as destructive as high-rise hotels. Over two thousand feral swine plagued Cumberland, and they feasted especially on the omelets buried in the dunes. Hundreds of endangered turtle nests were scavenged by hogs each season.

Pigs are smarter than dogs, as the fabled wolf knows too well. They can do a circus's worth of tricks, use mirrors, and play video games with their snouts. Hogs also live in long-term families that protect one another from predators. Their smarts and social bonds make them difficult to hunt or trap.

The National Park Service had made halfhearted attempts to remove hogs from the island through trapping yearly hunts, but their efforts failed miserably. Sows reach sexual maturity at six months and can farrow sixteen piglets a year. The park's annual hunt barely made a dent in the island's swelling population of swine.

So Carol launched her own hog eradication campaign. Every day, she followed tracks through the dunes to find a hog digging up a nest. She sighted her rifle, pulled the trigger, and watched the hog slump over. *One hog down. Two thousand to go*, she said to herself. Then she sliced open the hog, whose belly was loaded with dozens of turtle eggs.

But after a few years of hog hunting, she realized that her solo efforts were futile. The hogs bred and fed too fast for her to keep up. She needed the National Park Service's help to stop the turtle slaughter. Because sea turtles were an endangered species, the National Park Service and the state of Georgia were required to protect their nests from feral hogs. For nearly thirty years, Carol made a stink

about the hogs, but the National Park Service ignored her. Finally, she teamed up with a young attorney named Hal Wright, who quickly got the feds' attention by threatening a lawsuit.

In 2001, the National Park Service and Georgia's Department of Natural Resources agreed to hire hog hunters to patrol Cumberland beaches. During turtle nesting season, the hog hunters shot every hog that wandered onto the eighteen-mile stretch of beach. Hundreds of hogs still roamed the island's interior, but on the beach, the numbers of hog-raided nests dropped to nearly zero.

Another unexpected reprieve in the turtle holocaust arrived in 2005. The number of sea turtle carcasses washing ashore suddenly dropped dramatically. But it wasn't because of TEDs. Nor was it due to any of Carol's efforts. Ironically, it was caused by the collapse of commercial shrimping in the South. The demise of the industry has cost many shrimpers their livelihoods, but it has been saving sea turtles' lives and staving off their extinction.

Just offshore from Cumberland Island, Calvin Lang continued to trawl the waters, gathering lots of bycatch but few shrimp. All day long, he and his strikers sorted through a deck full of jellies and flopping fish for a few pounds of brown shrimp. The nets' harvests weren't nearly as bountiful as they used to be.

"It's cheaper to go to bed than to keep doing this," Calvin grumbled. He puttered back toward the dock after dark, slipping past other paint-chipped, barnacle-hulled shrimp boats bobbing idly along the river, tow arms folded up in prayer. Dozens of boats once trawled here. Now, *Lang's Pride* was the last.

The ebb tide flowed silently through the shadowed pilings as the strikers moored the boat for the night. A crescent moon cast the skipper's reflection onto the dark pilothouse window. Calvin Lang stared into the barren waters.

Shrimp harvests had crashed in the Atlantic after decades of overharvesting. Average hauls were down 50 percent, even with fewer boats trawling the waters. And with flattened ocean floors and far fewer sea turtles than ever before, many shrimpers caught more

jellyfish than shrimp. The explosion in jelly populations was leading some shrimpers to switch from shrimping to harvesting jellyfish, which commanded a high price in Asian markets.

Rising fuel prices had also walloped shrimpers. In a weeklong trip, *Lang's Pride* gulped about 1,500 gallons of diesel, which required catching 1,250 pounds of shrimp just to cover fuel, to say nothing of the TED-equipped nets and other equipment. Throw in 10 percent of the take for each striker, and it's easy to see why the boat owner sweats as much as the crew.

But the biggest blow to shrimpers had come from shrimp aquaculture, which didn't require boats or fuel. Shrimp ponds had undercut prices, especially the overseas shrimp farms, whose cheap labor and lack of government regulations enabled them to sell their shrimp at lower prices. Today, 90 percent of all shrimp consumed in the United States is imported, mostly from foreign shrimp ponds.

Shrimp farms don't snare sea turtles, but they are equally devastating to the health of the ocean. Shrimp aquaculture destroys saltwater marshes, wetlands, and mangroves—nurseries for wild shrimp and fish. The antibiotics and pesticides used by shrimp farmers poison the water, and pollution from shrimp farms devastates marine life, creating vast dead zones along the coast.

By 2010, most shrimpers in Georgia had pulled in their nets and sold their boats. Many went bankrupt. Shrimping boomtowns like Darien were quiet. Warehouses were shuttered, and piers rotted.

After sixty years of shrimping, Calvin Lang sold all but one of his seven trawlers. Fortunately, he hadn't put all of his shrimp in one net. Years before the big crash, he bought a two-story former brothel along the St. Marys harbor from Wild Bill Carnegie, who had been banished from Cumberland years ago by his mother, Lucy. Calvin renovated the building and opened a family-run seafood restaurant and marina.

He also became the National Park Service's exclusive concessionaire to ferry passengers to Cumberland Island. Twice a day, Calvin Lang's *Cumberland Queen II* shuttles visitors back and forth. He

and his sons pilot the ferry boat from the St. Marys dock, through the wind-dimpled marshes lining the river, past the paper mills and submarine base, and across the sound to Cumberland's docks. In between ferry trips, Calvin has spent many afternoons on Cumberland collecting shark's teeth and seashells.

"Being on Cumberland is like a religious experience," Calvin says. "It's a very strong feeling, like you're in the presence of God."

In a strange twist of fate, the shrimper king and turtle queen became accidental allies in saving Cumberland Island. Calvin had inadvertently played a crucial role in Carol's wilderness campaign. The three-hundred-person daily visitor limit to the island that Carol helped achieve was largely due to the carrying capacity of Calvin's ferry. In the end, it wasn't just Carol who saved wild Cumberland, but also the size of Calvin's boat.

The island had been preserved, but its sea turtles were still being slaughtered. Though the local shrimping industry was declining, international super-trawlers—some with nets large enough to hold thirteen jumbo jets—continued to plow the seafloor just a stone's throw from Cumberland. Turtles were vacuumed up in the giant nets. And it was completely legal. The National Marine Fisheries Service continues to issue special permits allowing trawlers to legally kill ten thousand endangered sea turtles each year and injure more than 344,000 others.

Beyond U.S. borders, turtles face more troubles. Turtle eggs are poached by gangs throughout Latin America, and dozens of turtle activists have been kidnapped or killed trying to protect nesting beaches. In coastal communities worldwide, sea turtles are still routinely hunted and eaten. Outside of American waters, shrimp trawlers drag the open ocean without TEDs or regard for turtles that end up in their nets.

Carol stopped eating shrimp, except the ones she caught off the dock with her handheld cast net, which did not threaten turtles. "When the buying stops, so will the killing," she said.

Carol squarely faced a hard truth of twenty-first-century environmentalism: there was nothing pristine left on the planet. Climate change and industrial pollution were global game changers. Already on Cumberland, sea levels were rising and freshwater lakes were drying up amid prolonged drought. Invasive species were migrating to the island while native species were disappearing. No wilderness—on land or at sea—was untouched by us.

However, that didn't mean we should tinker even more with the natural world, Carol believed. Give nature enough wild space so that animals and plants can adapt to changing conditions, and it can manage itself far better than we ever can.

"To save people, we must save nature," Carol maintained. Like fish without water, we won't survive long without the ecosystems that sustain us. But most folks are blind to this bare truth, she said. As a result, they see conservation as a minor amenity benefitting a small cadre of birdwatchers and backpackers rather than the best way to save humanity.

On Cumberland, Carol had achieved as much as she could hope for: a relatively undeveloped island, a federally protected wilderness, a global biosphere reserve, and a hog-free seashore. She had single-handedly launched a national turtle stranding network and had sounded the alarm on trawling and TEDs. She had amassed one of the country's largest collections of sea turtles in her hand-built museum. From her four thousand necropsies, she had gathered the most complete, continuous, and comprehensive data on what was killing the world's most ancient and endangered reptiles.

Just beyond the island's boundaries, however, new threats emerged. South of the island, a one-thousand-acre marsh was about to be buried beneath a gated community with million-dollar waterfront lots and an eight-hundred-boat marina. To the west, a private spacecraft pad was being built to launch rockets over the island year-round. Four Superfund sites on the adjacent mainland leaked radioactive waste into Cumberland's waterways.

"We're fouling our nest," Carol said.

And directly across from Cumberland, the U.S. Navy had built the world's largest nuclear submarine base. The sixteen-thousand-acre facility was nearly as immense as Cumberland Island. Eighteen submarines armed with Trident nuclear warheads docked there. They produced toxic nuclear waste and discharged radioactive water into the ocean. Bill Mankin, who had helped lobby for Cumberland's wilderness, called Kings Bay Nuclear Submarine Base "the greatest threat to the future of the Southern coast."

The nuclear sub base—one of only two in the country—created a gushing money pipeline from D.C. to south Georgia. It brought thousands of new jobs, boosted the local economy by a hefty $560 million each year, and ignited a development boom. Grover Henderson was one of the most prosperous locals who capitalized on the real estate rush that resulted from Kings Bay.

But it was hardly the wisest geographical location for a submarine base. Kings Bay is nestled in the Georgia Bight, an indented stretch of concave coast where the shallow continental shelf extends for sixty miles. Every six months, the navy must dredge out an eleven-mile, sediment-filled channel in order for the mammoth, missile-heavy submarines to reach Kings Bay.

The submarine base is also located directly in the path of the world's only known right whale calving grounds. Only eighty female right whales remain worldwide, and they all return to Cumberland Island's offshore waters to give birth each winter. Carol watched helplessly from shore one afternoon when a right whale was struck by a forty-foot boat. It thrashed the water with its wounded tail, bleeding into the ocean from a long gash inflicted by the boat's propeller.

She feared even more collisions in the future. In 2008, Kings Bay announced plans to construct a five-hundred-square-mile Undersea Warfare Training Center offshore from Cumberland Island, in the heart of right whale calving habitat. More ship strikes, entanglements, and whale casualties are expected. The world's most endangered whales will be dodging torpedoes, missiles, and sonar-pulsing subs as they give birth.

Sound is the most important sense for marine mammals. Whales, dolphins, and manatees use their voices to navigate, hunt, find mates, and sing to their calves. Sea turtles rely on underwater sound, too, transmitting low-frequency vibrations to communicate with each other.

The navy blasts nonstop sonar pulses at more than 235 decibels—louder than dynamite explosions—that travel across hundreds of miles of ocean, drowning out the songs and calls of these animals.

The navy admits that the sonar testing kills 6,000 whales and dolphins and thousands of other marine animals each year. Already, the navy's use of deafening sonar pulses in its submarines has been linked to several mass whale strandings. Cumberland Island has the most whale, dolphin, and turtle strandings of any island along the Southern coast.

Carol had hoped to live an untainted, self-reliant life on a wild island, away from the noise and pollution, apart from the mainland. But no woman is an island. The submarine base on the horizon reminded her every day that she couldn't escape the world beyond her island borders.

To save Cumberland, she would have to venture beyond the tide line. So, instead of an underwater navy battleground, Carol proposed a five-hundred-square-mile underwater wilderness.

Offshore, there is another United States larger than the one above sea level, extending two hundred miles from the coast. This continental shelf is a mostly undiscovered treasure of coral reefs, kelp forests, and sea grass meadows, with chasms deeper than the Grand Canyon and mountains taller and richer than the Appalachians. Turtles spend most of their adult lives foraging along the continental shelf. Almost all of it is open to trawling, mining, fishing, dredging, drilling, and dumping.

Carol hoped to create water wilderness areas along the continental shelf that were off-limits to trawling and commercial fishing, especially where turtles feed and breed. The United States has already established a patchwork of semi-protected areas, but nearly all of these so-called sanctuaries—including Gray's Reef, a

vast complex of underwater sandstone caves and outcroppings just forty miles north of Cumberland—still allow commercial fishing, and many even allow bottom trawling. "They're nothing but paper parks," said Carol.

Marine reserves are more protective—and more rare. They are true underwater wilderness areas. Less than a fraction of 1 percent of the world's oceans are currently protected as no-trawl marine reserves. But the tide seems to be turning. In the past decade, over a dozen countries have established no-trawl zones, protecting some 2.5 million acres of underwater habitat for sea turtles and other endangered marine species.

"Habitat is their only hope," Carol said.

After the 2010 oil spill in the Gulf of Mexico, tar-black sea turtles drowned in oil-coated waters, and hatchlings flapped across poisoned beaches. Thousands more turtles were torched alive as BP burned off the oil. Now, oil companies are eyeing the Atlantic and the offshore waters of Georgia for new drilling platforms. Their seismic underwater oil explorations fire air guns every ten seconds, nonstop, that are even louder and more deadly than the navy's whale-deafening sonar.

Meanwhile, Carol has turned up the volume on her call for a marine reserve along the Southeastern coast of the United States, home to the world's largest population of loggerhead sea turtles and their most prized nesting habitat, along with the nursery of the most endangered species of whales.

Many locals, including Grover Henderson, scoffed at Carol's idea of prioritizing sea life over submarines.

"Those subs are keeping this country safe. Are you willing to die for a bunch of whales and turtles?"

"Our security depends more on the health of the wild ocean than a bunch of blowhards playing underwater war games," Carol said.

"You oughta be shot for treason," he replied.

"We gotta look beyond our borders at the whole web."

Like wilderness boundaries on land, marine reserves are just dotted lines on a map. But at least they can buy time for whales,

dolphins, and other marine life to replenish their numbers. They can offer a trawl-free haven for turtles amid deeply troubled waters. And they can help us, too, Carol believed. Marine reserves can help restore fisheries and stabilize the ocean's health, which sustains our own.

"Our planet—and our bodies—are mostly ocean," Carol often observed. "Our blood has the same salinity and pH as seawater. Our fate is bound to the tides."

part five

beneath the shell

22

Most of us have opinions and principles that we argue and vote for, but we still live our everyday lives like everyone else: buying food at the grocery store, watching televison, driving to work for corporate America. Carol is different. She lives her convictions every day, without compromise.

She doesn't want much. She lives frugally and feeds herself from the island. She is straightforward and direct, and she doesn't play games—she says exactly what she thinks. It doesn't take a lot to make her happy: sunrise, silence, a sky full of stars.

She sums up the solution to all of the island's problems in three words: leave it alone. Let nature do the work, she says. Managing wildlife inevitably fails. Manipulating ecosystems invariably backfires. Vehicle tours are no substitute for a walk in the woods.

Her solution to the world's problems is also clear and straightforward: fewer people, more wilderness. People are still part of nature, but we have gobbled up too much of it. None of our little feel-good actions will save us unless we can share the planet with other species. Our only hope is working with Mother Nature rather than crowding her out.

Carol sees the world in black and white, but her own life is a gauzy gray. She isn't always as simple as she seems. She is too kaleidoscopic to fit neatly into categories, too paradoxical to be pegged by stereotypes. She will rescue an injured coon but will shoot a healthy one sneaking into her yard. She saves animals but doesn't think we should be saving humans who overbreed or overconsume.

She's not afraid of snakes or alligators, but driving in traffic makes her nervous. She is a bold, iconoclastic female, yet she has cooked and cleaned for every one of her men. She is fearlessly candid one on one, yet surprisingly shy in front of groups.

She wants the horses off the island, but she rides them, feeds them, and looks after them more than anyone, including the

National Park Service. She thinks hogs should be removed, too, but she relies on pork for most of her food and even has a pet pig named Priscilla. She fights for untrammeled wilderness yet lives and drives within it.

Publicly, she is strictly scientific. Privately, she is deeply soulful. Her arguments are grounded in logic and law, but her actions are guided by emotion, especially compassion. She doesn't hold out much hope for change, yet she has spent her whole life fighting for it.

Carol says she isn't lonely, but sometimes she is.

She says that people don't hurt her, but sometimes they do.

In 2009, turtles lost their voice. Soon after Carol uncovered the illegal construction in the park, the National Park Service revoked her permits and officially ended Carol's turtle research. After four decades of compiling the most comprehensive sea turtle stranding data in the world, Carol had been abruptly cut off. The new superintendent, Fred Boyles, claimed that her research permits were not renewed because Carol had been listening to confidential conversations on her park-issued radio. "She needed to learn that her actions have consequences," he said.

Her sea turtle research suddenly came to a screeching halt. Dead sea turtles rotted on the beach again. Carol buried her sorrow.

"More food for the vultures," she shrugged, her eyes wet.

Carol continued to follow vultures, as she had since childhood. They led her to other carcasses and kills. They helped her clean the flesh from bones. Carol whistled to them and called them by name.

Then Carol turned sixty-five and, suddenly, the vultures shadowed her. Feisty and fearless as ever, Carol was the only senior citizen in America wading in gator holes, tracking bobcats through midnight swamps, and climbing trees to check bald eagle nests. But age was catching up to the other people in her life.

Carol's mom was diagnosed with Alzheimer's. Helplessly, Carol watched her painful decline. She traveled back to Atlanta every weekend to be with her. In a sudden moment of clarity a few weeks before

her death, her mom looked Carol straight in the eye and asked, "What's happening to me?"

Carol wished she could end her mother's misery. "At least we take care of animals. We put them down when they're in pain or fading," she said to her father one afternoon.

"I'll kill myself before I ever get that sick," Earl vowed. "I plan on shooting myself as soon as I start going downhill."

"That's fine if you want to do that," Carol said. "But don't you dare leave without giving me a chance to say goodbye."

Anne died quietly in her sleep later that year. Earl fell apart after his wife's death. He stopped eating and leaving the house. For the next year, Carol spent more time in Atlanta than on Cumberland. She sat beside her father on the musty living room couch, listening to the wall clock ticking. She flipped through scrapbooks with him, hoping the old photographs—taken by cameras and film he had developed while working for Kodak—would pry open his shuttered heart. She confessed to skipping Sunday School to feed the feral cats in Rochester, and she reminisced about family swims and volcano hikes in Hawaii. Earl remained despondent.

While in Atlanta, Carol took a few trips to check on the Pigeon Mountain salamander she had discovered decades earlier. Many of the hollers where her salamander once thrived were being filled with vacation homes. Mamie, the mountain woman who had taught her backwoods skills, had moved to a housing project next to a four-lane highway. When Carol stopped by to visit, the first thing she noticed was Mamie's unnatural smile. "She had fake teeth that didn't fit right, so there was no way to feel that good gut-feeling warmth that comes from the smile of an old friend," Carol recalled. Mamie wore city clothes instead of dirty dresses with sweaty aprons. Her food came from the grocery store. "She seemed happy, but that wonderful essence, that strong driving spirit, that fierce independence which I so admired in her, is subdued. Gone are the woodstove ashes, the mounds of cathead biscuits, the rows of vegetables in mason jars. Mother is no longer personified in Mamie."

One afternoon, sick of sitting in the stale house, Carol drove her dad down to the Chattahoochee River. Her dad sat quietly on the bank while she rolled up her jeans and walked out shin-deep into the shoals.

Water rolled over rock. The cascades drowned out the noise of the interstate bridge a mile downstream. Earl took off his shoes and dipped his toes in the river. Carol sat next to him, skipping stones across the water.

"I thought I would be relieved when she was gone," Earl said. "I was wrong."

"I miss her, too," Carol said.

"I loved her so much," said Earl.

Carol looked out across the river. "Why didn't you tell her that when she was alive?"

Carol's father died soon after her mother's passing. He didn't end up shooting himself. He fought to the very end. He was eventually hospitalized for heart complications and kidney failure. A few days before he died, he held Carol's hand.

"I'm so proud of you," he whispered.

They were words she had waited a lifetime to hear.

Death was part of Carol's daily life. She faced it up close: swarming flies, rotten flesh, maggots crawling up her arm. She saw death as it was: not dressed up by a mortician, but rank, raw, and real.

Though death was necessary and natural, Carol wanted to minimize it. She avoided needless killing. She saved life wherever she could, rescuing wounded animals, relocating snakes, and even liberating moths from bug traps.

"There is nothing moral or altruistic about what I do," Carol wrote in her journal. "We all share the same flesh."

Death brought out the best in us, Carol believed. In the face of death, we discover what really matters. For Carol, daily contact with death provided perspective on her everyday life that was refreshingly candid and clear. Death's hot wind stripped away the veneer

and exposed deeper truth. Death didn't numb her to death. Just the opposite: it intensified her life.

Back on the mainland, death was pushed to the shoulder of the road or hidden in coffins. But on Cumberland, life and death bled out in the open, knitted together, stitched into the same fleshy fabric. Life didn't stop. It only changed form, like a windblown wave melting into the sea.

There were worse things than death, Carol believed. Suffering scared her more than dying. She had seen too many injured animals still clinging to life—writhing, gasping, bleeding the sand red.

Once, Carol had come upon a pilot whale stranded alive on the beach. It had already furrowed itself into a depression in the sand, where it was jerking and convulsing. The low tide was far from shore. She wrapped chains around its tail and tried to pull it with her jeep, but it wouldn't budge.

The whale's huge flopping anguish was unbearable. There was nothing she could do to save it. So she unsheathed her knife and sliced the whale's throat, working as quickly as possible to end its suffering. The whale thrashed as the knife went in. Once she gouged a hole, she shoved first her fist and then her arm into the whale, found its heart, and ripped it out. She watched the fire fade from its ink-black eyes. Pain—and life—left the whale. She knelt down in the sand beside the dead whale, its heart still twitching in her bloody hands, and whispered goodbye.

Dealing with death on a daily basis had made her unafraid of it. But she never got used to it. Her stomach still dropped every time a carcass washed ashore. She wept for days when Gator, her pet otter, was bitten by a rattlesnake and died in her arms. But then she dried her tears, steeled herself, and dissected the dead otter. She removed the otter's skull for the museum and tossed the carcass to the vultures.

Life ate itself. She faced this naked truth inside every dead turtle. Death fed life's insatiable appetite. We were all brief survivors of flesh, nibbled and pecked, eaten alive, devoured even as we dined. Not even the wealthiest could escape it. The rich died as plainly as

the poor, and, like every creature that has ever lived, they all decayed into the same earth.

Just before her father died, Carol and Bob stumbled upon a secret island deep in the tidal creeks near Hush Your Mouth. It was blanketed with large birds, especially pelicans, egrets, herons, ibises, and endangered wood storks. Their nests covered nearly every square inch of open ground. The stench of guano was overpowered only by the deafening shrieks of dive-bombing birds. Carol and Bob marveled at the fecundity of life crammed onto the tiny island.

"This is what the world must have looked like before we arrived," Bob said. "We have no idea what we're missing."

"A good mechanic doesn't throw away any parts," Carol said. "When I used to disassemble my dad's watches, he always asked: 'Did you save all the pieces? Do you know how to put that back together again? Can you make it work?'"

She gingerly tiptoed between nests counting birds and eggs.

"But my dad was no tree hugger," she continued. "He also used to ask me, 'Do we really need millions of species? Humans only use a few of them. Give me a few deer to shoot at and some trout to fish for. Everything else needs to get the hell out of the way.'"

It was a fair question, Carol acknowledged, and one that she had been asked often: do we really need so much nature? Can't we get by with fewer cockroaches? Surely some of the world's ten million species are superfluous. We can probably stand to lose a few of the twenty-seven hundred species of mosquitoes, forty thousand species of spiders, or three hundred thousand different kinds of beetles.

There's just one problem, Carol pointed out. We don't know which ones we need. Species are like the rivets holding together an airplane, she said. If a few pop out, the plane might rattle a bit, but it can keep flying. Lose a few more, and the plane goes down—along with all of its passengers.

Earth has already seen five big rivet-popping crashes, including the mass extinction around 250 million years ago that wiped out 95 percent of species on earth. The 5 percent of species that survived

may have seemed superfluous until they saved life itself from going extinct.

Life's diversity was the key to surviving these mass extinctions. Mother Nature was not just showing off with her jeweled squid, flamingo tongue snails, and glowing octopus. She was creating as many possibilities of life as possible, hoping that a few strange forms survive. We're alive today only because a handful of rare species hung on in the dark times. Diversity kept life going.

Diversity keeps life going today. It produces the oxygen we breathe, pollinates the food we eat, nourishes the soil for our crops, recycles nutrients, and filters our air and water. More species diversity means fewer disease outbreaks and pandemics.

Biodiversity is also our best medicine. Half of all pharmaceuticals come from plants, animals, and fungi, including aspirin and penicillin. It's our best investment, too. Economists calculate the total value of ecosystem services—such as water purification, soil building, and pollination of food crops—at over $33 trillion each year, twice as large as the entire world's economy. Nature does it all free of charge.

Life is a diversified portfolio, but we are drawing down our capital and stealing from the future. Our economy is consuming its planetary host. The end result is inevitable: bankruptcy. We're causing a sixth mass extinction. Frogs and salamanders are dying from a deadly fungus. So are bats. Bees—which pollinate one-third of the food we eat—are mysteriously disappearing. Sea turtle, whale, and dolphin populations are crashing. Even the seemingly ubiquitous songbirds are in serious trouble. Half of all species alive today will be gone by the end of the century.

"We're hogging the planet," Carol wrote in her journal. "We're reducing life's diversity to a single species and the handful of livestock and crops we've domesticated. There's only so much protoplasm our planet can support." There isn't room or resources for one hundred million species and seven billion people. It's either more of us or fewer of them.

On their way back from the bird haven, Carol drove past a dead armadillo on Cumberland's sandy main road. Carol thought about

stopping to pick it up, but Bob had a head-splitting migraine and wanted to get home.

The next morning, they ate a breakfast of marsh rabbit chili and lemon-drizzled watercress while watching the vultures drying their wings atop the museum roof like statued gargoyles. One glided down to peck a hunk of rabbit meat from Carol's palm. She admired his cinder body, ashen face, and long, curved bill.

"Vultures get such a bad rap," Carol said. "They are such beautiful, life-affirming birds."

The vulture glided over to the chicken yard to pick at table scraps that Carol had scattered for them, but one of Carol's hens pecked at him and chased him away.

"That hen—she's a C-C-Cumberland Island woman," Bob said.

"You haven't even had a drink yet, and you're already slurring your words," Carol said.

Bob stood to get another helping of chili. Woozily, he stumbled against the wall, dropping his plate and silverware. Then everything went black, and he collapsed to the porch.

Carol used his cell phone to call for help. He was transported to a Jacksonville hospital, where surgeons showed Carol the CT scans: over half of his brain was dark. A blood vessel had burst in his brain.

Carol sat beside his bed in the windowless hospital room and held his cold hand. For twenty-five years, he had stuck by her. She didn't realize how much she leaned on him until suddenly he was yanked away.

"Stay with me," she whispered.

Later that morning, the hemorrhage swelled, swallowing the rest of his brain. Bob died the next day.

A memorial was held at Plum Orchard. Carol went through the motions. There was nothing new to be said. All the old truisms and condolences were repeated, as they had to be. The first twinges of feeling didn't come until everyone left, and the sun sank into the marsh, and the frogs began to sing.

* * *

Carol returned home alone. Grief washed over her like the tides. In the span of less than two years, she had lost everyone who mattered—first her parents and now Bob.

Driving back to her cabin, Carol passed the same dead armadillo in the road from a few days earlier. A bed of leaves now surrounded the carcass. Puzzled, Carol pulled over for a closer look. The armadillo was wreathed by laurel leaves. *How did those get there?* she wondered. The carcass was in the middle of a pine forest, but the nearest laurel trees were a half-mile away.

She looked closer. Within the wreath, twigs were neatly arranged in a pattern around the dead armadillo. Then she heard a rustle. Hiding in the palmetto, a female armadillo watched through the fronds. She had been tending to her mate in something resembling a burial ritual.

Carol hunkered down behind a tree and observed. Eventually, the armadillo crept over to her partner, twigs and foliage in her mouth, and continued cloaking him in a leafy shroud. Was this armadillo mourning like her? Carol was awestruck. The armadillo ceremony opened a hairline crack in Carol's hardboiled relationship to the universe.

Her heart ached every evening at five o'clock, when the porch was empty, Bob's glass unfilled. Carol kept her wedding ring on a necklace and fingered it whenever she felt her sorrow swell.

Though the rest of her body felt benumbed, her heart continued to hurt, like a dull knife in her chest. Then she caught a cold that she couldn't shake and grew increasingly listless and lethargic. Her breathing became shallow and raspy. She moved glacially through her days.

After several months, she suspected something was seriously wrong. She was frail and bony, barely able to eat or drink. Finally, at age sixty-nine, for the first time since her dad had shot her, Carol went to the hospital as a patient. Doctors immediately rushed her into open heart surgery. One of her heart valves had become dangerously infected.

On her way to the operating room, Carol felt death slide over her. It hovered in the air, the way flocks of seagulls floated above a

boat adrift at sea. Death was unexplored terrain of the far shore, at once frightening and fascinating, and she let herself go there. She had nothing left to live for. The people she loved most had left her. The people on the island hated her. She was never good at relationships, but she loved more intensely than she let on—and hurt more deeply than anyone knew.

Now she was tired. Tired of bearing it away. Tired of fighting. For what? Nobody was willing to change. Nobody really cared about wilderness or sea turtles or anything except themselves. Nobody really cared about her, either.

Being tired made it easier to let go. Death descended closer, like a suffocatingly hot blanket. She wasn't afraid of death, but she hoped it would go quickly.

Her chest felt heavy. It was hard to breathe. She distracted herself with highlight reels of happy memories, and she kept looping back to one scene: her porch at sunset, Bob in the rocking chair beside her, hands laced behind his head, his floppy lips stretching into a wide, warm smile as he said softly: "Ain't life the greatest."

Amen, she uttered aloud.

Life was messy and mean, she realized, but mostly it was amazing. She still relished its faint hum, even as her heart sputtered to a stop. She loved being a part of it. And she wasn't ready to leave it after all. She wanted to stay. Every extra second was even more precious and made her want to stay even harder.

She didn't care about the meaning of life, but rather the experience of it—the sublime pleasure of a storm rolling in, the raw, jagged feeling of cutting into a carcass, the simple wonder of a crackling fire. There was no sentimentality to it—only an urgency to live.

She kicked and thrashed against the blanket. There was so much still to do. She still had some fight left in her. She clung to life, fierce as a barnacle.

The operating doors swung open. Down came the anesthesia mask. Carol wondered if the fluorescent bulbs overhead would be the last light she saw.

Her heart went silent. She was connected to a machine that pumped blood for her. Surgeons cut through her breastbone to reach

her damaged heart—just as she had dissevered thousands of turtle shells to examine their chest cavities.

Once they opened her heart, the surgeons removed the rotted valve and sewed a stainless steel one into place. After five hours, the surgeons closed up the foot-long incision in her chest. Carol would have loved to watch—to see how she was put together inside, to understand her inner workings, to examine the hole in her heart.

She survived the surgery, but surgeons worried about her recovery. The infection could have spread to other parts of her heart. Doctors kept her on life support.

Carol awoke one afternoon in a gray hospital room, breathing tube down her throat, feeding tube in her nose, machines controlling her breathing. The warm blanket had lifted. Her blurry vision came into focus.

I sat in the wooden chair beside her bed and pretended to be upbeat. She was a ragged skeleton with bulging eyes and limp skin hanging from her bones. Her hair was thin and frayed. Never had she seemed so vulnerable.

Rain strummed the window. Not knowing what to say, I just sat there, holding her bony, rope-veined hand. It was callused and coarse. Her hands had eviscerated turtles and stitched torn flesh, caressed lovers and wiped away tears. They were a map of her life.

We listened to the steady patter of the rain for a few more minutes.

"You can't die on me," I said finally. "This will make a shitty ending to the book."

Carol's cracked lips curved into a faint smile.

Unable to speak, Carol feebly lifted a finger. Wired to a buzzing, beeping life support system, she pointed out the window to the breathing trees, the pulsing wind, the wet sky.

23

One week after open heart surgery, Carol returned home to Cumberland Island. She ritually splashed the back of her neck with saltwater. Then she walked barefoot along the wide shore, the sun-warmed sand between her toes. Ahead, a flock of terns lifted as one cloud of wings, like white flames burning the sky. *What was the signal?* she wondered. How did they know when to rise together like mist from the beach?

Beside the sea, Carol felt stirrings of the heartbroken girl she once was, arriving on Cumberland's dark beach for the first time, carving her name in the wet sand. Now she had come home again, and once more her battered heart needed to heal.

She closed her eyes as she walked. With her eyes shut, her other senses were magnified: she tasted the salty breeze, felt the pings of windblown sand, and listened to the murmur of the tides growing louder with each step. She didn't open her eyes until her feet touched water.

An hour later, Gogo's husband, David, drove down the beach. He saw Carol and his jaw dropped to the dashboard. He slammed his brakes and skidded beside her.

"You're back?" he asked.

"Apparently so."

"I thought you—you're living here?"

"Got nowhere else to go."

"I mean, in your condition, I figured you might—is it wise? For how long—"

"For good."

He stared blankly at the steering wheel. They hadn't gotten rid of her. He shook his head, gunned his engine, and drove off.

Carol missed Gogo, but she had let go of the hurt. Now, instead of a hard knot, there was just a frayed end to a friendship.

* * *

Near Long Point, Carol came upon a dead sea turtle. She whistled, and soon a pair of vultures circled overhead. One alighted on the turtle carcass and watched her with unblinking eyes.

Carol had once been invincible. Now she felt the weight of her own mortality. Death's hot breath had brushed her cheek. Like everything else, she came with an expiration date. She still had fire in her blood. But soon enough, she would feed the vultures.

Carol loved life more than herself. Like gravity, she was drawn to it. She couldn't get enough of it, and she still was astonished by it every day. She hoped that it would never end, but she knew that it had to. She secretly longed for the eternal but was blood-bound to the earth.

Carol had lived close to the bone, engrossed in dead things. She went where no one else dared. She wallowed in the rank and rancid, picking fetid flesh from beneath her fingernails. She reveled in the raveling rot. She studied death to better understand life, and in the end, what she had learned was this: the greater the knowledge, the deeper the mystery.

She once had said that her religion was truth. And what was true? Death was true, and it was nothing to be afraid of. Her only fear was not fully living.

Carol was an unsentimental biologist who grounded herself in the messy sludge of reality. All she needed to get to heaven was a good pair of boots, she often said. She resisted mixing spirituality with science. But recently, she had felt the presence of something larger in her life and work.

"I don't fool myself into any talk about an afterlife or immortality," she wrote in her journal. "But when I am waist-deep in a gator hole or elbow-deep in turtle guts, all I can say is: I feel a deep, visceral connection to the Source." It couldn't be talked about, prayed to, hoped for, understood, or even sought. In rare moments, it revealed itself—in the shadows of an old-growth forest, the morning fog ghosting over the ocean, and the flickering light in the eye of a whale. It was ordinary as sunlight—and as luminous.

The armadillo funeral pointed toward something deeper, too. There was a current flowing through all of life, an undertow of awe

that swept her away. She felt it on a bareback turtle ride into the depths and in quiet moments on the dock, throwing a cast net like Jesse had taught her.

She felt it again nights later, alone on the dark beach, a dripping wet lemon moon rising over the water behind a scrim of cloud. She held her hand over her scarred, steeled heart and felt it ticking.

"Well, here I am," she said aloud. It was all she knew for certain. And it was enough.

The tide was like a metronome marking the now. In the glassy moon-glow of the sea, she beheld a reflection of herself, oscillating like the ocean between ferociousness and tenderness. Human nature was not hopelessly selfish, as she once thought. The ocean had violent tempests and dark depths. And yet the ocean could be gentle and lucent, too. So could she. Carol had killed a man and saved an island. She was oceanic: brutal and benevolent, savage and sympathetic, cutthroat and compassionate. Both were part of the ebb and flow of the human heart.

The most meaningful men in her life were long gone. Jim Kemph died of a heart attack years ago. Charlie Wharton passed away in his mountain cabin in 2003. John Pennington died of colon cancer in 1980, only a few years after leaving Cumberland, and Jimmy Carter had visited his hospital room to say goodbye. Now her dad was dead, and Bob was gone, too.

She and Bob had often locked horns, but the old bastard was right about one thing: nobody goes it alone, not even a self-sufficient naturalist living in the wilderness. She cut her own firewood and gathered her own food, but that didn't make her any less dependent on the world around her. She had always relied on a community of animals and plants—and people. Her mom changed her diapers. Her dad taught her how to hunt. Jesse taught her how to live. Bob taught her how to love.

Love. It was a word she never heard from her family and only rarely from the men in her life. But it was love that had helped her crawl out from her hiding place. Love reconnected her to life.

She had wrung every drop out of life. Each day she immersed herself in its natural wonders. But there was one wonder that had

passed her by: she had missed her chance to have kids. It was one of her biggest regrets and deepest sorrows.

Instead of children, Carol had devoted her life to parenting the island and protecting its wildlife. Yet by her reckoning, she had failed there, too. Species were disappearing faster than ever. The island wilderness was fragmented and its future uncertain. The wood storks beside Lake Whitney were gone. The island's freshwater was drying up, and its ponds were shrinking. There were only a few big gators left. She hadn't saved the sea turtles, either. All five island species were still endangered, and carcasses continued to wash ashore.

Then Carol saw a wet-backed glimmer in the moonlit surf. A sea turtle was crawling out of the water. The turtle pressed her beak into the sand and tasted home.

The turtle climbed into the dunes, dug a nest, and buried her hundred embryos. Salty tears trickled from her eyes.

Before heading back to sea, the turtle stopped to look at Carol. A breath of wind stirred the sand between them.

Carol couldn't prove it, but she knew: one of the hatchlings that she had rescued thirty years ago had come home to nest. She didn't measure the turtle or count the eggs this time. She just watched her crawl back to the ocean.

Then, in a moment of scientific weakness, Carol etched a word in the wet sand below the nest. Using the back of her heel, she wrote: THANKS.

Her turtle heart was still beating. She stood beside the sea, her bare feet sinking into the sand, whispering to no one in particular: Thank you. Thank you. Thank you.

epilogue
stubborn sand

Genetic tests confirmed that at least two additional hatchlings born on Cumberland Island during Carol's tenure have returned home to nest.

Ray, the blind alligator living in the wilderness, has grown to fourteen feet, thanks to plentiful meals of feral hog.

The Carnegies at Greyfield Inn continue to run commercial tours to Plum Orchard mansion and the First African Baptist Church. So does the National Park Service.

Over 53,000 sea turtles drowned in shrimp nets last year in the United States. In 2014, conservation groups filed a lawsuit against the National Marine Fisheries Service for allowing the shrimp industry to continue to kill tens of thousands of endangered species each year.

In 2014, the feds designated 739 miles of beach—nearly the entire Southeastern coastline—as critical habitat for sea turtles. Their offshore waters remain unprotected.

The navy will open its underwater warfare range in 2014. In 2013, a judge ruled against twelve conservation organizations seeking to halt construction.

At age seventy-two, Carol continues to study sea turtles, wade into gator holes, and fight for wilderness on land and in the ocean.

author's note

In writing this book, I conducted numerous interviews, attended countless island gatherings, and undertook extensive research for nineteen years.

Carol Ruckdeschel endured hundreds of hours of interviews and tolerated a tagalong for nearly two decades. She also provided unfettered access to decades of field notes, journals, photographs, publications, and correspondence.

I also spent a lot of time with Bob Shoop, both in the field searching for critters and on the porch drinking White Peggies. He is deeply missed.

I am indebted to the Carnegie, Rockefeller, and Candler families for sharing their stories. I listened to audio recordings that Lucy Ferguson made a few years before her death, and I interviewed dozens of island residents and Carnegie heirs; some asked to remain anonymous.

I interviewed U.S. Congressman Jack Kingston in his D.C. office, and I consulted National Park Service regional directors and staffers at the Atlanta headquarters. I met with several park superintendents in St. Marys, including Art Frederick, Jerre Brumbelow, Denis Davis, and Fred Boyles. Many park rangers also contributed on-the-ground experiences and anecdotes, especially Charlotte Fries, Renee Noe, Pauline Saville, Newton Sikes, Don Starkey, and Zack Kirkland.

Betty McKee bravely recounted a painful chapter of her life. Patti Hagan also powerfully recapitulated her experiences with Louie McKee.

Atlanta Journal-Constitution reporters Charlie Seabrook and Robert Coram—and *Florida Times-Union* reporter Gordon Jackson —were invaluable sources of island insight. Dr. Steven Hochman helped immensely with the Jimmy Carter material. Mark Dodd and

Brad Winn at the Georgia Department of Natural Resources were also treasure troves of knowledge and experience, and so were renowned sea turtle experts Dr. Jim Richardson, Dr. Jeanette Wyneken, Dr. Terry Norton, Dr. Jeff Seminoff, and Brian Shamblin. I tagged along with several Cumberland Island turtle technicians on daily beach patrols, and their firsthand observations from the field were essential.

Calvin Lang, Dr. Lisa Ligouri, the Boone family, Clint Guidry, and John Wallace generously offered generations of shrimping wisdom and experience.

Hans Neuhauser, Bill Mankin, and Hal Wright patiently persevered through many interviews untangling the island's political history.

Lum Pennington offered candid and heartfelt remembrances of John Pennington. Mike Kemph was immensely helpful in describing his father's relationship with Carol.

Carol's closest friends—Ann Mahoney, Jim Henry, Linda Armstrong, Creighton Cutts, Moses Funderburk, Roger Buerki, Sheila Willis, and Rebecca Bell—were extraordinarily generous in sharing their thoughts and correspondence. So were Carolyn Rader and Leslie Henry.

Many others—both on and off the record—related their stories, experiences, and insights.

I relied heavily on Joyce Seward's oral histories of island residents, recorded for the National Park Service. I used legal records on file with the Camden County District Courthouse, Camden County Sheriff's Department, the United States District Court, the National Park Service, and the National Marine Fisheries Service. I also used historical documents and records on file at Cumberland Island National Seashore, the Georgia Department of Archives, the Georgia Department of Natural Resources, the Georgia Division for Historic Preservation, the University of Georgia Library, the Carter Center, the National Park Service's Southeast Regional Office, and two decades of my own notes and recordings.

Some of the other material in this book was taken from direct interviews and conversations while I lived on Cumberland Island in

the mid-1990s as a volunteer park ranger and from numerous subsequent visits. Other material was taken from oral histories, written accounts, and other sources. The fact that a particular individual is quoted or discussed in this book should not be taken as an indication that any such individual approves of, endorses, or is otherwise associated with the author, the publisher, or the book.

Please respect the privacy of Carol Ruckdeschel and other island residents. If you're interested in helping Carol protect sea turtles and wilderness on Cumberland Island, visit wildcumberland.org.

acknowledgments

Thanks to Christopher McDougall, Larry Weissman, and Sascha Alper for believing in this book, and to Morgan Entrekin for making it happen. Morgan's guidance and the deft, thoughtful editing of Jamison Stoltz helped shape and sharpen the story.

Alan Cattier first encouraged me to visit Cumberland, and Bill Fox inspired me to write a book about it. Dan Sadowsky and Ken Edelstein eviscerated my first Cumberland feature and dared me to go deeper.

The encouragement of Eric Diener, Christie Posner, Andy Runkle, Mark and Anne Lundblad, Thomas Crowe, Rick Bass, Melissa Walker, Becky Bitzer, Jill Rios, Robert McGee, Rod Murphy, Mickey Mahaffey, Laura Dominkovic, Evan Bowers, and my colleagues at *Blue Ridge Outdoors Magazine* buoyed me through stormy seas. Julia Green's pointed critiques honored the narrative.

Dale Youngkin dragged me out of bed before sunrise to witness my first sea turtle hatch, and Gene Nicholson pushed me through all-night hikes to watch turtles nest. Sasha Greenspan was heroic, and her island insights were critical.

My family—especially Bill and Elaine Harlan, Barry and Betty Diznoff, and Jill Youse—has been incredibly patient and supportive. So has my five-year-old son, River, who skipped baseball games and birthday parties to hike with his dad on Cumberland.

My deepest gratitude goes to Carol, who courageously allowed me to rip the scabs off old wounds, splay open her innards, and dissect her life.

If there is any woman as strong as Carol, it is my wife, Emily, whose name was also written in the Cumberland sand when I proposed to her there fourteen years ago. Emily read countless versions of the manuscript, endured endless island treks, and anchored me throughout this book's journey. Ultimately, she reminded me, this is a love story.